SPIRITUAL LIVES

General Editor
Timothy Larsen

SPIRITUAL LIVES

General Editor
Timothy Larsen

The *Spiritual Lives* series features biographies of prominent men and women whose eminence is not primarily based on a specifically religious contribution. Each volume provides a general account of the figure's life and thought, while giving special attention to his or her religious contexts, convictions, doubts, objections, ideas, and actions. Many leading politicians, writers, musicians, philosophers, and scientists have engaged deeply with religion in significant and resonant ways that have often been overlooked or underexplored. Some of the volumes will even focus on men and women who were lifelong unbelievers, attending to how they navigated and resisted religious questions, assumptions, and settings. The books in this series will therefore recast important figures in fresh and thought-provoking ways.

Titles in the series include:

W. T. Stead
Nonconformist and Newspaper Prophet
Stewart J. Brown

Margaret Mead
A Twentieth-Century Faith
Elesha J. Coffman

Theodore Roosevelt
Preaching from the Bully Pulpit
Benjamin J. Wetzel

Queen Victoria
This Thorny Crown
Michael Ledger-Lomas

Benjamin Franklin
Cultural Protestant
D. G. Hart

Arthur Sullivan

A Life of Divine Emollient

IAN BRADLEY

OXFORD
UNIVERSITY PRESS

OXFORD
UNIVERSITY PRESS

Great Clarendon Street, Oxford, OX2 6DP,
United Kingdom

Oxford University Press is a department of the University of Oxford.
It furthers the University's objective of excellence in research, scholarship,
and education by publishing worldwide. Oxford is a registered trade mark of
Oxford University Press in the UK and in certain other countries

© Ian Bradley 2021

First Edition published in 2021

Impression: 1

Published in the United States of America by Oxford University Press
198 Madison Avenue, New York, NY 10016, United States of America

British Library Cataloguing in Publication Data
Data available

Library of Congress Control Number: 2020949752

ISBN 978-0-19-886326-7

Printed and bound by
CPI Group (UK) Ltd, Croydon, CR0 4YY

In fond memory of Ian Smith
born 21 June 1939 died 22 November 2019
like Arthur Sullivan, a lover of life

Acknowledgements

This book has been a labour of love and can perhaps be regarded as the consummation of a life-long love affair with the works of Arthur Sullivan. I have benefitted hugely over the last twenty-five years from the friendship, encouragement, and help of fellow members of the Sir Arthur Sullivan Society, notably the late David Eden, Martin Yates, William Parry, Doreen Harris, Robin Gordon-Powell, Elaine and Chris Richardson, Chris O'Brien, Steve Skinner, Arthur Barrett, and John Balls. My greatest debt is to the society's indefatigable and knowledgeable secretary, Stephen Turnbull, who has been a constant source of support and has read this book in manuscript, saving me from several egregious errors.

I must also record thanks to those responsible for the International Gilbert and Sullivan Festival who have allowed me to preach, talk, and exchange views on Sullivan's sacred music over the last twenty-five years, chief among them the late Ian Smith, together with Neil, Janet, Oliver, Henry, and Charles Smith. It has been a joy to collaborate with my good friend Stephen Shipley in church services associated with the festival in Buxton and Harrogate featuring Sullivan's church music and exploring his faith and spirituality.

Dr Peter Hawig opened my eyes to the religious works of Jacques Offenbach and also gave me useful information on the training in church music experienced by Franz von Suppé and a number of French operetta composers. Jeff Clarke alerted me to the pastiches of church music in Offenbach's operettas and to Léo Delibes' training as chorister and organist. Dr Paul Seeley shared with me his PhD thesis on the life and music of Franz Lehár and Dr Anne Stanyon very kindly let me quote from her fascinating PhD thesis on the 1898 Leeds Musical Festival. I have also profited from email exchanges with Dr Stanyon. I am indebted to Chris Crowcroft and Andrew Nunn for information on Thomas Sullivan's time at the Royal Military Asylum and his subsequent career. It has been a privilege to meet and talk with Arthur Sullivan's great-great-nephew, Scott Hayes, and his great-great niece, Katie Treherne.

In the course of my research, I have received much help from the staff of the Pierpont Morgan Library, New York, where most of Sullivan's correspondence is deposited; the Beinecke Rare Book and Manuscript Library at Yale University, which holds most of his diaries, made available to me in microfilm form; the D'Oyly Carte Opera Trust (where I consulted material before it was acquired by the British Library); the British Library; and the archives of Hymns Ancient and Modern in Norwich.

I have received much help and encouragement from the editor of this series, Timothy Larsen, and from Tom Perridge and Karen Raith at Oxford University Press.

Contents

List of Abbreviations

AS	Arthur Sullivan
BL	British Library
BRB	Beinecke Rare Book and Manuscript Library, Yale University
HAM	Hymns Ancient and Modern
PML	Pierpont Morgan Library, New York
RMA	Royal Military Asylum
SASS	The Sir Arthur Sullivan Society

Introduction

In November 2018 the independent record label Dutton released the first ever professional recording of Arthur Sullivan's oratorio, *The Light of The World*, based on Biblical texts and focused on the life and teaching of Jesus. Unusually, those reviewing the recording, which featured the BBC Concert Orchestra, the BBC Symphony Chorus, and a distinguished group of soloists conducted by John Andrews, focused as much on the piece as on the performance. The critical reaction to this work, which had been largely ignored and rarely performed for over 140 years, was extraordinary. Classical music magazines and websites hailed 'a truly revelatory discovery', commenting that 'this music touches greatness' and 'there is an engaging freshness and directness to Sullivan's writing'. There was enthusiasm for 'the intrinsic merits of this extraordinary score', and admiration for 'a splendidly distinctive, unstuffy achievement, brimful of captivating melodic charm, communicative flair and technical confidence', and 'a piece of theatre as well as a religious experience . . . everything is lived rather than just narrated'.[1]

What particularly excited and impressed critics was the handling of the character of Jesus. As one put it, '*The Light of the World* has Jesus speaking to us directly—something which few composers had been willing to entertain'.[2] Radically, Sullivan dispensed with the usual narrator and made Jesus a real character who interacted with others but was also set apart from them both in terms of vocal range and also through the accompaniment of his recitative-like arias by an inner orchestra made up of cor anglais, clarinet, bass clarinet, bassoon, contra-bassoon, and divided violas and cellos. There was general agreement among those reviewing the recording that this treatment of Jesus as a human figure with emotions gave *The Light of the World* a real spiritual depth contrasting with the pious sentimentality of most Victorian oratorios. As one put it: 'An extraordinary feature of Sullivan's genius is the sensitivity of word setting to the emotional as well as the religious meanings of given phrases. At times, he is fully prepared to unsettle as well as to comfort'.[3]

These tributes represent an overdue acknowledgment of the talents of a very different figure from the familiar master of the patter songs, rumpty-tumpty choruses, and light, lilting waltzes of the Savoy operas. They are part of a welcome rehabilitation and appreciation of Arthur Sullivan's sacred music and of the spiritual sensitivity as well as the artistic competence and daring innovation that underlay it. After more than a century of almost total neglect, this significant part of his overall output is coming to be appreciated not just in its own right but also in terms of its influence on Edward Elgar, Benjamin Britten, and other twentieth-century British composers. Thanks in large part to the efforts of the Sir Arthur Sullivan Society, founded in 1977, there are now both regular performances and excellent professional record-ings of his cantatas, oratorios, *Te Deums*, and other sacred pieces. The advocacy of a number of academic musicologists has also done much to restore his reputation as a serious composer.

Benedict Taylor, who has played a significant part in this process of rehabilitation, rightly asserts that Sullivan is 'probably the most loved and widely performed British composer in history'.[4] This is almost entirely thanks to the comic operas which he wrote with W.S. Gilbert and which continue to be widely performed by both professionals and amateurs across the English-speaking world. The Savoy operas will always remain his most enduring legacy. Yet they are not what he wanted to be remembered for. In a newspaper interview during a visit to the United States in 1885, he said: 'My sacred music is that on which I base my reputation as a composer. These works are the offspring of my liveliest fancy, the children of my greatest strength, the products of my most earnest thought and most incessant toil.'[5] This statement is corroborated by family lore among his descendants. Some years ago I met his great-great niece at a graduation garden party in St Andrews where I regularly led student members of the University Gilbert and Sullivan Society in impromptu singing. I invited her over to listen to our somewhat raucous rendering of choruses from the Savoy operas composed by her illustrious ancestor. She politely declined saying, 'We were always told in the family that it was his sacred music that meant more to him'.

Sullivan was schooled in the Christian faith and more specifically in the world of Anglican church music. As a young boy he attended the parish church where his father seems to have had some responsibility for the music. Between the ages of 12 and 15 he sang as a chorister in the Chapel Royal, steeping himself in the Anglican choral tradition of hymns, anthems, and plainchant. While making his way as a composer and conductor, he served as organist in two fashionable churches in the West End of London. He wrote numerous hymn tunes and served as the music editor for a major Anglican hymn book. His closest friends were church musicians and he developed a particularly intimate relationship with one of the leading amateur Biblical scholars of the Victorian age.

Church music was Sullivan's most abiding love. His first and last compositions were settings of a Biblical and a liturgical text respectively. At the age of 8, he wrote an anthem setting the opening verses of Psalm 137, 'By the waters of Babylon'. At the age of 58, when his strength was ebbing fast, he wrote a *Te Deum* to celebrate the end of the Boer War, devoting himself to this sacred piece to the detriment of an operetta which remained unfinished at his death. In the fifty years between these two compositions, he produced a formidable corpus of sacred music encompassing two Biblically based oratorios, *The Prodigal Son* and *The Light of the World*; a sacred musical drama, *The Martyr of Antioch*; a sacred cantata, *The Golden Legend*; three *Te Deum*s; twenty-six sacred part songs and ballads; nineteen anthems; and over sixty original hymn tunes, including ST GERTRUDE, written to accompany 'Onward, Christian soldiers', and NOEL, the melody to which the Christmas carol 'It came upon the midnight clear' is universally sung in Britain. Several of these religious works were every bit as well-known and popular with his contemporaries as his comic operas and other lighter pieces. His sacred ballad 'The Lost Chord' sold an average of 20,000 copies annually for twenty-five years, making it the best-selling song of the last quarter of the nineteenth century. For more than two decades, *The Golden Legend* was the second most performed choral work in the United Kingdom after Handel's *Messiah*.

Sullivan's earliest biographers were agreed in their acknowledgement of the importance of his church and sacred music and the extent of his own commitment to it. The first substantial biographical essay on him appeared in 1893 in a volume on *Masters of English Music*. The author, Charles Willeby, accorded Sullivan the first and longest entry in his book, which covered four other composers, including C.H. Parry and C.V. Stanford, noting that he was generally regarded as 'the greatest musician of his country'.[6] He emphasized Sullivan's training in church music, making much of the influence of his mentor, the Anglican priest, Thomas Helmore, and devoted particular attention to his solemn overture *In Memoriam* and to *The Golden Legend*.

The other biography which appeared in Sullivan's lifetime, written in 1899 by the journalist Arthur Lawrence and based on interviews with the composer, also made much of his church upbringing. It included the complete text of his important Birmingham lecture on music with its many Biblical and religious references (see pp. 145–9) and a substantial concluding essay on 'Sullivan as a Composer' by Benjamin Findon which had two separate sections of equal length on his sacred music and his secular and dramatic music. Writing about the former, Findon noted:

> It was in the domain of church art that he first displayed those signs of creative talent which was afterwards to bear such rich fruit, and which has to a certain extent coloured all his subsequent endeavours. Even in his operas we find it sprouting forth, sometimes with a peculiarly touching effect.[7]

Findon went on in 1904 to write his own biography of Sullivan, to whom he was related twice over (his grandmother was Sullivan's aunt and he married the daughter of the composer's uncle). In it, he noted that:

> Arthur Sullivan was peculiarly sensitive to the subtle and moving influence of the Christian life. The ecclesiastical character of so much of his music is as much a part of the nature of the man as the outcome of his early training and his association with the Church in after years.[8]

In 1927, Sullivan's nephew Herbert, whom he had treated almost as a son, collaborated with Newman Flower, a distinguished publisher and author, on a life which once again portrayed church music as the composer's first and greatest love. Pointing out how much he enjoyed the church choirs which he led, they observed:

> His later composing of church music proved how full was his under-standing of religious thought in music. He once said that his music was really intended for the Church. Lying somewhere in his brain was an inexhaustible store of melody upon which he drew to express religion as

no contemporary composer could express it, except perhaps Stainer and Gounod.[9]

The almost complete disappearance of Sullivan's serious music, and particularly of his religious compositions, from the repertoire throughout the twentieth century was partly due to the general reaction against Victorian taste and values but it was also the consequence of a sustained campaign by music critics and commentators. During his lifetime, Sullivan faced considerable criticism for devoting too much of his time and talent to lightweight theatrical pieces and not fulfilling his youthful potential as a composer of serious and sacred works on a par with Brahms. In the twentieth century, while his comic operas won many accolades and continued to be performed, criticism shifted to his sacred and church music which was denigrated for being dull, affected, insincere, vulgarly populist, and over-sentimental. The tone was set by Ernest Walker in his influential *History of Music in England* published in 1907. While acknowledging that 'Sullivan was, beyond all question, the most widely popular English composer of the nineteenth century' and that 'the comic operas written to the libretti of W.S. Gilbert made his reputation and form his chief title to fame', he dismissed him as 'merely the idle singer of an empty evening—a mere popularity-hunting trifler' and poured particular scorn on his sacred works:

> We can never recollect without shame that the composer who stood for contemporary English music in the eyes of the world could put his name to disgraceful rubbish like 'The lost chord' or . . . sink to the abysmally cheap sentimentality of the opening tune of the *In Memoriam* overture or the 'O pure in heart' chorus in *The Golden Legend*; and indeed there is a pitiful amount of this kind of thing. The sacred cantata *The Martyr of Antioch* . . . alternates between dullness and vulgarity, and sometimes attains both at once; while the more ambitious oratorio *The Light of the World* has hardly enough vitality even to be vulgar.[10]

This assault was continued by the eminent hymnologist, Erik Routley. Writing in the 1940s, he asserted that 'none of Sullivan's church music anywhere rises above the second-rate' and described it as being characterized by 'a shameless secularism' and 'a dreary dullness'.[11] For him, Sullivan was fundamentally unsuited to write sacred music:

Sullivan's genius was not in the least religious; it was too light for the graver themes. We can imagine the relief with which he escaped from his early occupation with church music, in which he was not at home, into that wholly congenial field of light opera in which, along with his twin genius, W.S. Gilbert, he was to achieve his artistic immortality.[12]

Other musicologists writing in the mid-twentieth century echoed these themes. Gervase Hughes, in the first book devoted to the study of Sullivan's music, published in 1959, launched attack after attack on his church and sacred compositions. Having dismissed the anthems, hymn tunes and part songs as 'trifles' of no worth, he turned on the oratorios:

It is in vain that we search the pages of *The Prodigal Son* for any sign of initiative; one of the first choruses is a setting of the words 'Let us eat and drink, for tomorrow we die', and as we wade through the rest of the work, half-submerged in a bog of conventional clichés, this strikes us as having been sound advice. *The Light of the World* is not much better.

The choruses in *The Golden Legend* were criticized for being 'in his worst Moody-and-Sankey tradition', the *Festival Te Deum* castigated for its brassy vulgarity and more than once Hughes delivered his damning verdict that Sullivan's entire corpus of oratorios, sacred cantatas, and liturgical works should be allowed to 'rest in peace'.[13]

The assault on Sullivan's sacred music continued unabated in the 1960s and 1970s. In the context of a more general attack on the Victorian hymn tune in 1967 Arthur Hutchings singled out Sullivan for his self-conscious and contrived religiosity:

It is not in the deeply religious Dykes that one finds revolting sanctim-osity but in the charmingly worldly Sullivan . . . If he had not felt the need to be a different Sullivan on Sundays, he might have contributed something enduring to church music . . . Sullivan's church music is best forgotten; from it we can but illustrate only the nadir of sanctimo-nious vulgarity.[14]

Kenneth Long, writing in 1972 about the history of English church music, pursued the same theme:

It is sad that his creative life was torn between two irreconcilable ideals. On the one hand his genius expressed itself naturally in the way most congenial to it—the operettas: on the other, feeling somehow that such frivolities were unworthy of a musician and unbecoming in a gentleman, he yearned to excel in 'serious' music, especially sacred music. It is not surprising then that many of his sacred pieces seem merely an extension of the operettas; indeed, if Katisha were to make a dramatic entry (assisted by the Chorus) in several of his anthems, the effect would in no way seem incongruous. Actually it would improve most of them.

Long further dug in the knife by observing that 'Sullivan was one of those people who thought that so long as the words were sacred—or at least vaguely religious—their aura automatically makes the music itself sacred'.[15]

Underlying these criticisms of Sullivan's religious music was a widely shared view that he was not himself a person of any great faith or spiritual depth. This has been the consensus among his more recent biographers, in marked contrast to the strong emphasis on his religious impulses and sensitivity in the early biographies written during his lifetime by those who knew or interviewed him. Percy Young makes no mention of faith or theology in his generally sympathetic study of Sullivan published in 1971. Arthur Jacobs, whose 1984 biography, revised in 1992, remains the standard work, much more emphatically portrays him as an essentially secular figure without any real Christian faith:

> His religion hardly went beyond a superficial conformity to the Church of England: neither on the threshold of death nor earlier in his mature years is there evidence of 'spiritual' guidance sought or offered. A strong family piety together with a deep commitment to friendship and to his art—these purely human values were, perhaps, enough.[16]

Jacobs returned to this theme in a radio interview in 1992:

> Sullivan conformed to the normal practice of someone who was brought up in the Chapel Royal and in a conventional home. He would have considered it to be very odd not to have been able as someone who mixed in royal and official circles to take part in official church celebrations and so on. He set biblical texts. But there is no evidence that he had any personal fervour. It is rather odd that even towards the end of his life and even when he knew he was dying or about to die he did not seek what we would call spiritual or church consolation.[17]

In a lecture the same year, he was even more emphatic, describing Sullivan as 'a man probably without any religious faith notwithstanding his output of sacred music'.[18]

David Eden, a key figure in the Sullivan Society and a considerable enthusiast for Sullivan (and denigrator of Gilbert) wrote in similar terms in his book *The Creative Conflict*, noting that 'Sullivan's Christianity was of the most summary Anglican kind . . . Theology meant nothing to him'.[19] He amplified this assessment in a talk at a Sullivan Society Conference in Ely in 1995:

> I think we can conclude with some safety that he was a person for whom the inner life of Christianity had little if any meaning. There is no suggestion that he ever experienced the pain of separation from God, or felt that the burden of his sins had been lifted by the atonement. On the contrary he lived an almost completely secular life. His real religion was probably sun worship . . . if he had a cathedral at all it was probably the casino at Monte Carlo.[20]

Those who have contributed to the recent rehabilitation of Sullivan's serious music have taken a broadly similar view, downplaying his religious commitment and his sacred works. In his 2002 study of the English Musical Renaissance, Meirion Hughes, while being broadly supportive of Sullivan in his tussles with critics, notes 'his lack of Christian zeal' and writes that 'His lack of any deep religious conviction meant that he brought little spiritual conviction to the composition of devotional works'.[21] In his important revisionist study, *Arthur Sullivan: A Musical Reappraisal* (2018), Benedict Taylor concentrates almost entirely on secular compositions, limiting his analysis of the sacred corpus to the two *Te Deums* and ignoring *The Prodigal Son*, *The Light of the World*, *The Martyr of Antioch*, and the hymn tunes, anthems, and sacred songs. He portrays Sullivan's character in entirely secular terms, reinforcing the impression given in the film *Topsy-Turvy* that his natural and preferred milieu was the brothel or the casino rather than the church organ loft. In his words: 'The composer would rather spend his days at the races and roulette wheel, within the upper echelons of society and charming female company, leaving the realization of musical commissions to the last possible minute'.[22]

Sullivan did undoubtedly have a lazy streak. He was a *bon viveur* who lived life to the full. David Eden was to some extent right to describe him as a sun worshipper—a friend writing anonymously after his death recalled him saying, 'What sun worshippers we are! And no wonder, for the sun means light and warmth, and that is life and love, while its absence means dark and hatred'.[23] But that remark does not betoken any attachment to paganism. Sullivan was someone who was naturally discreet and private about his own deep beliefs and thoughts. Edward Dicey, the editor of the *Observer*, who was a close friend for nearly forty years, remarked that he 'was not the kind of man who wears his heart upon his sleeve: he had a certain reluctance in putting himself forward.'[24] He did not often write or talk about spiritual or theological matters. But there is clear evidence, from his diaries and letters, which has been ignored or overlooked by his more recent biographers, that he had a consistent and simple Christian faith, which was shaped in a liberal Broad Church direction by his close friendship with George Grove and others that he met through him. One of the areas where this faith expressed itself was in his attitude to death. Arthur Lawrence recalled a conversation where the subject of death had come up and in which Sullivan had simply said, 'Death has absolutely no terrors for me'.[25] He had something of that 'sweet unmurmuring faith, obedient and resigned to Thee in life and death' which James Drummond Burns commended in the hymn 'Hushed was the evening hymn' that he set so beautifully and sensitively in his tune SAMUEL. Sullivan believed in heaven as a place of eternal rest where family and friends would be re-united. He also believed that Christian faith was best expressed in practical charity and in the exercise of generosity, forbearance, and mercy. He emphasized the theological themes of forgiveness and assurance in the texts that he chose to set and the way that he set them. He remained loyal to the church in which he had been nurtured, and retained a lifelong affection for the Anglican choral tradition with its roots in Byrd, Gibbons, and Tallis and later development by Purcell and Croft.

This book explores Sullivan's faith, its formation, the influences on it, and how it impacted on his character and work. Ultimately, it was a faith expressed through music, both via the works of others, notably Bach, who most inspired him, and in his own compositions. It was through music that he found and expressed the divine. It was also through music, as well as through his personality and character, that he expressed that softening, uplifting, life-affirming quality that made his life one of divine emollient.

Notes

1. Extracts from reviews gathered together in 'Celebrating The Light of the World', *SASS Magazine* 99 (Spring 2019), p.5.
2. http://www.musicweb-international.com/classrev/2019/Feb/Sullivan_light_2CDLX7356.htm Accessed 21 May 2020.
3. http://www.musicweb-international.com/classrev/2019/Feb/Sullivan_light_2CDLX7356.htm
4. Benedict Taylor, *Arthur Sullivan: A Musical Reappraisal* (London: Routledge, 2018), p.1. Other musicologists who have made a significant contribution to the rehabilitation of the 'serious' Sullivan include Nigel Burton, Meinhard Saremba, Richard Silverman, and Martin Yates. Their work can be found in the three volumes of *Sullivan Perspecktiven* edited by Albert Gier, Benedict Taylor, and Meinhard Saremba (Essen: Odlib Verlag, 2012, 2014, and 2017).
5. 'Sir Arthur Sullivan: A Talk with the Composer of "Pinafore"', *San Francisco Chronicle*, 22 July 1885.
6. Charles Willeby, *Masters of English Music* (London, James Osgood, 1893), p.1.
7. Arthur Sullivan [hereafter AS], *Sir Arthur Sullivan: Life Story, Letters and Reminiscences* (London: James Bowden, 1899), p.299.
8. Benjamin Findon, *Sir Arthur Sullivan: His Life and Music* (London: James Nisbet, 1904), p.62.
9. Herbert Sullivan and Newman Flower, *Sir Arthur Sullivan* (London: Cassell & Co., 1927), p.39.
10. Ernest Walker, *A History of Music in England* (Oxford: Clarendon Press, 1907), pp.293–4.
11. *Bulletin of the Hymn Society of Great Britain and Ireland* 27 (April 1949), p.105.
12. *Bulletin of the Hymn Society of Great Britain and Ireland* 20 (July 1942), p.7.
13. Gervase Hughes, *The Music of Arthur Sullivan* (London: Macmillan, 1960), pp.13, 16, 66, 82, 162, 166.
14. Arthur Hutchings, *Church Music in the Nineteenth Century* (London: Herbert Jenkins, 1967), pp.151, 18, 109.

15. Kenneth Long, *The Music of the English Church* (London: Hodder and Stoughton, 1972), p.366.
16. Arthur Jacobs, *Arthur Sullivan*, 2nd edn. (Aldershot: Scolar Press, 1992), p.410.
17. Quoted by Meinhard Saremba, 'Edward Elgar and Arthur Sullivan', *Elgar Society Journal* 17:4 (April 2012), p.1.3.
18. Quoted in 'Round and About', *DC Magazine*, Spring 1993 (Birmingham, The Friends of the D'Oyly Carte), p.7.
19. David Eden, *Gilbert and Sullivan: The Creative Conflict* (London: Associated University Presses, 1986), p.174.
20. David Eden, 'Sullivan's Christianity', *SASS Magazine* 41 (Autumn 1995), p.25.
21. Meirion Hughes, *The English Musical Renaissance and the Press 1850–1914*, paperback edn. (London: Routledge, 2017), p.123.
22. Taylor, *Sullivan*, p.214.
23. 'Sir Arthur Seymour Sullivan as an old Friend Knew Him', *Argosy* 73 (February 1901), p.163.
24. Edward Dicey, 'Recollections of Arthur Sullivan', *Fortnightly Review* January 1905, p.78.
25. *Masonic Illustrated* January 1901, p.69.

1

1842–1852

Ancestry, Early Upbringing, and Family Ties

Arthur Sullivan was born on 13 May 1842. There is some slight doubt as to his actual place of birth. Both his birth certificate and baptismal register give it as his parents' home at 8 Bolwell Terrace, Lambeth, south London, but the 1851 census records it as Frimley in Surrey, the parish which included the Royal Military College at Sandhurst where both his parents had previously worked. It is possible that his mother was staying with friends or family there when she gave birth to him. Both sides of his family had Irish and Catholic roots and it is fitting to begin this spiritual life with an exploration of his immediate ancestry in terms of ethnicity and religious persuasion.

Ancestry

Sullivan's paternal grandfather, Thomas (hereafter referred to as Thomas Sullivan Snr), was born near Tralee in County Kerry in the southwest of Ireland in 1776 and married his wife Mary, whose maiden name was also Sullivan, in Bandon, County Cork, around 1804. David Eden concluded after undertaking considerable research on the family that 'it is safe to assume that Thomas Sullivan was a Catholic' and that 'we may assume that the happy couple were married according to the Roman Catholic rite'.[1] Unfortunately no record survives of the marriage, nor of the subsequent birth or baptism of their oldest son Thomas (Thomas Sullivan Jnr), Arthur Sullivan's father, although documents relating to his time at the Royal Military Asylum (RMA) suggest that he was born in Cork on 4 June 1805 and baptized there by the Rev John Reardon. There is a very faint possibility that Mary might have been a Protestant. Bandon, the town from which she hailed and in which she seems to have met and married her husband, was famous for being the most staunchly Protestant town in Ireland, 'the inhabitants not permitting papists to reside there as they had been so cruelly treated by men of that persuasion.'[2] However, it seems most likely that she, too, was a Catholic.

Thomas Sullivan Snr was press ganged into the British army at the age of 30. According to family tradition, it happened when he was drunk after winning a horse race. He awoke from a heavy hangover to find that he had been enlisted. He served as a foot soldier in the British army from 1806 to 1821, deserting twice but also seeing active service in Portugal, Spain, and France against Napoleon's forces in the Peninsular War, going to Canada to support the war against the United States, and later guarding Napoleon during his imprisonment on St Helena. He was invalided out of the army 'worn out and undersize' at the age of 43 and settled in London, spending the latter years of his life from 1830 to 1838 as a pensioner in the Royal Hospital, Chelsea, where his wife, who had lived in London with her growing family throughout most of his time in the army, seems to have practised as a nurse. There was no requirement on him to convert to Anglicanism during his time serving the British Crown. The Papists Act of 1778 allowed Roman Catholics to join the British army and a large number of Irish Catholics served in it without renouncing their faith. Irish soldiers, many of whom were Roman Catholics, made up around one-third of the British army in the early decades of the nineteenth century.

There is, indeed, strong evidence to suggest that Thomas and Mary Sullivan remained Roman Catholic. The youngest of their four children, John, Arthur Sullivan's uncle, who was born in 1824, was baptised in St Mary's Roman Catholic Church in Cadogan Street, Chelsea, presumably his parents' place of worship at the time. Newman Flower and Herbert Sullivan state that another child, Elizabeth, also known as Ellen, who was born in 1809, became a nun and ended up as mother superior of a convent in Bruges, Belgium. This is incorrect as records show that she married in the Anglican church of St Luke's, Chelsea, in 1835. It may be that her younger sister, Margaret, born in 1811, became a nun but this cannot be established for certain.

There is unfortunately no record of the early religious affiliations of Thomas Sullivan Jnr. In 1813, his mother petitioned to have him admitted to the RMA, Chelsea, later known as the Duke of York's School, a tough educational establishment which had been founded ten years earlier for children of soldiers serving abroad by Prince Frederick, the second son of George III, commander-in-chief of the British Army and the 'Grand Old Duke of York' immortalized in the nursery rhyme. In her petition, Mary Sullivan described herself as being in bad health and having no means of support for her children 'save what arises from a day's washing when she is able to procure it'.[3] Thomas Sullivan Snr was at this time serving in Spain under the Duke of Wellington in the Peninsular campaign. Mary Sullivan gave the family's address as George Alley, Field Lane, Holborn. This was a notoriously poor part of London where Oliver Twist was taken by the Artful Dodger on his first visit to London and where Fagin had his lair. Charles Dickens noted that 'The sole places that seemed to prosper amid the general blight of the place, were the public-houses; and in them, the lowest orders of Irish were wrangling with might and main.'[4] Thomas Sullivan Jnr was admitted to the RMA at the age of 9 in 1814, by which time his father was on his way across the Atlantic to fight in the American war. He spent five years as a pupil there, several of them in the RMA annex in Southampton which was opened because of over-crowding in Chelsea on account of the number of orphaned children being admitted whose fathers had been killed in the Napoleonic Wars. He clearly showed an early aptitude for music and left the RMA to become a trainee army bandsman. Religious instruction at the RMA was according to the tenets of the Church of England and it was probably while there that Thomas Sullivan Jnr moved away from his Catholic roots towards the Anglicanism which he seems to have espoused in adult life.[5]

Arthur Sullivan's maternal ancestry was a mixture of Irish and Italian and possibly encompassed Protestant as well as Catholic influences. His maternal grandfather, James Coghlan (1773–1815), although born in Ireland, seems to have come to England relatively early in life and worked as a legal stationer. In 1802, he married Mary Louise Margaret Righy (1786–1829) in St Marylebone Parish Church in Marylebone Road, London. Arthur Sullivan claimed that his grandmother came of 'an old Italian family' and a note on a family tree that she compiled identified her father, Joseph Righy (1745–1808), as Italian.[6] In fact, he seems to have been born in Nice when it was part of the Kingdom of Sardinia. David Eden speculated that Joseph Righy may have been a Huguenot (i.e. Protestant) who came to England as a religious refugee via Berne and Florence (where Mary Louise was born) but there is no evidence for this. Why he landed up in England is not clear but once there he worked as a schoolmaster, latterly in Great Marlow in Buckinghamshire, where he seems to have taught French in the newly opened Royal Military College.[7] Following their marriage, James and Mary Louise Coghlan also settled in Great Marlow, where James taught in the junior department of the college. It was there that Arthur Sullivan's mother, Mary Clementina, was born in 1811. When the college relocated to Sandhurst in 1812 the family moved there. James Coghlan died in Sandhurst in 1815 and was buried in the churchyard of St Michael's Parish Church. His widow, Mary Louise, who seems to have worked in the college laundry, married again and died in 1829, being buried in the college cemetery.

Mary Clementina grew up in Sandhurst and it was there in 1820 that she met Thomas Sullivan Jnr who had just come to the Royal Military College at the age of 15 as a trainee bandsman. Although she was only 9, they seem to have struck up an immediate and close friendship. Thomas remained at Sandhurst until 1834 when he moved to London to embark on a freelance career as a clarinetist, music teacher, and music copyist. He and Mary Clementina married on 26 November 1836 in the Anglican church of St John the Evangelist in what is now Hyde Park Crescent in Paddington. Their first child, Frederic, known in the family as Fred, was born on Christmas morning 1837 when they were living in Chelsea. Thomas subsequently took up a position as clarinetist in the Surrey Theatre at the lower end of Blackfriars Road and the family moved to Bolwell Terrace, Lambeth. As already noted, Arthur was born while they were living there and was baptised Arthur Seymour Sullivan at the nearby (Anglican) parish church of St Mary's, Lambeth, on 30 July 1842.

So there was a strong Roman Catholic element in Sullivan's genetic make-up. Before exploring its possible effect it is worth disposing of two widely circulated canards about his ethnic and religious antecedents. The first is the suggestion which appeared in several publications during his lifetime and shortly after his death that he had Jewish ancestry. He appeared in a list of 'Jewish celebrities of the nineteenth century' in successive editions of the *Jewish Year Book* which began publication in 1897 and drew on a list originally compiled in 1885. *The Jewish Chronicle* confidently asserted Sullivan's Jewish ancestry in its review of his 1891 opera *Ivanhoe* and the novelist Samuel Butler described him in his posthumously published *Notebooks* as 'the Irish Jew'.[8] A correspondent to the *Jewish Chronicle* in November 1900 claimed to have been told by Fred Sullivan that the family were of Jewish descent, an ancestor having changed his name from Solomon to Sullivan on enlisting in the army.[9] Percy Young perpetuated this idea, noting in respect of a visit to the Jewish quarter of Prague in October 1867 that 'Like Mendelssohn, Sullivan occasionally paid respects to his Jewish antecedents.'[10] In fact, this whole notion seems to be without any foundation. I concur with Arthur Jacobs, who undertook considerable research on this topic and devoted an entire appendix to it in his biography, that 'there is no evidence for that supposition and indeed a strong presumption against it'.[11]

Even more bizarre is the suggestion that Sullivan had black African ancestry. His striking dark features and olive skin were often attributed to his supposed Italian antecedents, as were his eyes, described by Benjamin Findon as possessing 'the lustrous depth of Southern darkness'.[12] However, one contemporary maintained that they derived from negroid origins. Robert Francillon, a prolific author and poet whose sister-in-law Clara took a fancy to Sullivan when they were fellow students at Leipzig, wrote that there was 'a strong strain of African blood that became increasingly perceptible with increasing age. He was, in fact, an Octoroon [a person of one-eighth black ancestry]'. Francillon went on to suggest that this had led Sullivan to be 'subjected to inconveniences and annoyances during his visit to the United States which permanently embittered him against Americans and American ways.'[13] This appears to be a total fabrication unsupported by any evidence.

What is incontestable is the strong Irish strain in Sullivan's genetic make-up. Did the fact that three of his four grandparents were Irish give him a strong sense of Irish identity? This aspect of his ancestry was clearly important to him, as demonstrated by the name that he chose for his one and only symphony, which had been conceived when he was on holiday in northern Ireland, although he referred to it publicly as 'the Irish Symphony' only towards the end of his life, having modestly wanted to avoid comparisons with Mendelssohn's Scottish Symphony. Several of his contemporaries made much of his Irishness and suggested that it was a major contributory factor in his genial and generous temperament. Herman Klein, the *Sunday Times* music critic who became a good friend, commented that: 'Sullivan was a man of singularly sweet and amiable disposition. There was much more impulsive warmth and emotional depth to his Irish nature than one would have judged from his manner, which impressed most people as cold and reserved.'[14] Henry Lytton, who first joined a D'Oyly Carte Opera Company tour in 1884 and went on to be a leading exponent of the 'patter' roles in the Savoy operas, described Sullivan as 'a warm-hearted Irishman, he was always ready to do a good turn for anyone.'[15] Louis Engel, a music journalist, reckoned that he combined 'the vivacity of the Irish with the more solid intellectual qualities of the Italian'.[16] The Irish influence in his music is perhaps most apparent at the very end of his life in his unfinished comic opera, *The Emerald Isle.* Those who engage in ethnic stereotyping might point to some of Sullivan's most notable characteristics, such as his easy charm, generosity, lack of commitment, and tendency to leave everything to the last minute as characteristic of the Irish temperament. It is clear, however, that he saw himself first and foremost as British, if not, indeed, English, as manifested by his fervent support for the Crown, his affection for the Church of England and his staunch championship of English music—he made a point of employing only British musicians in every orchestra that he auditioned and assembled. He would not, of course, be the first or the last Irishman to outdo native Englishmen in terms of proud British patriotic sentiment.

The Roman Catholic influence on Sullivan is more intriguing and more difficult to quantify. His paternal Sullivan grandparents seem to have remained staunch Roman Catholics but his father espoused Anglicanism and attended the local parish church at Sandhurst. His mother's religious upbringing and faith is more difficult to discern. The evidence tends to point to the Coghlan family being at least nominally Anglican, as suggested by their marriage in a Church of

England church, but several sources claim that Mary Clementina grew up as a Roman Catholic, or at least with strong Roman Catholic influences. According to Benjamin Findon, she was educated at a Catholic convent in Hampstead.[17] In his biography of the composer, Percy Young wrote that 'it appears that she retained, or at least was loth wholly to lose contact with, the faith of her forefathers.'[18]

If Mary Sullivan did have Roman Catholic inclinations, they did not stop her marrying and having her sons christened in Church of England parish churches. She does appear to have attended Roman Catholic church services later in life, perhaps after her husband had died. Francis Burnand, the editor of *Punch* and himself a convert to Catholicism under the influence of John Henry Newman, recalled in a letter written in 1901 that Arthur Sullivan, a good friend with whom he collaborated on several comic operas, occasionally accompanied his mother to the Roman Catholic Church of St Peter and St Edward in Palace Street, Westminster. This was almost certainly out of filial devotion. Burnand's letter was written to rebut an erroneous story that he and Sullivan had initially planned their first collaboration, *Cox and Box*, while walking back together from church one Sunday morning in 1866. 'I should never have been going on a Sunday to a Protestant Church with him nor would he have been going with me to a Catholic Church', he wrote, 'moreover my early hours for going to Mass would never have suited Arthur S. who if he ever visited a Catholic Church would have visited it on account of the music, that is at High Mass at 11am'.[19] Burnand's letter provides the only extant evidence of Mary Sullivan's Catholic faith in adult life. Against it must be set the fact that following her death she had an Anglican funeral taken by Thomas Helmore.

Did the Catholic faith of his forbears have any significant influence on Arthur Sullivan's own religious beliefs and practice or on his sacred music? The only evidence of possible pro-Catholic sympathies that I can find is in a letter written at the age of 14 to his parents in which he reports learning about the Crimean War and also about plans to abandon the virulently anti-Catholic commemoration of Guy Fawkes Day, celebrating the foiling of a plot in 1605 to assassinate James I while opening Parliament and restore a Catholic monarch to the throne:

They talk of doing away with the services for that day altogether, and let the poor fellow sleep in his grave in peace, and only remember that it was the day the battle of Inkerman was fought, since the Roman Catholics helped us to win the day, and we speak so badly of them in the service.[20]

These sentiments are, however, clearly expressed from an Anglican, or at least a non-Catholic point of view. The sacred music that he most admired and which was most clearly influential on his own work, the anthems of the English Tudor composers and the oratorios of Bach, Handel, and Mendelssohn, was very clearly Protestant and rooted in Anglicanism and Lutheranism respectively. The only places in his own work where there is perhaps an echo of the Catholic faith of his mother and his Irish ancestors are in his particularly sensitive settings of prayers to the Virgin Mary in *The Golden Legend* and in his 1898 opera *The Beauty Stone*.

An Anglican Upbringing

Anglicanism was a much more important influence and presence than Roman Catholicism in Sullivan's early childhood. He grew up in Sandhurst where his father had returned in 1845 on being appointed band sergeant at the Royal Military College, a post which he held for the next twelve years. Thomas Sullivan seems to have been involved with the music in the parish church and young Arthur attended services there from a young age, as he recalled to his first biographer, Arthur Lawrence:

Sometimes I used to go to Sunday afternoon service at the old church at Sandhurst. The church was old in every respect: old-fashioned, high-backed, whitewashed pews, with a gallery at one end for the musicians. What used to interest me most was the little ceremony that the clerk performed so solemnly in regard to the hymns. After he had, from his desk, given out the hymn, always from Tate and Brady's Psalter, he would walk solemnly to the other end of the church, mount to the large empty gallery by means of a ladder, and picking up his clarionet, would lead the musical accompaniment, which consisted only of his own instrument, the clarionet, a bassoon and a violoncello.[21]

This early reminiscence from around 1850 provides a vivid description of the old ways of singing in the Church of England with the Tate and Brady psalms and west gallery band so beloved of Thomas Hardy that were about to be swept away by the arrival of organs and hymns. As a church organist and writer of hymns and anthems, Sullivan himself was to be in the van of the mid-Victorian movement which supplanted the old instrumental bands and replaced them with robed choirs. His youthful affection for the old style of church music probably had much to do with his early love of the instruments found in the west gallery bands. The military band which his father conducted was made up of wind players and as a boy he learned to play every single instrument in it. His familiarity with their particular strengths and weaknesses helped to make him a master of orchestration. More broadly, his early exposure to military bands gave him his life-long love of melody and of oom-pah-pah march rhythms which became a characteristic feature of so many of his compositions, not least his hymn tunes.

The music that he heard in the parish church enthused and excited young Arthur Sullivan even more than the marches played by the military bands on the Sandhurst parade ground. It is significant that his first composition, written at the age of 8 in 1850, was an anthem setting words from Psalm 137, 'By the waters of Babylon'. Having initially attended the local national (Church of England) school in Frimley, he continued his education in a small private school in the village. Here, as he recalled many years later, he fell under the influence of a young master who had been at one of the new national training colleges, set up to train teachers with a strong emphasis on music:

> He was for ever talking to me about the lovely music of Westminster Abbey and the Chapel Royal, and what splendid musical training the choirs had. Well, that simply turned my brain. I was mad on choirs; I read about them, thought about them, and even dreamed about them.

> My father was very much against my going to a choir school, but I was bent on it. I remember as well as if it was only yesterday jumping out of bed one morning with what seemed to me an inspiration. I ran into my father's room, and found him dressing.

'Father', I said triumphantly, 'Purcell was at a choir school.' I thought that was an unanswerable argument, and was much disappointed that my father did not think so too. On the contrary, he thought it was high time I was moved away from the influence of my choir talking school-master. So at the age of eleven I was moved to a boarding school in Bayswater. But here I stuck to my old determination. I had set my heart on a musical career, and my new master wrote to my father and said he had much better allow me to follow my inclination.[22]

The 'new master' referred to here was William Plees who ran an academy in Bayswater where Sullivan was enrolled as a boarder in 1853. He was far from being an exemplary pupil. By his own admission he hated Latin and Greek and the only subjects which engaged his interest were history and geography. He became ever more resolved to sing in the choir of either the Chapel Royal or Westminster Abbey and pestered both his father and Mr Plees to let him audition. It was the uniforms worn by the children of the Chapel Royal—scarlet and gold coats for special occasions and navy blue jackets and trousers with red cord stripes and crown buttons at other times—that determined his choice. Having been told about them by Plees, he set his heart on going there. His parents were uneasy about the quality of education that would be offered but he was adamant and in April 1854, a month before his 12th birthday, he prevailed on Plees to take him to see Sir George Smart, organist and composer to the Chapels Royal. Sullivan sang the aria 'With verdure clad' from Haydn's *Creation*, accompanying himself on the piano. Smart was impressed by the quality of his voice and told him to report immediately to Thomas Helmore, the Master of the Children of the Chapel Royal. He sang the same song to Helmore who quizzed him about the basics of the Christian faith, it being a rule that no boy was to be admitted as a chorister who could not answer the questions in the Church Catechism.

The fact that Sullivan was able to impress with his religious knowledge as well as his musical ability confirms that he must have had more than just a peremptory upbringing in the Church of England. Helmore was also doubtless influenced by a letter of recommendation from Percy Smith, the vicar of Sandhurst, who wrote at the request of Thomas Sullivan, 'a parishioner of mine', and described Arthur as 'a most highly principled boy . . . amiable and obedient and gentle in his manner'.[23] Choristers were not usually admitted beyond the age of 9 and Helmore was concerned that Sullivan's voice would soon break. The Bishop of London was consulted and agreed that although Arthur was just short of his 12th birthday and well above the usual age of admission, he should be allowed in and he was enrolled as a boy treble on 12 April 1854. It was to be one of the most important events of his life, both in terms of determining his career as a musician and also of confirming him in the Anglican faith and liturgical tradition.

Family Affections

Before closing this chapter on Sullivan's ancestry and early upbringing, it would be wrong not to reflect on the huge importance that family had on him and on his faith throughout his life. Arthur Jacobs has already been quoted as saying that his religion was expressed in terms of 'a strong family piety' (p. 7). It is certainly true that he showed an exceptional level of devotion to his father and mother, his brother Fred, his sister-in-law, and his nieces and nephews, all of whom he treated with great generosity and kindness. It is in his dealings with his family that he most obviously showed his simple and straightforward Christian faith. His letters to family members invariably ended with the words 'God bless you'. This could just be taken as a kind of formulaic valediction not necessarily illustrative of any real religious belief. Yet the cumulative effect of reading them reinforces the sense that they were a genuine expression of faith. His relationship with his mother was particularly close. She lived with him for many years and effectively acted as a combination of secretary, housekeeper, and valet. When he was away he wrote to her on an almost daily basis. In a letter to her on her 46th birthday in November 1857, he wrote that he and Fred had been ruminating on what to say to her and had settled on the words 'May God bless you and keep you'.[24] He addressed his father in similar terms, writing to him on his 55th birthday, 'You know that I thank God He has spared you for so many years in health, and also that I pray He will continue to do so for many years to come.'[25]

It was the death of family members that particularly brought out the faith that Sullivan was otherwise often very reticent about expressing. When his father died in September 1866, he noted that he found it particularly hard to think that never again would he 'hear his cheery voice saying, "God bless you, my boy"'. He went on to reflect that 'although he is gone for ever, perhaps he can look upon me and see all I do; and please God I will try and never do anything that will make him turn away his head and regret that he left me alone here.'[26] Characteristically, he expressed both his grief and his faith in music through the hymn-like motif which runs through his *In Memoriam* overture. His brother Fred's fatal illness and death in 1877 similarly inspired his setting of 'The Lost Chord'. Following the death of his mother in May 1882, he wrote in his diary 'I was alone in the room, alone that is with dear Mother's lifeless body. Her soul had gone to God' and he noted the words that he had said to her: 'God bless you, and take you to eternal rest'.[27] When his sister-in-law Charlotte died in 1885 he wrote to his young nephews and nieces: 'Now, in your prayers night and morning, pray that your dear mother may have joined your father in God's eternal Rest, and that you all may lead such lives on earth, that hereafter you may be taken to where our hope is they are.'[28]

These letter and diary extracts indicate a simple, trusting, Christian hope that family members would be re-united in death, conceived of in terms of eternal rest with God. They also express a view that entrance to heaven depends on how we live our lives here on earth and that human conduct is a more important indicator of true religion than credal subscription, extreme piety, or a personal sense of salvation. Both these beliefs were marked aspects of Sullivan's religious faith and it is significant that they were worked out and expressed primarily in the context of family attachments and bereavements.

Notes

1. David Eden, *Kyrie Eleison: The Ancestry of Sir Arthur Sullivan* (Retford: SASS, 2016), pp.7–8.
2. *Gazetteer and New Daily Advertiser*, 6 March 1772, quoted by David Eden, 'From York Town to Bolwell', *SASS Magazine* 79 (Summer 2012), pp.21–5.
3. Petition dated 24 July 1813 for entry of Thomas Sullivan to RMA in archives of the Duke of York's Royal Military School, Dover.
4. Charles Dickens, *The Adventures of Oliver Twist* (London: Chapman & Hall, 1866), p.58.

5. I am indebted for information on Thomas Sullivan's time at the RMA to Chris Crowcroft and Andrew Nunn.

6. Arthur Jacobs, *Arthur Sullivan*, 2nd edn. (Aldershot: Scolar Press, 1992), pp.5–6; the annotated family tree is in a scrapbook in the Pierpont Morgan Library, New York [hereafter PML].

7. Eden, *Kyrie Eleison*, pp.38–42.

8. *Jewish Chronicle*, 6 February 1891; Samuel Butler, *Notebooks* (Auckland: The Floating Press, 2014), p.169.

9. *Jewish Chronicle*, 30 November 1900.

10. Percy Young, *George Grove* (London: Macmillan, 1980), p.100.

11. Jacobs, *Sullivan*, p.6.

12. Benjamin Findon, *Sir Arthur Sullivan: His Life and Music* (London: James Nisbet, 1904), p.182.

13. Robert Francillon, *Mid-Victorian Memories* (London: Hodder & Stoughton, 1914), p.194.

14. Herman Klein, *Thirty Years of Musical Life in London* (New York: The Century Co., 1903), p.201.

15. Henry Lytton, *Secrets of a Savoyard* (London: Jarrolds, n.d.), p.62. *The World*, 13 November 1879, p.3.

16. *The World*, 13 November 1879, p.3.

17. Findon, *Sullivan*, p.10.

18. Percy Young, *Sir Arthur Sullivan* (London: J.M. Dent, 1971), p.2

19. Young, *Sullivan*, p.54.

20. Letter of 6 October 1856, quoted in Arthur Lawrence, *Sir Arthur Sullivan: Life Story, Letters and Reminiscences* (London: James Bowden, 1899), p.11.

21. Lawrence, *Sullivan*, pp.236–7.

22. 'Sir Arthur Sullivan Speaks for *Chums*', *Chums* 69 (3 January 1894), pp.295–6.

23. Leslie Baily, *The Gilbert & Sullivan Book*, revised edn. (London: Cassell & Co, 1956), p.34.

24. Herbert Sullivan and Newman Flower, *Sir Arthur Sullivan* (London: Cassell & Co., 1927), p.18.

25. Arthur Sullivan [hereafter AS] to his father, 5 June 1860: PML.

26. Henry Saxe Wyndham, *Arthur Seymour Sullivan* (London: Kegan, Paul, Trench, Trubner & Co., 1926), p.88.

27. Jacobs, *Sullivan*, p.178.

28. AS to nieces and nephews, 31 January 1885: PML.

2

1852–1861

Musical and Spiritual Formation

Arthur Sullivan's musical formation was effected during his teenage
years in three institutions: the Chapel Royal, where he was a chorister
between the ages of 12 and 15; the Royal Academy of Music, where
he studied from 14 to 16 as the first Mendelssohn scholar; and the
Conservatory of Music in Leipzig, which he attended from the age of
16 until just before his 19th birthday. Each of these places had a
considerable impact on him, deepening his childhood love of church
music and laying the foundations for his later career as a composer
and conductor of sacred works.

The Chapel Royal

Sullivan's time as a chorister in the Chapel Royal, which lasted from
April 1854 to June 1857, was the most formative period of his life in
terms of the influence that it had on both his musical career and his
faith. Its importance is acknowledged equally by those who regarded it
as a benign influence and by those for whom it was a malign one.
Thomas Helmore's brother Frederick believed that 'being established
in his new abode, the future Sir Arthur found himself in an atmosphere of music in accordance with his own spiritual longings.'[1] For
David Eden, by contrast, 'his entry into the Chapel Royal may be
regarded as the most grievous blow ever suffered by English music,
for it tainted him with the spiritual bankruptcy of Victorian
Anglicanism.'[2] His time there reinforced his early love of church
music and especially of the great Anglican choral tradition which
stretched from the mid-sixteenth century to his own time. It brought
him in touch with many of the leading church musicians of the day

and with fellow students who would be among the most important church composers of the later Victorian period. It also grounded him in the liturgical and theological traditions of the Church of England as well as giving him a particular love of royal occasions and ceremonial. It was his experience and enjoyment of church music while singing in the Chapel Royal that led him into this area of composition and profoundly influenced his style and choice of subject matter. Performing for royalty and at great state occasions undoubtedly fostered in him the unmistakable sense of patriotic Protestantism that characterizes so much of his sacred and secular music.

Tracing its origins back to Anglo-Saxon times and still in existence today, the Chapel Royal essentially makes up the monarch's ecclesiastical household and is one of the key links between the British Crown and the Established Church. In Sullivan's time its choir, which sang in services at the private royal chapels and at royal and state occasions, was made up of ten boys and sixteen gentlemen, split into two eight-man divisions who sang during alternate months. As one of the children of the Chapel Royal, Sullivan not only gained a superb grounding in English church music, comparable if not superior to what he would have received as a cathedral chorister, but found himself at the heart of the establishment with easy access to leading musicians and churchmen as well as to others in high society and Court circles. He also joined a long line of distinguished musicians who had sung in the Chapel Royal, either as boys or gentlemen, among them Thomas Tallis, Thomas Morley, Thomas Attwood, John Blow, and William Croft as well as contemporary composers like George Smart, John Goss, and Edward John Hopkins.[3]

The choristers' principal task was to sing at Sunday morning and evening services in the chapel at St James' Palace. The boys had to walk there from Thomas Helmore's house in 6 Cheyne Walk, Chelsea, where they boarded. It was a round trip of over 5 miles which they had to make in their heavy and conspicuous gold and scarlet coats. On at least one occasion they were accosted by a group of young hooligans and had to hitch up their coats and take to their heels. Helmore recalled that Sullivan, who had delicate health throughout his life, had to lie down every Sunday afternoon, exhausted by the morning service and the walk to and from the Chapel, before facing the rigours of repeating it in the evening. On weekdays the boys frequently sang in the morning services at St Mark's Training College for schoolmasters where Thomas Helmore was precentor and vice-principal. They were also expected to attend and perform in London motet and madrigal societies where boy trebles and male altos were still preferred to female singers. There were further opportunities to perform with the Sacred Harmonic Society and at the regular musical matinées held at Helmore's house. The boys' services were additionally required at royal christenings, weddings, and funerals, other state occasions, and major Christian festivals, including Christmas. This last commitment meant young Arthur missing the family celebrations. A touching letter from his mother written on 23 December 1855 notes: 'I shall miss your happy little face and black eyes at my dinner table'.[4]

From the first it was clear that Arthur Sullivan had an exceptional voice. The day after joining the Chapel Royal choir he was singing the duet in James Nares' anthem, 'Blessed is he that considereth the poor and the needy' at the Maundy Thursday service at the Royal Chapel in Whitehall and twelve days later he sang the soprano aria 'Rejoice greatly' from the *Messiah* in a concert at St Mark's College. Christopher Bridgman, a fellow treble, recalled many years later: 'His voice was a very pure high soprano. His top A or B flat used to ring out with brilliant effect, and apparently without effort. The enunciation of his words was very distinct and, moreover, he sang from his heart'.[5] Thomas Helmore noted that 'his voice was very sweet and his style of singing far more sympathetic than that of most boys'.[6] Charles Corfe, one of the first batch of choristers at St Michael's College, Tenbury Wells, a training school set up by Frederick Ouseley to promote choral music throughout the Church of England, could still vividly remember more than fifty years later Sullivan's treble solo in the verse, 'O pray for the peace of Jerusalem' from John Goss' anthem 'Praise the Lord' at the college's service of consecration in September 1856. 'I can hear it now', he wrote in 1918, 'the voice, wonderfully preserved and developed was then at its best'.[7] A month after singing in that service Sullivan became the first (i.e. senior) boy in the Chapel Royal choir.

It is difficult to judge what effect membership of the Chapel Royal had on Arthur Sullivan's own emerging religious beliefs. As master of the choristers, Thomas Helmore was specifically charged with presiding 'not only over the Musical, but over the general, and above all the moral and Christian education of the Children' and it was a duty that he took very seriously.[8] Twice every year all the boy choristers were examined by the sub-dean as to their Scriptural knowledge. It is clear that this side of their education was taken seriously by their teachers, if not necessarily by the boys themselves. A letter home in January 1855 records 'We have had the Gospel to write out ten times for not knowing it'.[9] Another letter written a few weeks earlier to his mother could be taken to indicate either Arthur's early interest in the female sex or his proficiency in and enthusiasm for his religious studies. It promises that he will give some unspecified young ladies 'a lesson or two in Religious Instruction when I go home'.[10] More exciting was the opportunity to be involved in state occasions full of ceremonial and pageantry and to mix with high society, both activities which he developed a taste for and continued to relish in adult life. He regularly performed before members of the royal family and prominent public figures and was rewarded for his singing with half a sovereign by both Prince Albert and the second Duke of Wellington.

Sullivan's years in the Chapel Royal contributed hugely to his musical education and exposed him to a wide range of sacred music with a specific focus on the Anglican choral tradition. Helmore himself was an enthusiastic devotee of plainsong and Anglican chant which consequently featured prominently in the services both at St James' Chapel and at St Mark's College. The anthems of the leading Tudor composers, Orlando Gibbons, Thomas Tallis, and William Byrd, featured prominently in the choir's repertoire, as did pieces by their lesser-known early-sixteenth-century predecessors and their eighteenth-century successors, William Boyce and George Frederick Handel. Arias and choruses from the *Messiah* were a staple of the public concerts given by the Chapel Royal choir. Sullivan was in the 1,500-strong chorus that performed the Hallelujah chorus when Queen Victoria re-opened the Crystal Palace at its new site in Sydenham, South London, in June 1854. Some months later he sang the soprano solos in Handel's *Judas Maccabeus* in a concert in Battersea.

He was also introduced to more recent works. Extracts from Mendelssohn's *Elijah* were a staple of the musical matinées held at 6 Cheyne Walk, which the composer himself had attended before his early death in 1847, and where the famous Swedish opera singer Jenny Lind often sang the soprano arias, entrancing Sullivan by her vocal quality and sensitive interpretation. Following her death in 1887 he told her widower, Otto Goldschmidt, 'She it was who made me feel that music was divine'.[11] The compositions of contemporary English church musicians also had a strong impact on him. He was much taken with the work of John Goss, who took over as composer to the Chapel Royal in 1856, enthusing to his father about 'Praise the Lord, O my soul', the piece in which he sang the treble solo at St Michael's College, Tenbury Wells: 'I like Mr Goss' anthem very much; it is very fine'.[12] He was also impressed by Frederick Gore Ouseley's oratorio *The Martyrdom of St Polycarp* in which he sang the solo soprano part at its first performance in the Sheldonian Theatre, Oxford, on 9 December 1854. Written as an exercise for the composer's doctoral thesis, it appealed to Sullivan so much that he copied the trio from it into his music book. Returning home some time later for the Christmas holidays, he recommended to his father the march which accompanied the advance of the heathens and copied it out from memory with full band parts.

Arthur Sullivan developed a youthful passion for oratorios, amassing a collection of scores using the money that he received for singing. A letter to his father, probably written in 1857, reported that he had put half a crown given to him by the bishop of London for singing 'With verdure clad' towards buying a copy of Handel's *Samson* at Novello's. On the same expedition he also bought a score of *Judas Maccabeus*. Noting that the cover of the Novello editions 'is scarlet cloth and gold', rather like the Chapel Royal children's coats, he gleefully pointed out 'Shan't we be well stocked with oratorios?' before signing off with his customary 'God bless you'.[13] In rather more serious vein, at the age of 17 he reprimanded his brother Fred for making frivolous remarks about the most famous of all sacred oratorios: 'The slighting manner in which you speak of Handel's *Messiah* is an insult to sacred music—and besides it is no fault [of his] if it is not exactly lively. Perhaps you would have liked him to have interpolated a few comic songs in each act.'[14] Ironically, in later years Sullivan would be accused by his sterner critics of doing exactly that in his own sacred works.

If the scolding of his brother shows how seriously Sullivan took sacred music, he was not above having a little fun with it as well. On a wet half-holiday, Bridgman recalled, he would compose impromptu pieces and conduct his fellow choristers, each equipped with a comb covered with paper:

> It was a great delight to him to take some popular comic song or common tune of the day and turn it into a psalm or hymn tune. Some of his best hymn tunes, if played in appropriate time and method, will be found to have originated in this way. He was very clever at fugue. He would frequently say to one of us, 'Now, like a good chap, hum or whistle me something', and his request being complied with, he would rush off to the pianoforte and make a good fugue from the subject given him.[15]

Sullivan's efforts at composing during his three years in the Chapel Royal were not confined to these parodies and light-hearted fugues. He wrote three sacred pieces which set him off on his career as a composer of church music. The first, an anthem, 'Sing unto the Lord and bless his name', was written when he was just 12. He showed it to George Smart who was sufficiently impressed to tell him to copy out the parts. In May 1855, Smart conducted a performance of it in the Chapel Royal. Afterwards Charles James Blomfield, the dean of the Chapel Royal, then as now an office undertaken by the bishop of London, called the young composer into the vestry, congratulated him, and told him that perhaps he would be writing an oratorio some day. Sullivan recalled that Blomfield was anxious to strike a spiritual as well as a musical note and 'said that there was something higher to attend to, and then Mr Helmore said that I was a very good boy indeed. Whereupon he [Blomfield] shook hands with me, with a half sovereign.'[16] This episcopal reward for his moral as well as his musical prowess was Sullivan's first recorded earning from composition.

The second sacred piece that Sullivan composed during his time at the Chapel Royal, which was to be his first published work, was written when he was just 13. It was a song based on the two opening verses of Hosea 14 as they appear in the Authorized Version of the Bible, 'O Israel, return unto the Lord thy God; for thou hast fallen by thine iniquity. Take with you words, and turn to the Lord. Say unto him, Take away all iniquity and receive us graciously.' It is an unusual text for a composer to choose, let alone such a young one—I am not aware of these verses being used as the basis for any other song or anthem. Sullivan may have been influenced by the great soprano aria that begins part two of Mendelssohn's *Elijah*, 'Hear ye, Israel' which he had heard Jenny Lind singing. Based on verses from Isaiah, it has a somewhat similar message both about Israel not heeding God's commandments and also of God being 'He that comforteth'. There are undoubtedly echoes of Mendelssohn in Sullivan's setting of the verses from Hosea, although it is altogether simpler, gentler, and more wistful than 'Hear ye, Israel'. Set for boy soprano voices, it begins on a high F sharp and goes up to a high A, giving it a floating, ethereal quality. It also has an underlying sense of reassurance. It is interesting that Sullivan chose a text which is about rebelliousness, backsliding, and falling through iniquity but which also asks the Lord to 'receive us graciously' and which, in his setting, emphasizes and repeats the theme of returning to God. His youthful choice of verses about a wayward people returning to a gracious God provides an early hint of a theological motif, the forgiving, merciful nature of God and his embrace of the repentant sinner, which would recur several times in his sacred works. He wrote it in Tavistock while staying with his fellow chorister, Christopher Bridgman, to whose mother he dedicated it. Thomas Helmore arranged for a small quantity of copies to be printed and published by Novello in November 1855.

His third sacred composition was a setting of Psalm 103, 'Bless the Lord, O my soul, and all that is within me bless his holy name'. Composed in 1856, it was unpublished but is contained in an autograph manuscript book sold at Sotheby's in 1966. An undated letter to his father almost certainly written shortly after its composition, asking 'When are you going to sing my Psalm?' suggests that Thomas Sullivan had some involvement in the music at Sandhurst Parish Church.[17]

The most important and abiding influence during Sullivan's time at the Chapel Royal was Thomas Helmore (1811–90). The son of a Congregational minister, he was attracted to Anglicanism through the Tractarian movement's emphasis on liturgy and recovering ancient church music and was ordained into the Church of England. He served as vice-principal and precentor of St Mark's College, Chelsea, the first Church of England teacher training college, where, under his direction, prayers and responses were intoned and psalms sung unaccompanied either to Gregorian or Anglican chant by the entire student body gathered every morning in the Chapel. He retained the precentorship when in 1846 he became master of the children of the Chapel Royal, with responsibility for the choristers' education and pastoral care. He was the first clergyman to hold this office since the Reformation and did much to improve the boys' moral and physical welfare following a lax and cruel regime under his predecessor.

A distinguished musician in his own right, Helmore played a decisive role in raising the standards and changing the face of Victorian church music. Together with his younger brother, Frederick, he was largely instrumental in establishing choral services, with sung anthems and chanted psalms and responses, in parish churches throughout the Church of England. His own particular passion was for plainsong which he believed to be the perfect form of congregational singing. As Sullivan himself noted, Helmore 'was enthusiastic for the revival of old Church music, and was at the head of the movement for the use of Gregorian music in the Church'.[18] Central to his efforts to restore its use were his publications *The Psalter Noted* (1849), *A Manual of Plainsong* (1850), and the *Hymnal Noted* which appeared in two parts in 1851 and 1856. This last volume was a collection of plainsong melodies attached to translations of early Latin hymn texts by John Mason Neale, which included 'Of the Father's love begotten' and 'O come, O come, Emmanuel'. Helmore and Neale also collaborated on a volume of *Carols for Christmastide* which appeared in 1853 and launched 'Good King Wenceslas' on the world.

Helmore recognized Sullivan's potential as both a performer and a composer, and did much to establish the foundations of his career. He was particularly taken with the sensitivity of his interpretation of sacred music, writing after a service at St Neots Church in Cambridgeshire: 'Arthur sang a very elaborate solo in church today . . . his expression was beautiful. It brought tears very near my eyes . . . but as I was immediately to enter the pulpit, I was obliged to restrain myself'.[19] Helmore gave Sullivan a good deal of solo work and encouraged him greatly, not just with singing but with composing, telling his mother that, as well as getting on with his Latin and not neglecting his general education, every week 'he should compose a little something, a song or a sanctus, or an anthem of his own. This is the practical way of testing his industry'.[20]

It was Helmore more than anyone else who kindled and nurtured Sullivan's love of church music. He had three specific influences on both the nature and style of his pupil's future work in this area of composition. The first came through immersion in plainsong and Anglican chant. Helmore was renowned for the beauty and purity of his chanting on one note. George Elvey, organist of St George's Chapel, Windsor, heard him intoning a service on a day when there was no choir or organ and remarked, 'I never in my life heard anything to approach the grandeur and solemnity of that monotone service'.[21] Sullivan employed plainchant in several of his anthems and liturgical settings. Its influence may also lie at the root of his frequent use of a string of repeated notes, particularly at the beginning of pieces, a practice especially noticeable in his hymn tunes and sacred songs. More generally, I wonder if the grounding in plainsong and its virtues which he received from Helmore was a factor in making him such a master of word setting. Plainchant follows the natural rhythms and cadences of speech. It is, indeed, in some senses an enhanced form of speaking. Sullivan's schooling in this particular technique gave him a particular concern with setting words clearly and economically, generally eschewing melisma, lengthy trills, and cadenzas. It also made him the master of the patter song.

The second area where Helmore made a distinctive and lasting contribution to Sullivan's musical style was through introducing him to the work of the early-sixteenth-century English composers who featured prominently in the Chapel Royal repertoire. Their influence can be heard in the clean, bright, straightforwardness of so much of Sullivan's music, both in the secular and the sacred spheres, the quality which makes it so English. In the lecture which he delivered on music in Birmingham in 1888 he enthused about the superiority of the English predecessors of Tallis and Byrd—he cited specifically Edwards, Redford, Shepperd, Tye, White, Johnson, and Merbecke—over the Continental predecessors of Palestrina:

> They were their equals in science, and they far surpassed them in the tunefulness and what I may call the common sense of their music. Their compositions display a 'sweet reasonableness', a human feeling, a suitability to the words, and a determination to be something more than a mere scientific and mechanical puzzle, which few, if any, of the Continental composers before 1550 can be said to exhibit.[22]

The attributes which Sullivan singled out as distinguishing the work of these early Tudor composers—sweet reasonableness, human feeling, and suitability of setting to the words—were precisely those which characterized so much of his own music.

The third major way in which Helmore influenced his talented young pupil musically was more direct and immediate, through getting him started on the business of writing and arranging hymn tunes. Arthur contributed four harmonized accompaniments to plainsong melodies for an edition of the *Hymnal Noted*, published in 1858. It was his first commission and his first experience of working in this genre. He later wrote that the knowledge and experience gained in this early venture 'assisted me materially in making my big collection of hymn tunes for the Society for the Promotion of Christian Knowledge, entitled "Church Hymns".'[23]

Helmore shaped Sullivan's character as well as his musical tastes and direction. It could hardly be otherwise when he was for three years effectively a second father, as he was for the other choristers living in Cheyne Walk who saw considerably more of him than of their own parents during their time in the Chapel Royal. Although High Church in his attitude to worship and music, in other respects Helmore held to the liberal creed of his Congregationalist father. He had a broad theological outlook and a generous spirit, and he almost certainly recognized and nurtured these same qualities in the gifted young chorister under his care. A deep and genuine bond of mutual affection and admiration developed between them. In a moving and heartfelt letter sent to his old master in 1862, when he was back from studies at Leipzig and setting out on his professional career as composer and conductor, Sullivan wrote:

> To you I owe more than to anyone else perhaps. The high principles and elevated tone applying equally to Art as to morals with which you strove more by example than by precept to imbue me (God grant that it may have been with some success), the care and attention bestowed upon every branch of my education, and the constant and kindly interest taken in my progress, have been in no small manner influential in making me what I am—viz: an earnest labourer in the cause of true Art.[24]

Sullivan continued to revere Helmore after he had become a highly successful composer and achieved fame and fortune. Writing to his mother in 1875, he described him as 'good in every sense—a thoroughly good, religious man, and a kindly man of the world as well' and he told Arthur Lawrence that he had been greatly influenced throughout his life by Helmore's 'great idea of relying on the boys' sense of honour'.[25] Helmore officiated at Fred Sullivan's wedding at St Margaret's, Westminster, in September 1862, and Arthur asked him to take the funeral services of both his father and his mother. For his part, Helmore sought to keep his former pupil true to the Christian faith which he had played an important role in instilling into him. The year before he died, he sent Sullivan as a Christmas present a copy of a new translation of Thomas à Kempis' classic of spiritual devotion, *The Imitation of Christ*. In his letter of thanks, written in the midst of rehearsals for the American premiere of *The Gondoliers*, Sullivan wrote: 'It seems to me, from the hasty glance that I have been able to throw at the book, that the lines require no music—the rhythm itself is music, and of a most beautiful character'.[26]

Two other older musicians had an important formative influence on Sullivan in his Chapel Royal days. George Smart (1776–1867), who first heard him sing and recommended him to Helmore, had himself been a chorister in the Chapel Royal in the 1780s. He had sung in the first great Handel commemoration in 1784, played the drums for Josef Haydn, and known Beethoven, Weber, and Mendelssohn. He was organist to the Chapel Royal from 1822 to 1856 and composer there from 1838 to 1856. Smart greatly encouraged Sullivan, conducting his first anthem and showing a keen interest in his work. He was chairman of the committee which awarded him the first Mendelssohn scholarship which sent him initially to the Royal Academy of Music and then to Leipzig. He sent a glowing testimonial to the professors there and did all he could to further the young composer's career. Sullivan characteristically reciprocated this kindness, continuing to visit his old benefactor when he was well into his 80s and writing a moving letter to his widow after his death (p. 76).

John Goss (1800–80), another former Chapel Royal chorister, went on to become professor of harmony at the Royal Academy of Music and organist of St Paul's Cathedral from 1838 to 1872. In 1856, he succeeded Smart as composer to the Chapel Royal and it was in this capacity that he got to know and admire Sullivan, although he probably also met him socially as he was a near neighbour of

Helmore, living two doors away in Cheyne Walk. Goss was among the leading church composers in mid-Victorian Britain, turning out a stream of anthems and hymn tunes, his best-known and most enduring being 'Praise my soul', written for Henry Lyte's 'Praise my soul, the King of heaven' in 1869, and 'Humility' for 'See amid the winter's snow' in 1871. Goss, like Helmore, was a strong Christian influence on Sullivan, seeking in later years to remind him of his faith. In a letter written in July 1866, he wrote: 'you and I have been taught and believe in Him whose hands and guidance are in all things'.[27] The two men were great admirers of each other's work and it was fitting that despite the forty-year age gap between them they received their Cambridge doctorates of music together in 1876. If Goss had a particular influence on Sullivan it was perhaps in reinforcing the importance of taking great care over setting the words of hymns and anthems. This was a characteristic that both teacher and pupil shared. The judgement that W.A. Barrett made about Goss in 1882 could equally have applied to his pupil: 'his music is always melodious and beautifully written for the voice, and is remarkable for a union of solidity and grace, with a certain unaffected native charm'.[28]

Alongside these contacts with leading church musicians of the day, Sullivan also forged close relationships with young musicians of his own generation. Joseph Barnby (1838–96) was a boy chorister at York Minister and came to London in 1854 to study at the Royal Academy of Music. It is not entirely clear when he first met Sullivan but they became and remained friends, despite Barnby being pipped at the post for the Mendelssohn scholarship by his younger competitor. Barnby went on to have a distinguished musical career as precentor (head of music) at Eton College and principal of the Guildhall School of Music.

Another contemporary with whom Sullivan became very friendly was John Stainer (1840–1901). The two almost certainly met through singing together at the grand occasions which brought together the choirs of the Chapel Royal, St Paul's Cathedral, where Stainer was a chorister, Westminster Abbey, St Michael's College, Tenbury Wells, and Oxford and Cambridge college chapels. Sullivan's obituary in the *Musical Times* noted that 'the two lads, when off duty, were wont to delight in penny trips together on Thames steamboats, their enjoyment of those water excursions being considerably enhanced by a copious consumption of nuts and oranges'.[29] Stainer later recalled a hilarious incident in either 1855 or 1856, when both he and Sullivan were up in the organ loft at St Paul's. John Goss inadvertently walked across the pedals in the middle of a service, sending a sustained roar of 'alarming thunderings' which frightened the congregation and put a temporary stop to the sermon.[30] Around the same time the two teenagers sought to assist Frederick Ouseley's efforts to build a new organ in the chapel of St Michael's College using gutta-percha, a natural form of rubber obtained from trees in southeast Asia, for the pipes. The experiment was abandoned when Ouseley complained about the strong smell. Stainer, who succeeded Goss as organist at St Paul's Cathedral in 1872, remained a close friend and supporter of Sullivan throughout his life and was one of the pall bearers at his funeral.

These mentors and friends whom Sullivan acquired during his formative years in the Chapel Royal were all first and foremost church musicians. Helmore, Smart, Goss, and Stainer hardly wrote a note of secular music between them. Barnby did turn his hand to part songs and parlour ballads but devoted most of his efforts to sacred works. Sullivan retained very close friendships with these and other church musicians in later life, and they were often his strongest champions and defenders when he was assailed by critics. Perhaps it is not so strange that it was those who grew up, as he had, steeped in church music and who shared his early fascination and love for it who became his natural soul mates.

Sullivan himself looked back to his days in the scarlet and gold uniform, which came to an end when his voice broke in June 1857 shortly after his 15th birthday, as among the happiest of his life. His three years as a chorister in the Chapel Royal greatly influenced his style and direction as a composer as well as initiating several of his deepest and most enduring friendships. They immersed him in the world of church music which he relished as a singer, a listener, and, increasingly, as a composer. Did they also 'taint him with the spiritual bankruptcy of Victorian Anglicanism' as David Eden suggested? Were they the source of that artificially sanctimonious style and the dull religiosity which critics identified as his besetting sin? A relatively early biographer, Henry Saxe Wyndham, suggested that 'Sullivan's early musical education . . . had been much too exclusively ecclesiastical'.[31] It is true that he was exposed to little other than liturgical and sacred music in these formative teenage years. As we have seen, however, it was music of a broad and varied scope, encompassing plainsong, chant, the work of the English composers of the sixteenth century, the oratorios of Handel and Mendelssohn, as well as contemporary compositions.

There was undoubtedly both a sentimentality and an ethereal strain in several of Sullivan's sacred compositions that can be traced directly to the influence of his time as a choirboy. Perhaps the most directly obvious legacy of his Chapel Royal training was his tendency to employ a high soprano line floating over the other voices at the end of his part-songs, rather in the manner of Allegri's *Miserere*, a work which he greatly admired. This device, which perhaps had its origins in his own exceptionally high vocal reach, conveys an impression of angelic voices expressing a sense of peace, calm, and reassurance. It can sometimes seem cloying, as can the hushed almost sepulchral tones which he so often employed in his sacred songs, but as in everything he wrote, it came from the heart and was sincere rather than contrived or affected.

Herbert Sullivan was surely right to say that it was the Chapel Royal which gave his uncle 'the note of religious melody which coloured his own composing in later years and often stole, as if unaware, into his operas'.[32] There was undoubtedly a religious note in much of Sullivan's subsequent work but it was hardly spiritually bankrupt or dull. Rather it was highly melodic and often distinctly theatrical—too much so for his many rather po-faced and disapproving critics. Those latter qualities owed much to his early years listening to and learning to play the instruments in his father's military band, but they also came in part from his experience as a chorister. Through the Chapel Royal as much as through the Sandhurst band room, his introduction to music was by way of melody, a quality which continued to infuse his own work, both sacred and secular.

What of the lasting spiritual legacy of his three years there? Former choirboys are not always renowned for the strength of their faith and piety in later life but in Sullivan's case the biblical texts and precepts to which he was exposed daily as a chorister did stay with him and informed his personal as well as his professional development.

The Chapel Royal experience deepened his Christian faith as well as his attachment to the church.

Continental Parallels

It is worth pausing briefly here to set Arthur Sullivan's early training in and lasting attachment to church music in a European context. Several of his Continental contemporaries who went on to become leading operetta composers had similar youthful exposure to sacred music and continued, like him, to write in this genre even though their main work was for the theatre.

Jacques Offenbach (1819–80), rightly described as 'composer of some of the most exhilaratingly gay and tuneful music ever written' and founder of the French tradition of *opéra bouffe* of which the Savoy operas have often been seen as the English equivalent, was the son of the cantor in the Cologne synagogue.[33] Jacob, as he then was, sang in the choir of a synagogue in Paris while attending the Conservatoire there from the age of 14. Some of his earliest compositions were Jewish chants and songs written for the synagogue. They are now in the manuscript collection of the library of the Hebrew Union College in New York.

Offenbach converted to Roman Catholicism when he married his devoutly Catholic Spanish wife, Herminie, in 1844. He subsequently composed Masses for the marriages of two of his daughters. Although the manuscripts have remained in private family archives, two *Ave Marias* and an *Agnus Dei* which have been published probably come from them. He also wrote a soprano aria, *Gloire à Dieu*, and *Litanies de la Vierge* for tenor and organ. Like Sullivan, he put religious themes and music into his stage works. There are invocations to the Virgin Mary in *Les Trois baisers du Diable*, a one-act operetta of 1857; in *La haine*, a historic drama for which he wrote the music in 1874; in pastiches of church music in the anthem sung by the Crusoe family after Robinson has run off to sea in *Robinson Crusoe*; and in the introit which accompanies Helen of Troy's first entrance in *La belle Hélène*. He also composed a sacred song, *Espère, enfant, demain*, which became a choir piece, *Espoir en Dieu*, in an unfinished symphony that he wrote in 1871 and was eventually used for the finale of *Les contes d'Hoffmann*, 'Des cendres de ton coeur'.

Offenbach suffered similar criticism to Sullivan for abandoning the sacred and serious music in which he had been brought up in favour of light frivolous pieces for the theatre. As one of his biographers pointedly commented, 'the father preached the gospel of God, and the son preached the gospel of joy'.[34] But behind his love of life and happy, optimistic disposition there was a more serious and spiritual dimension. In an interesting essay on his childhood, Richard Fischer has argued that Offenbach retained something of the strong Jewish faith in which he was raised and specifically that he was gripped by the Biblical theme of expulsion from Paradise and loss of childhood innocence which he returned to several times in his works. For Fischer, this was heightened by the sense of loneliness that Offenbach felt when he was sent away from home at the age of 14 to study in the Paris Conservatoire, giving much of his more sentimental music a wistful sense of memory.[35]

Franz von Suppé (1819–95), who composed around thirty operettas and 180 farces, ballets, and other stage works, had an even more similar upbringing to Sullivan, being schooled in church music while singing as a boy in the choir of the cathedral in the Dalmatian city of Zara (now Zadar). Encouraged by the choirmaster, he started writing his first musical work, a Mass, at the age of 13. He extended and completed it three years later following the death of his father—as in the case of Sullivan, family tragedy triggered a religious composition. An ambitious work, incorporating a *Gloria* lasting twenty-one minutes, it was revised and extended three times before being published much later in his life. Suppé also wrote a *Requiem* following the death of his friend and mentor, Franz Pokorny, director of several theatres in Austria where he had worked as conductor and composer. It was performed at a memorial service for Pokorny in 1855. He later extended it to form an oratorio, *Extremum judicium*, which could be performed as a concert piece. Towards the end of his life, Suppé returned to sacred music, composing single works for use in church. Sullivan's exact contemporary, the Austrian operetta composer, Carl Zeller (1842–98), most famous for *Der Vogelhändler*, was recruited at the age of 11 into the choir of the Imperial Chapel in the Hofburg in Vienna, an institution similar to the Chapel Royal in many ways. Like Sullivan, he had an exceptionally pure boy soprano voice and went on to write choral works as well as operettas and songs.

Several leading French operetta composers received their musical education at the École de Musique Religieuse et Classique established in Paris by Louis Niedermeyer in 1853. Niedermeyer, a Swiss composer who had switched from opera to sacred music, was, like Thomas Helmore, an enthusiast for plainsong and Gregorian chant. The curriculum in his boarding school for boys from the age of 11 included the principles of liturgical music, organ studies, and sixteenth-century counterpoint. Among the pupils at the École Niedermeyer were two near-contemporaries of Sullivan, Edmond Audran (1840–1901), a church organist who wrote a Mass in 1873 and then switched to writing numerous operettas, and Léon Vasseur (1844–1917), who resigned his post as organist at Notre-Dame church in Versailles to concentrate on writing for the theatre. His output included two Masses, two motets, a Magnificat, and several anthems as well as twenty operettas. Later students included Victor Roger (1853–1903), composer of successful operettas like *Joséphine vendue par ses soeurs* and *Les Vingt-huit jours de Clairette*; and André Messager (1853–1929), who was organist and choirmaster at the prestigious St Sulpice church in Paris before becoming stage composer at the Folies-Bergère and later musical director of the Opéra Comique. Although not educated at the École de Musique Religieuse et Classique, Léo Delibes (1836–91), who wrote several comic operas and operettas, started out as a boy chorister at the church of La Madeleine in Paris and later became organist of St Pierre de Chaillot.

In European terms, therefore, Sullivan was far from being alone or even unusual as a composer of light or comic opera who had been schooled in church music and who crossed over between the stage and the sanctuary in his compositions. The fact that so many leading nineteenth-century operetta composers had similar training raises interesting questions about the possible religious roots of this type of music. The importance of Jewish influences on the development of musical theatre has long been acknowledged and is the subject of several recent monographs.[36] The Christian influences have not been so well explored although I have myself suggested that while the music-led genre of nineteenth-century and early-twentieth-century Continental operetta may have Catholic roots, the emphasis on the primacy of the word which distinguishes both Gilbert and Sullivan and twentieth-century musicals is a distinctly Protestant phenomenon.[37] Sullivan's sound and thorough schooling in the Anglican choral tradition and English church music had a bigger impact on the tone and ethos of the Savoy operas than is at first apparent.

It is appropriate to conclude this short digression on Continental parallels with the reflections of perhaps the most famous of all operetta composers, Franz Lehár (1870–1948). Like Sullivan, he was the son of an army bandmaster and grew up surrounded by military music. Unlike him, he was not schooled in church music and, as far as I can discern, he did not write any sacred pieces, unless one counts a 'Preludium religioso' in his early and unperformed one-act opera, *Rodrigo*. He was, however, a devout Roman Catholic and he had a great sense of the spiritual power of music. Towards the end of his life, in 1944, he reflected on the impact made on him as a young boy by a performance of Franz Liszt's oratorio *Christus* conducted by the composer and in which his father was among the violinists in the orchestra:

> At that moment there was awakened for the first time within my childlike soul the realisation that music, the archetype of all the arts, is more than a means of entertainment or livelihood, but a gift from God to uplift, cheer and comfort the heart, and that the vocation of musician means ministering to man's affirmation of life and his zest for life.[38]

Sullivan's reaction on hearing Jenny Lind singing the arias from Mendelssohn's *Elijah* at Helmore's house in Cheyne Walk comes to mind. He shared Franz Lehár's sense of the musician's vocation to uplift, comfort, and affirm life. Both composers in their very different ways infused their writing for the stage with a spiritual dimension.

The Royal Academy of Music

Arthur Sullivan's formal musical education took place at the Royal Academy of Music where he began his studies in September 1856, aged just 14, having won the Mendelssohn scholarship. He was the first recipient of this prestigious award, founded in memory of the German composer who was so popular in Britain and who had died in 1847, and designed to enable a promising young British or Irish musician to study in both London and Leipzig. The youngest of the seventeen candidates for the award (only qualifying by six weeks for the minimum age of application which was 14—the maximum was 20), he won out in the final elimination examination against the oldest candidate, Joseph Barnby, who was just a month off his 18th birthday. The award of the scholarship, which was subject to annual renewal on the basis of good academic performance, was a godsend to someone whose family did not have the financial means to support this level of education. His father's emotional response on hearing the news from Thomas Helmore expressed Christian faith as well as paternal pride: 'I could not suppress my tears that accompanied my prayer to the Almighty for His goodness . . . Should the Almighty spare him I think he will at no distant day achieve much greater things'.[39]

At this stage of its history, the Academy was essentially a specialist musical secondary school, admitting gifted pupils from the ages of 10 to 15, rather than a full-blown conservatory. Arthur studied the theoretical rudiments of music, including harmony and counterpoint, in which his teacher was John Goss, as well as piano and violin, and basic composition. For his first year of study, he continued to sing in the Chapel Royal and live with the Helmores at Cheyne Walk. After his voice broke in June 1857, forcing him to leave the ranks of the Chapel Royal choristers, he took up residence at the new family home in Ponsonby Street, Pimlico, to which his parents had just moved on his father's appointment at the newly opened Royal Military School of Music at Kneller Hall in Twickenham. Originally hired to teach the clarinet, Thomas Sullivan switched to the larger brass instruments, particularly the bombardon, the military band equivalent of the E Flat tuba in an orchestra, in which he came to specialize. An unnamed student provided a pen-portrait which suggests that he had both the genial temperament and the musical versatility inherited by his son:

> He welcomed one with a smile and generally had a little joke to crack or tale to tell which made the lesson all the brighter. Sometimes he would give a dissertation on the violin during the lunch hour to those who cared to avail themselves of it, and the opportunity was readily seized. He also took the beginners on the clarinet—in fact nothing came amiss to him, for he was at much at home teaching on the trombone or bombardon as the clarinet or violin.[40]

In his first year at the Academy, Arthur set Shakespeare's 'It was a lover and his lass' for duet and chorus, the beginning of a life-long love

Arthur Sullivan

affair with the works of the Bard which bore fruit in both song settings and orchestral pieces. His leaving concert in July 1858 included the performance of an overture in D minor which he dedicated to John Goss.

Leipzig

In September 1858, Arthur Sullivan moved to Germany to continue his studies at the Conservatory of Music in Leipzig. Founded in 1843 by Felix Mendelssohn as the Conservatorium der Musik and based in the Gewandhaus, home of the Leipzig Symphony Orchestra, it is the oldest university school of music in Germany. The teachers at the Leipzig Conservatory were famous for their conservative classical preferences. Devoted to the works of Mendelssohn, Schubert, and Beethoven, they were uneasy about Brahms, Schumann, and Liszt, and deeply suspicious of Wagner. Sullivan never much liked the works of Wagner, and to that extent he followed his mentors, but in other respects he was more modern and open-minded. He loved Schumann's music and came greatly to admire and promote the sacred corpus of Liszt, whom he met several times in Leipzig. He had a very high regard for Schubert, but his greatest affection, perhaps not surprisingly, was reserved for Mendelssohn, the composer who almost certainly influenced him most and with whom his own sacred works were most often compared.

The teacher who had most impact on Sullivan at Leipzig was Ignaz Moscheles (1794–1870), his principal piano tutor. Born in Prague to an affluent Jewish family, he had converted to Anglicanism on settling in England in 1822 and come to teach at the Leipzig Conservatorium at his friend Mendelssohn's request in 1846. As a young man, while still a practising Jew and living in Vienna, he had collaborated with Beethoven who had entrusted him with the preparation of the piano score for *Fidelio*. On the last page of his manuscript, before presenting it to Beethoven, Moscheles wrote *Fine mit gottes Hülfe* (*Finished with God's Help*). Beethoven later appended the words *O Mensch, hilf dir selber!* (*O Man, Help Thyself!*). Another teacher who left his mark was Moritz Hauptmann, cantor of the Thomaskirche, who taught harmony and fugue classes in the room in which Johann Sebastian Bach, a previous cantor, had written some of his greatest sacred works.

As well as taking classes in the principles of music, composition, performing, and conducting, and pursuing studies on their chosen instruments (in Sullivan's case, violin and piano), students were expected to attend the regular orchestral concerts in the Gewandhaus. These raised a religious difficulty for Sullivan. In his first month in Leipzig he wrote to his mother saying that he would not be attending the first two Gewandhaus concerts 'as they are on a Sunday'.[41] He stuck to these strict Sabbatarian principles throughout his time there, giving a negative answer to the first question that George Smart put to him on his return home, 'Did you go to any concerts on a Sunday?' thereby delighting his pious patron.[42] Later in life, he dropped these youthful puritan scruples and became a strong advocate of Sunday afternoon concerts in London.

Smart, who was chairman of the Mendelssohn scholarship committee, provided financial support to help his young protegée extend his time at Leipzig for a further year beyond the two that the scholarship covered. Thomas Sullivan also contributed substantially to his son's education and expenses there, working four evenings a week teaching at the piano makers, Broadwoods, to supplement his earnings at Kneller Hall. A grateful Sullivan dedicated to Smart the one religious piece which he seems to have composed during his time in Leipzig, an anthem entitled 'We have heard with our ears'. He sent him an additional copy to be passed on to Helmore, and the anthem was performed at the Chapel Royal in January 1860.

Sullivan's other compositions while studying in Leipzig included a string quartet in D minor; an overture in E major, *Der Rosenfest*, based on a scene from Thomas Moore's Oriental romance; *Lalla Rookh*, about the daughter of a seventeenth-century mogul emperor; and incidental music to Shakespeare's *The Tempest* which was performed at his graduation concert on 7 April 1861 with Mendelssohn's brother in the audience. Outside his musical studies, he took the chance to extend his language skills by acquiring fluency in German. He also extended his religious knowledge and experience by going several times to the Leipzig synagogue, albeit primarily for musical rather than spiritual reasons. He was struck by the repeated use there of a particular melody chanted by the minister (as he described him) involving 'a quaint progression in the minor'.[43] More than thirty years later he used this for the aria 'Lord of our chosen race' sung

by the Jewish character Rebecca in his grand opera *Ivanhoe*. One of
Offenbach's earliest compositions, a waltz entitled *Rebecca* published in
1837, was similarly based on traditional synagogue melodies.

The charm and sociability which were to be so marked a feature of
Sullivan's adult character were much on display during his time at
Leipzig, as were his fondness for females and tendency to flirt. A fellow
student, John Barnett, observed that his 'genial and delightful manner' and 'charming boyish ways' made him very popular with his
fellow students.[44] Barnett's cousins, Rosamond and Clara, who were
also students at the Conservatory, were the first of many young ladies
to succumb to the Sullivan charm. He was particularly taken with
Rosamond, to whom he dedicated a German song, 'Ich möchte
hinaus es jauchzen', but it was her younger sister, Clara, who fell
for him in a big way, being bowled over by 'the smiling youth with
an oval, olive-tinted face, dark eyes, a large generous mouth and the
crop of dark curly hair . . . the sight of him excited in me a strange
emotion, never before experienced'.[45] The 14-year-old Clara was
convinced that she was in love but disturbed by Sullivan's constant
flirting with other girls, not just her sister but also many others
who came his way, including 'a little Irish girl' whom he was all
over when she felt he should have been paying attention to her.
She later came to realize that his passions and flirtations were 'only
ripples on the surface of his feelings' and 'fires of straw which quickly
burnt out'.[46]

Although she was troubled by his 'flirtatious propensity', Clara
Barnett was also struck by Sullivan's acts of kindness. One such
occurred when, having secretly copied out the parts of a string quartet
which she had composed, he gathered some of the best players at the
conservatory to rehearse and play it at a surprise party for her. For
that she could forgive him for the fickleness of his affections. Writing
her memoirs more than fifty years later, she could still recall vividly the
effect that the assured, poised 16-year-old had had on her. She also
remembered how she had been struck by his ability to make whoever
he was talking to feel that they were the sole focus of his attention, and
by the way that he used his natural charm to make influential friends.
Whenever distinguished visitors came to the Gewandhaus, he always
somehow managed to be in the front row to meet them while others
just observed from a distance:

It was part of Sullivan's nature to ingratiate himself with everyone that crossed his path. He always wanted to make an impression, and what is more, he always succeeded in doing it . . . It was this instinct, followed on a larger scale, that had much to do with his subsequent social success in high quarters and his intimacy at the court of England. He was a natural courtier; which did not prevent him, however, from being a very lovable person.[47]

This was a shrewd and prescient observation. Sullivan had a particular talent for making friends with those who were influential and important in society and who were in a position to help him along in his career and his rise up the social ladder. On his return from Leipzig, he assiduously cultivated his contacts with those who had been involved with the Mendelssohn scholarship committee, notably Otto Goldschmidt and his wife Jenny Lind, and Henry Chorley, one of the leading music and literary critics of the time, with whom he was to collaborate on his first opera, *The Sapphire Necklace*, which was never performed, and on a masque entitled *Kenilworth* based on Walter Scott's novel. Sullivan was something of a social climber and Clara Barnett was right that he was also a natural courtier. But she was right, too, in saying that he was also a very lovable person who was genuinely devoted to friends and family, and would go out of his way to help them. His charm and sociability were not just a smooth, cynical veneer. They were integral to his generous and sympathetic personality. He felt genuine affection and admiration as well as gratitude towards those who helped him on his way. When Karl Klingemann, another member of the Mendelssohn scholarship committee, who had himself been a pupil of Mendelssohn, died in 1862, Sullivan wrote a moving and heartfelt letter to his widow describing him as 'an upright man and true Christian'.[48]

In addition to greatly improving his own conducting, composing, and performing skills, Sullivan's period of study in Leipzig broadened his musical appreciation. Towards the end of his time there, he wrote that 'Besides increasing and maturing my judgment of music it has taught me how good works ought to be done'.[49] Despite forsaking their Sabbath concerts, he was bowled over by the orchestral playing he heard at the Gewandhaus, being especially moved by a performance of Beethoven's C Minor Symphony. He was also impressed by the respect accorded to the sacred music of Leipzig's most famous former resident, J.S. Bach. Sullivan went to several services at the Thomaskirche where many of Bach's works had first been performed and where they were undergoing a significant revival in the 1850s. It is not clear whether he attended the first fully complete performance of the B Minor Mass which took place there on 3 June 1859, conducted by Carl Riedel. There is no reference to it in his diary or his letters, but it seems strange that he would have missed the opportunity to have heard a work which he later described as containing his own favourite piece of music and of which he would himself conduct the first complete performance in Britain twenty-seven years later (p. 133). Whether or not he was in the audience in the Thomaskirche for that celebrated performance in 1859, there is no doubt that other concerts which he did attend during his time in Leipzig laid the foundations for his life-long love of Bach's sacred works.

Not all the performances that Sullivan attended while he was in Germany impressed him. The centenary of Handel's death led him to make a pilgrimage to Halle in August 1859 where he was deeply disappointed by a performance of *Samson* in a church there, as he told Smart:

> A more wretched performance it was never my good fortune to hear. All the tempi were taken wrong, many of the best things left out, and altogether is quite unworthy of the occasion. The fact is that they do not understand Handel in Germany and have not the traditional reading of it like we have . . . I think without pride I may venture to assert it would have been otherwise in England.[50]

This is an early sign of Sullivan's staunch patriotism and strong belief in the British musical tradition. Although his own musical formation was distinctly Germanic, as were the composers he admired and emulated, he felt that no one trumped the British when it came to church and choral music.

Leipzig, that most Protestant of German cities with its associations with Martin Luther as well as Bach and Mendelssohn, reinforced the patriotic Protestantism and commitment to sacred music that Sullivan had imbibed at the Chapel Royal. It did not, however, imbue him with a Protestant work ethic. By temperament he was inclined to be lazy, easily distracted, and tending to work in short bursts, often at the last moment. Perhaps it was the technique that he learned as a boy chorister of having quickly to learn new repertoire that enabled him to work fast and to achieve so much when he also devoted much time to pleasure and socializing.

But this was for the future. He left Leipzig still just 18 with his teachers convinced that he had the talent and potential to be a great conductor, a great classical composer, perhaps even a concert pianist, and the expectation that he would make his mark in at least one of these fields, if not in all three. Yet it was as a church musician that he would initially work on his return to London, partly for economic reasons but also because of his training and his own interests and enthusiasms.

Notes

1. Frederick Helmore, *Memoir of the Rev Thomas Helmore* (London: J. Masters, 1891), p.73.
2. David Eden, *Gilbert and Sullivan: The Creative Conflict* (Madison: Farleigh Dickinson University Press,1986), p.175.
3. For the history of the institution, see David Baldwin, *The Chapel Royal* (London: Duckworth, 1990).
4. Arthur Jacobs, *Arthur Sullivan*, 2nd edn. (Aldershot: Scolar Press, 1992), p.12.
5. 'The Chapel Royal Days of Arthur Sullivan', *Musical Times*, 1 March 1901, p.167.
6. *Musical Times*, 1 December 1900, p.785.
7. *St Michael's College Magazine*, December 1918, re-printed in *SASS Magazine* 72 (Spring 2010), p.22.
8. Report of Commission on the Chapel Royal, quoted in Percy Young, *Sir Arthur Sullivan* (London: J.M. Dent, 1971), p.13.
9. Arthur Sullivan [hereafter AS] to his parents, 29 January 1855: Pierpont Morgan Library, New York [hereafter PML].
10. AS to his mother, 1 November 1854: PML.
11. Young, *Sullivan*, p.9.
12. Herbert Sullivan and Newman Flower, *Sir Arthur Sullivan* (London: Cassell & Co., 1927), p.13.
13. Jacobs, *Sullivan*, p.16.
14. Sullivan and Flower, *Sullivan*, p.28.
15. *Musical Times*, 1 March 1901, p.167.

16. Arthur Lawrence, *Sir Arthur Sullivan: Life Story, Letters and Reminiscences* (London: James Bowden, 1899), p.12.

17. Jacobs, *Sullivan*, p.12.

18. Benjamin Findon, *Sir Arthur Sullivan: His Life and Music* (London: James Nisbet, 1904), p.14.

19. Jacobs, *Sullivan*, p.15.

20. Sullivan and Flower, *Sullivan*, p.13.

21. Quoted in David Owen Norris, 'Art Songs', *Opera Now* April 2017, p.48.

22. Lawrence, *Sullivan*, p.269.

23. Findon, *Sullivan*, p.15.

24. AS to Thomas Helmore, 9 April 1882: PML.

25. AS to his mother, Sunday, November 1875: PML; Lawrence, *Sullivan*, p.238.

26. AS to Thomas Helmore, 26 December 1889: PML.

27. John Goss to AS, 16 July 1866: PML.

28. William Barrett, *English Church Composers* (London: Sampson, Low, Marston 1882), p.173.

29. *Musical Times*, 1 December 1900, p.785

30. Jeremy Dibble, *John Stainer: A Life in Music* (Woodbridge: Boydell Press, 2007), p.35.

31. Henry Saxe Wyndham, *Arthur Seymour Sullivan* (London: Kegan, Paul, Trench, Trubner & Co., 1926), p.49.

32. Sullivan and Flower, *Sullivan*, p.1.

33. Stanley Sadie (ed.), *New Grove Dictionary of Music and Musicians* (London: Macmillan, 1980), Vol.18, p.347.

34. Siegfried Kracauer, *Jacques Offenbach und das Paris seiner Zeit* (Amsterdam: Albert de Lange, 1937), p.157.

35. Ralph Fischer, *Aus Jacques Offenbach's Kindergarten* (Bad Emse Hefte Nr. 169, 1997).

36. See, for example, Andrea Most, *Making Americans: Jews and the Broadway Musical* (Cambridge, MA: Harvard University Press, 2004) and Stuart Hecht, *Transposing Broadway: Jews, Assimilation, and the American Musical* (New York: Palgrave Macmillan, 2011).

37. Ian Bradley, *You've Got to Have a Dream: The Message of the Musical* (London: SCM Press, 2004), pp.43–4.

38. Franz Lehár, 'Musik—mein Leben', *Neues Wiener Tagblatt*, 23 September 1944.

39. Leslie Baily, *The Gilbert & Sullivan Book*, revised edn. (London: Cassell & Co, 1956), p.43; Saxe Wyndham, *Sullivan*, p.14.

40. Percy Binns, *A Hundred Years of Military Music* (Shaftesbury: The Blackmore Press, 1959), pp.60–1.

41. Jacobs, *Sullivan*, p.21.

42. Lawrence, *Sullivan*, p.27.

43. Hermann Klein, *Thirty Years of Musical Life in London* (London: William Heinemann, 1903), p.336.

44. John Francis Barnett, *Musical Reminiscences and Impressions* (London: Hodder & Stoughton, 1906), p.38.

45. Clara Rogers, *Memories of a Musical Career* (Boston: Little Brown & Co., 1919), p.156.

46. Rogers, *Memories*, pp.168, 186.

47. Rogers, *Memories*, p.168.

48. Young, *Sullivan*, p.13.

49. Lawrence, *Sullivan*, p.43.

50. Jacobs, *Sullivan*, p.22.

3

The 1860s

The Influence of George Grove

Arthur Sullivan returned home from Leipzig in late April 1861, just short of his 19th birthday, loaded with great expectations. Was he the one who would scotch the Germans' disdainful view of Britain as *Das Land ohne Musik*, widely held throughout the nineteenth century and famously expressed in a book with that title by Oskar Schmitz published in 1904? He came back to a country where musical life was dominated by Continental conductors and composers, notably the German-born Julius Benedict (1804–55), Charles Hallé (1819–95), and August Manns (1825–1907); and the Italian, Michael Costa (1808–84). He was determined to rise to the challenge and do his bit to raise the musical profile of his native land, especially in his chosen field of composition. As he wrote later:

> I was ready to undertake anything that came my way, symphonies, overtures, ballets, anthems, hymn tunes, songs, part songs, a concerto for the cello, and eventually comic and light operas—nothing came amiss to me, and I gladly accepted what the publishers offered me, so long as I could get the things published.[1]

Over the next ten years, he did indeed achieve a prodigious output, writing a symphony, a cello concerto, an oratorio, ballet music, overtures, choral pieces, comic operas, and numerous songs, including some sensitive settings of Shakespeare. But first he had to resort to more mundane ways of making a living and paying off his debts to his parents who had helped him through his studies. Now back living with them in Pimlico, he advertised for piano pupils and was hired by Thomas Helmore to teach reading, writing, and arithmetic to the children of the Chapel Royal. One of the main opportunities for an aspiring professional musician to make money was through becoming a church organist. As soon as he returned to London, with a view to gaining a suitable church post, he took up organ lessons with George Cooper, who had succeeded George Smart as organist at the Chapel Royal in 1856.

Church Organist and Composer of Anthems

Did Sullivan become a church organist simply to make money or did he feel some sense of vocation to this particular branch of the musical profession? It is telling that he turned down the first organist's job that was offered to him, just a month after his return from Leipzig, 'on religious grounds'.[2] It was at the German Lutheran Church in London, where his name had been suggested by Jenny Lind's husband Otto Goldschmidt. Presumably Sullivan declined it because of his strong Anglican affiliations. With his early upbringing in the Church of England, his Chapel Royal schooling, his veneration for and close friendship with Goss and Smart, it was unthinkable that he would not attach himself to an Anglican church. For him, playing the organ in church was not just a matter of financial reward. It was an opportunity to engage in the church music that was his first love and to be part of the great Anglican choral tradition in which he had been nurtured. He did not have to wait long to find a suitable post. In the late summer of 1861 he was recommended by a friend of Helmore's to Joseph Hamilton, vicar of St Michael's Church, Chester Square, just half a mile from his parents' home in Pimlico.

At his audition for the vacant organist's post there, Sullivan scored an immediate hit with the vicar's daughter, Mary, who later confessed that she 'was quite enthralled by the performance of the E minor fugue of Bach, one of the pieces played by the slim, curly-headed, black-eyed youth'.[3] She went on to become Sullivan's organ pupil, to deputize for him at Wednesday morning and Sunday afternoon services at St Michael's, and to 'save his life' by copying out the violin parts of his first comic opera, *Cox and Box*, on the morning of its first band rehearsal. A strong bond developed between the new organist and the vicar's daughter, and they maintained a lifelong friendship. Mary, who went on to marry a clergyman, Walter Carr, was not the only one to be captivated by Sullivan's attractive personality and winning ways. In a moving tribute published shortly after his death, she wrote of 'the charm that he exercised over the church officials at St Michael's' and the 'affectionate intimacy between himself and the vicar.'[4]

St Michael's had a mixed congregation which included MPs, barristers, surgeons, and army officers as well as bricklayers, butlers, engine-drivers, and grooms. According to Percy Young, Sullivan received an annual stipend of £80. If this figure is correct, he was receiving considerably more than other, better qualified London organists; Joseph Barnby received only £30 at St Andrew's, Wells Street, which was in the van of the choral revival in the Church of England and prided itself on having entirely sung services. St Michael's had a three manual organ which occupied three-quarters of the west gallery. Edward Mills, who acted as Sullivan's deputy at the church from 1867, has left this description of his talents as an organist:

> His style of playing was eminently legato and quiet, and scrupulously in keeping with the general feeling of the words; but when occasion required, the louder portions of the instrument would gradually be drawn upon for a well-conceived climax, such as is found in Haydn's tune 'Austria'. He rightly considered his thoughtful accompaniment of the service to be his strongest point as an organist.[5]

Others agreed that Sullivan's greatest strength as a church organist lay in his sensitive accompaniment of hymns. His skills as a conductor were also much appreciated, as Mary Carr pointed out:

> Arthur Sullivan's conducting power was shown still more in what he could make the congregation do. As a rule, the hymns were sung very heartily by everybody in the congregation, but he could subdue the whole body of voices to a whisper when he chose; as, for instance, in such passages as the last verse of 'Rock of Ages' sung to a German tune named 'Cassell'.[6]

The choir at St Michael's gave Sullivan his first experience of choral conducting and a good deal of pleasure and amusement, as he later recalled:

> We were well off for soprani and contralti but at first I was at my wit's end for tenors and basses. However, close by St Michael's Church was Cottage Row police station, and here I completed my choir. The Chief

Superintendent threw himself heartily into my scheme, and from the police I gathered six tenors, and six basses, with a small reserve. And capital fellows they were. However tired they might be when they came off duty, they never missed a practice. I used to think of them sometimes when I was composing the music for the *Pirates of Penzance*.[7]

Although Sullivan described himself as being 'tired to death with teaching my gallant constables a tune', his persistence and patience paid off and, in the judgment of Mary Carr, the '"harmonious Bluebottles" . . . made an efficient and steady choir, if not one distinguished for beauty of tone'.[8] Sullivan's close friend, Joseph Bennett, music critic of the *Daily Telegraph* and organist at the Westminster Chapel who sometimes attended rehearsals at St Michael's, gives this lovely picture of Sullivan's relations with his constabulary choir:

I never ceased to admire the way in which he kept the constables at the boiling point of enthusiasm, as well as on brink of laughter. The organist's good spirits were infectious, and though, as he himself sang in after years,

> Taking one consideration with another,
> A policeman's life [sic] is not a happy one,

I would be bound that the 'able-bodied' of St Michael's were, during rehearsal, as cheerful as all the birds in the air. They could not help it, neither could their musical chief help it either, so ebullient was his good nature, and so captivating his charm.[9]

Sullivan was conscientious in his duties as a church organist and gave them priority over social engagements. In November 1862, he turned down a dinner invitation from one of his many female admirers, telling her that 'I have a Church Service to attend to (being poor and striving to earn an honest livelihood) and twelve of the police force . . . to crack in choral matters for the church of S. Michael on Thursday'.[10] His organ playing skills were not just displayed in church. In 1863 he was appointed organist with the Royal Italian Opera Company at Covent Garden. It was his first experience of working in a theatrical environment and his critics would later point to it as an early sign of where his true musical sympathies and preferences lay. This early flirtation with the theatre was short-lived, however, lasting for just two seasons, whereas he remained a regular church organist for another nine years, taking on a further commitment from June 1867 at the newly built St Peter's Church in Cranley Gardens in South Kensington. He had designed the organ there and volunteered to play for two or three Sundays until a new permanent organist could be found. In the event, Sullivan remained as organist of St Peter's until 1872. He retained his post at St Michael's until 1869, regularly using Edward Mills as his deputy there but increasingly it was St Peter's that received most of his attention.

In contrast to St Michael's where, in Mills' words, 'the services were of a very plain type', the more fashionable St Peter's, despite being designed by its architect, Charles Freake, to be 'evangelical in religious observance and arrangement', had a surpliced choir in the chancel, where the organ was sited, and put on full Cathedral-style choral services of the kind that Sullivan had experienced under Helmore's direction at St Mark's Training College.[11] Although its musical standards were considerably higher than those displayed by the singing police constables at St Michael's, St Peter's presented its own challenges to the organist, not least at the consecration service in June 1867 for which the Bishop of London was an hour late in arriving:

> I had to play the organ the whole time in order to occupy the attention of the congregation. As the minutes went by and the Bishop didn't arrive I began to play appropriate music. First I played 'I waited for the Lord', and then went on with a song of mine which is entitled 'Will he come?' The appropriateness of the pieces was perfectly apprehended by the congregation.[12]

During his five years as organist at Peter's, Cranley Gardens, Sullivan made good use of his contacts in the church music world. For the consecration service he augmented the church choir with boys from the Chapel Royal and chose John Goss' 'Praise the Lord', the anthem that he had sung as a 14-year-old soloist at St Michael's College, Tenbury Wells, and later praised to his father. Goss was present for the consecration and quite often attended the evening service at St Peter's. On one occasion when he came up to the organ at the end, Sullivan got the choir to sing the hymn 'Praise my soul, the King of Heaven' to Goss' recently composed tune PRAISE

MY SOUL which Sullivan described as the 'finest hymn tune in existence'.[13] The choir then sang Sullivan's anthem 'The strain upraise' which Goss praised in similarly effusive terms.

Sullivan's work as a church organist brought him into contact with clergy as well as with fellow church musicians and he struck up a particularly close friendship with three clergymen. The most colourful was the Rev and Hon Francis Byng (1835–1919), the vicar of St Peter's, Cranley Gardens, from 1867 to 1889. A chaplain to both the queen and the speaker of the House of Commons, his imposing presence, mellifluous voice, and aristocratic origins made him a favourite with couples wanting to be married in a fashionable London church. He was an active Freemason and was elected in 1889 as the grand chaplain of the United Kingdom Lodge. Later that year, however, he suddenly resigned from his ecclesiastical appointments and left London, supposedly because of a gambling debt. He was said to be 'addicted to cards', an affliction that he perhaps passed on to and certainly shared with his organist, who was a keen gambler throughout his adult life. In 1899, Byng became the fifth earl of Strafford when his brother, the fourth earl, was decapitated in a railway accident. He remained a friend of Sullivan who jokingly pointed out his musical limitations in a letter written just a year before his own death:

> In endeavouring to intone, you led choir, congregation, and organist an exciting chase over a gamut of about two octaves, we vainly doing our utmost to follow you. You were heroic—we never could run you to earth; that is, pin you to the same note for two consecutive prayers or collects.[14]

A rather more musically accomplished clergyman with whom Sullivan struck up a close friendship at this time was Robert Brown (1840–94), known as Brown-Borthwick after his marriage at Westminster Abbey in 1868 at which Sullivan was a groomsman and for which he wrote a four part unaccompanied anthem, 'Rejoice in the Lord' based on Psalm 33. Curate at the Quebec Chapel, Marble Arch, Brown-Borthwick was a leading hymnologist and gave Sullivan his first substantial commission for hymn tunes in 1869. A third clerical friend during this period was Clement Cotterill Scholefield (1839–1904), who served as curate at St Peter's from 1870 to 1879 and went on to become chaplain of Eton College. Although lacking any formal musical education, he was commissioned by Sullivan to write several tunes for the hymn book that he edited in 1874, among them the immortal ST CLEMENT for 'The day, Thou gavest, Lord, is ended'.

Inspired by his time in the organ loft and his experience in conducting church choirs, Sullivan composed several liturgical pieces during the 1860s, notably a *Jubilate*, *Kyrie*, and *Te Deum* in D in 1866 and seven anthems, all of which were settings of the Psalms: 'O love the Lord' (Psalm 31) in 1864; 'We have heard with our ears' (Psalm 44) dedicated to Helmore and based on a plainsong motif, originally written in 1860 and revised in 1865; 'O taste and see' (Psalm 34) in 1867; 'O God, Thou art worthy' (Psalm 20) in 1867; 'I will lay me down in peace' (Psalm 4) and 'Rejoice in the Lord' (Psalm 33) in 1868; and 'Sing, o heavens', dedicated to Byng with a composite text drawn from Isaiah chapters 49 and 25 and Psalms 85 and 45, in 1869. Although there were further anthems to come, this was Sullivan's most prolific period for writing this type of church music. The anthems drew a mixed response. The *Musical Times* described 'O taste and see' as having a pleasing quality of gracefulness but being 'rather secular in style, perhaps, considering the purpose of its composition'.[15] This was an early expression of what was to become a common criticism directed at Sullivan's sacred music, that it was altogether too shallow, vulgar, and secular in character. Others might have used the word accessible.

Friendship with George Grove

Not long after his return to London from Leipzig, Sullivan began what was to be the most intimate and enduring friendship of his lifetime. George Grove, a Victorian polymath, was the founder and editor of the multi-volume *Dictionary of Music and Musicians* which still bears his name in its current eighth edition, now online. The two men first met early in 1862, either at a concert in St James's Hall in the West End of London or at the home of the music critic, Henry Chorley. Despite an age gap of more than twenty years—Sullivan was still just 19 and Grove 41—they hit it off immediately and were soon spending a good deal of time together. Writing to his mother from Grove's home in October 1862, Sullivan reported that

'Mr Grove and I write on till two every morning, & then have a cigarette & go to bed'.[16] In an enthusiastic exchange of letters the following May, Grove wrote of 'the happy year we have had since we knew each other' and Sullivan responded 'I have learned more from being with and talking to you than you can ever know . . . Long may our friendship last!'.[17]

Like Sullivan, George Grove was a Londoner, although of a slightly higher social station. His father, a devout but broad-minded Congregationalist, had a thriving business as a fishmonger and venison dealer in Charing Cross. The seventh of ten children, George grew up in Clapham where he attended two small private schools and the newly established grammar school. He then trained and worked as a civil engineer, supervising the construction of a lighthouse in Jamaica, Chester Railway Station, and the Britannia Bridge spanning the Menai Straits between North Wales and Anglesey. In 1850, he left civil engineering to become secretary of the Society of Arts, the co-ordinating body behind the Great Exhibition of 1851. In 1852, he went on to be the first secretary of the Crystal Palace Company, which had been set up to move Joseph Paxton's great glass palace built for the exhibition from Hyde Park to Sydenham in South London, and to run it as a cultural venue.

Grove's main task was to organize concerts and other events at the Crystal Palace, which opened for business in its new location in June 1854 with the concert attended by Queen Victoria in which Sullivan had sung in his early days at the Chapel Royal. It was a job to which Grove was admirably suited. Music had been his consuming passion since childhood. He was brought up on the great choral classics, especially the works of Bach and Handel. Like Sullivan, he was an enthusiast for English church music, with a special fondness for the works of the great Tudor composers like Morley, Byrd, and Gibbons, and of their seventeenth-century successor, Henry Purcell. His other great passion in life was biblical scholarship and particularly researching the geography of the lands and places mentioned in the Bible. He was a keen disciple of the new movement of Biblical criticism emanating from Germany, which treated the Bible not as the revealed word of God to be accepted literally but rather as an ancient text to be subjected to scholarly analysis. Grove immersed himself in the history, geography, and religion of the Holy Land which he visited in 1858 and 1861. His work in this area encompassed the preparation of an atlas of the Bible, support for projects to map and carry out archaeological surveys in Palestine, and substantial involvement in a three-volume *Dictionary of the Bible*, edited by William Smith, published in 1863 and still in print today, of which he was effectively co-editor and author of more than half the content.

George Grove's interest in biblical criticism and scholarship owed much to the encouragement of Arthur Stanley, one of the leading churchmen of Victorian England who went on to be regius professor of ecclesiastical history at Oxford University from 1856 to 1863 and dean of Westminster Abbey from 1864 to 1881. The two first met in 1854, when Stanley was a canon at Canterbury Cathedral. In 1856, Grove and Stanley collaborated on a book about Sinai and Palestine based on the latter's travels there. Stanley was one of the leading exponents of liberal theology in the nineteenth-century Church of England. It was he who in an article in the *Edinburgh Review* in 1850 coined the term 'Broad Church' to describe what he saw as its natural position in contrast to the High and Low Church extremes. Under the influence of Stanley, Grove became markedly more liberal in his theological outlook through the 1850s and early 1860s. He was also influenced in this direction by his close friendship with Frederick Denison Maurice, the former Unitarian turned Anglican who was dismissed from his professorship at King's College, London, for rejecting the doctrine of eternal punishment or, as Grove put it, 'for venturing to hope that God was good enough not to let men burn for ever and ever'.[18] Maurice emphasized Christ's headship over all humanity which, rather than being divided into the elect and the damned as Evangelicals insisted, he saw as forming one organic whole, often struggling and suffering, and worthy of profound sympathy and care rather than narrow judgement. Grove regarded Stanley and Maurice as 'the two greatest men in the Church of England'.[19]

By 1862, when he first met Sullivan, George Grove was well-established as a leading figure in London's cultural and intellectual life. He had thrown open his house in Sydenham as a kind of salon for gatherings of those involved in the worlds of art and literature as well as musicians and theologians. He was a close friend of Alfred Tennyson, the Poet Laureate, and had more than a nodding acquaintance with the novelists Wilkie Collins and Charles Dickens, the Pre-Raphaelite painters John Millais and William Holman Hunt, and the rising Liberal politician, William Ewart Gladstone. The Saturday concerts which he organized at the Crystal Palace, featuring a full symphony orchestra conducted by August Manns, had established themselves as a major feature of the musical life of the capital.

From the start of their friendship, Grove actively promoted Sullivan's work and acted as his chief patron and impresario. He put on the full music to *The Tempest*, of which only a selection had been performed at Leipzig, at the Crystal Palace on 5 April 1862. It received rapturous reviews and effectively launched Sullivan's career as Britain's foremost young classical composer. Grove went on to showcase nearly all of Sullivan's major compositions at the Crystal Palace Saturday afternoon concerts. His choral masque, *Kenilworth*, was performed there in November 1864 and in 1866 both his symphony and his cello concerto received their premieres there. It was thanks to Grove that Sullivan received the first of many commissions to write music for royal occasions. For the celebrations surrounding the marriage of Albert Edward, Prince of Wales, to Princess Alexandra of Denmark in March 1863, he composed *The Princess of Wales' March*, and a song, 'Bride from the North', with words by Henry Chorley. Both were premiered at a 'Wedding Festival Concert' held at the Crystal Palace, at which Sullivan was introduced to the Prince of Wales and his younger brother, Alfred, Duke of Edinburgh, who was to become a close personal friend. This effectively put him on track to take up the unofficial position that he held for much of his adult life as 'Composer Laureate' producing music for royal occasions. Grove further helped his career by appointing him as professor of pianoforte and ballad singing at the Crystal Palace Company's School of Art, Science and Literature. This in turn led to an appointment on the staff of the National College of Music and later, in 1869, to a professorship at the Royal Academy of Music.

Almost as helpful to furthering the budding composer's reputation and career was Grove's introduction of Sullivan to some of the leading cultural figures of the day, including Tennyson, Dickens, Millais, and Gladstone, as well as to fellow liberal theologians. In an early sign of the closeness of their friendship, Grove made Sullivan godfather to his youngest son who was born in 1864. The other godfather was Arthur Stanley. The boy was named Arthur in a tribute to the two men whom

Grove often later bracketed together as his two dearest friends. His eldest son had been named Maurice after F.D. Maurice who was a regular guest in Grove's house in Sydenham. Another frequent visitor there was Nina Lehmann, the daughter of the Edinburgh publisher Robert Chambers and wife of a prosperous German-born merchant. Eleven years Sullivan's senior, she was the first of a number of older married women to whom he became close and who served as his travelling companions and confidantes. In 1865, he made the first of many visits to Paris, accompanied by Nina Lehmann and her husband, and Henry Chorley. There they met up with Charles Dickens and with Gioachino Rossini whom Sullivan cajoled into joining him in playing a piano duet version of *The Tempest*.

Sullivan owed more to Grove than the promotion of his work and the introduction to influential people, important though both of those were to his burgeoning career. In a letter that he penned on his 21st birthday to his older friend and mentor to 'acknowledge with gratitude the immense advantage which your friendship has been to me', he wrote: 'I have learnt more from being with and talking to you than you can ever well know, for you have taken good care not to let my Art alone absorb me, but have interested me in other equally, if not more instructive matters'.[20] Those other 'more instructive matters' aside from music included questions of faith and belief. Grove may not have turned his young friend and protégé into a serious amateur theologian and biblical scholar like himself, but he encouraged him to think and talk about these subjects. This is clear from an account that he gave of an evening which he and Sullivan spent with Tennyson at the poet's home in Freshwater, Isle of Wight, in October 1866:

> We had as much music as we could on a *very tinkling* piano, but very much out of tune, and then retired to his room at the top of the house . . . and talked till two o'clock in a very fine way about the things which I always get around to sooner or later—death and the next world, and God and man, etc.[21]

In fact, the conversation between poet and composer on the eternal verities was rather more of a success than their subsequent collaboration, engineered by Grove, on a song cycle, similar to Schumann's *Liederkreis*, which was designed to beat the Germans at their own game and show that the British could succeed in this field. Although they did eventually produce a collection of eleven songs, published in 1871 as *The Window*, Tennyson regretted his involvement in the project and was less than gracious about it. Maybe this rather unhappy early experience with a literary lion was what led Sullivan six years later to turn down a request from Lewis Carroll to collaborate on a musical version of *Alice in Wonderland*.

Sullivan and Grove's close relationship, which continued throughout their lives, was at its most intense in its early years. For a time Sullivan took rooms over a shop in Sydenham Road to be near Grove and he seems sometimes to have lodged at Grove's house, not just overnight after a convivial evening but for periods of several days. Looking back thirty years later on this period, Grove wrote, 'for 4 or 5 years [Sullivan] almost lived here and was on the most intimate terms with us both (more so than anyone else).'[22] Sullivan was among the select group of intimate friends who met in Grove's house on Sunday evenings and, in the words of the local vicar, 'held sweet converse on the highest and deepest subjects'.[23] Despite the workaholic Grove taking on yet another task with his assumption of the assistant editorship of *Macmillan's Magazine* in 1866, the two men continued to see a lot of each other and to exchange letters of deep intimacy. Writing in September 1866 following the death of Sullivan's father, Grove concluded: 'God help you my dear fellow; and thank you over and over for all your kindness to me and for your love—which is like a well of light every time I come near you'.[24] A few days later he adopted an even more intimate tone: 'I do long for you so—there is no man I care to be with so much . . . do come and smile on me now and then my dear'.[25] In July 1867, they travelled together to Paris for the International Exposition, prompting Sullivan to write to his mother about his travelling companion, 'It would be painting the lily to try to describe his goodness and charm, so I refrain. We take great care of each other, are very economical, haggle over centimes and get on famously'.[26]

The best known venture which the two men undertook together, and which further deepened their friendship, was a trip to Vienna in October 1867 to search for lost manuscripts of Schubert's music and specifically the score of his ballet *Rosamunde*. They took eight days to travel there via Baden-Baden, Munich, and Salzburg. As well as much sightseeing and visiting eminent musicians, like Clara Schumann,

Grove managed to squeeze in at least one theological encounter, meeting with Ignaz von Döllinger, a liberal Roman Catholic priest who strongly opposed the doctrine of papal infallibility. He had two hours' conversation with 'the great professor and champion of liberty and toleration'.[27] There is no mention of Sullivan's presence at the meeting, and maybe on this occasion he did absent himself from theological discussion, although the two men were usually inseparable—Arthur told his mother, 'the chief difficulty I have felt has been the impossibility of detaching myself from Grove'.[28] During their travels, both men wrote regularly to Mary Sullivan, showering compliments on each other and also assuring her of their frugality and thrift. Sullivan wrote of Grove, 'The charm of that remarkable man is so great, his versatility, his energy, his good looks, his dress, his admirable German and above all his singular modesty form a combination which, as I can safely affirm, the world has never before seen'.[29] Grove reciprocated, telling her, 'we have had the pleasantest time and agreed like soap and water or bread and honey or any other agreeing things . . . We are very economical. I don't mention this out of pride—but to give you pleasure'.[30]

In Vienna the two friends attended Mass in the Dominican Church and paid their respects at the graves of Beethoven and Schubert in the *Zentralfriedhof* before setting about their main task of searching for the Schubert manuscripts. They found two symphonies, two overtures, a string trio and quartet, and several songs, but feared that they were going to come away empty-handed in respect of the main purpose of their visit until, on their last afternoon in the city, they unearthed a dusty bundle in the far corner of a cupboard in the home of the composer's nephew, Eduard Schneider. It turned out to contain part books of the whole score of *Rosamunde*. Sullivan and Grove set about copying out the missing accompaniments, a task that took them until two in the morning. When they had finished, they celebrated by playing leap-frog in the street outside.

What was it that drew these two men together so closely and intensely? Their letters display a more than usual level of affection. In the biographies that he wrote of both figures, Percy Young suggested there was a sexual element in their relationship and described Sullivan as 'strongly homo-erotic'.[31] I am more inclined to agree with Arthur Jacobs' assessment that they 'expressed mutual affection in terms which are not in the least inconsistent with Victorian manly sentiment, and in which a subsequent age would be quite wrong to suspect homosexuality'.[32] There was possibly an element of physical attraction on Grove's part. According to the reminiscences of a friend, their first meeting came about when Grove espied Sullivan peering through the door of the gallery in St James' Hall and asked 'Who is that engaging looking young man?'[33] Undoubtedly both men had a strong sexual urge but they were vigorously heterosexual, with a similarly jaundiced view of marriage and a shared tendency to become infatuated with much younger women in their later years. Their relationship was certainly deep and intense but there is no evidence that it was sexual.

They were attracted to each other first and foremost by their mutual love of music and also by a recognition that they were kindred spirits. Both were open, warm, gregarious, romantic idealists with a love of life but also with a more serious spiritual side. Grove had a darker and more depressive nature and more hidden demons, although Sullivan was not without them. They appreciated and drew much from each other's warmth, sympathy, generosity, and liveliness. There were differences between them, not least in political outlook. Sullivan was a staunch Tory—he wrote before one election that he would vote for 'any Unionist or Conservative who holds right views about things generally'.[34] Grove was on the radical wing of the Liberal Party, although he ultimately left it over Irish Home Rule. The two men were also somewhat different in their theological and religious beliefs. While both were deeply embedded in and devoted to the Church of England, Grove was a modernist and Sullivan a traditionalist. Grove was much more of a theologian, and wrote and spoke much more freely about spiritual matters. He was also much more tormented by religious doubts.

There are, in fact, grounds for thinking that it was at a deep spiritual level that the bond between them was really forged and that each gave the other something significant and helpful in this area. Grove made Sullivan more theologically and biblically aware and reinforced his naturally liberal Christian faith of forgiveness and assurance, while Sullivan helped to bolster Grove's flagging faith and assuage his growing religious doubts through the simplicity of his own faith and through his music.

In the years when their relationship was at its most intense, Grove was moving in a steadily more liberal direction theologically and was also beginning to succumb to the doubts that would assail him ever more keenly in subsequent decades. He had travelled a long way from the flirtation with High Church ritualism which had briefly engaged him as a young man, perhaps in youthful reaction to his father's plain and simple Congregationalism. As he wrote in a revealing letter in 1866, 'Though once a great ritualist and High Churchman, I was more so in taste than doctrine, and *now* have left the doctrine altogether'.[35] Indeed, he had come to have a profound distaste for High Church ritualistic churchmanship of the kind represented by the Oxford Movement and the Roman Catholic church. A visit to Catholic churches in Italy in 1869 reinforced his distaste for idolatry and miracles, and prompted the observation that there was little to distinguish the learned and pious Hindu praying before 'a rude and obscene symbol' and the Christian doing the same before an image of Christ: 'One rises from the consideration of the question with an uneasy feeling that the symbols and documents of Christianity may be as baseless as those of the Hindoo'.[36] His opposition to what he took to be the superstition, magic, and mumbo-jumbo at the heart of Roman Catholic and High Church Anglican practices increased and in later life he was to mount a stinging attack on John Henry Newman, the darling of the Oxford Movement who had quit the Church of England for Rome in 1845:

> To him we owe the flood of ritualism and material worship and magic that now fills the Church, and I for one don't feel very grateful . . . Our church is fast becoming, from the reasonable Service which was the pride of the country, a mere magic mill for the production of Sacraments which are to act as charms.[37]

If Grove intensely disliked the High Church Catholic element in the church of his time, he was equally opposed to its strong Evangelical wing—he described High Church and Low Church Anglicanism as 'the two great sects'.[38] His work as a biblical scholar made him deeply antagonistic to the view that the Bible was the inspired word of God to be taken literally. He was delighted when in 1864 the Judicial Committee of the Privy Council overturned the convictions of heresy imposed by the Church of England's Court of Arches on a group of liberal churchmen who had written in support of Biblical criticism and questioned the doctrine of eternal punishment in their controversial collection of *Essays and Reviews* published four years earlier. For Grove, their acquittal confirmed that 'the Church of England does not require its members to hold every word and letter of the Scriptures as absolutely and infallibly dictated by God, and that there may be differences of opinion as to the everlasting duration of future punishment'.[39] He went on to adopt even more radical views, writing in 1865 of the 'harm which slavish devotion to the Bible has done' and calling for the production of what would effectively be a new 'modern Bible of our own' in which 'the conceptions of God, and of the next world, formed in a dark ignorant age would be superseded by others more in accordance with the progress of the world and the continual revelation which God is making to us through nature and life and events'. He continued:

> Everything in the world seems to advance—science, philosophy, metaphysics—all are miles ahead of where they were 1000 years ago—and yet not one of them may be applied to religion because the Bible is set up as an idol, or as a final gauge and measure for all times to come. It's only because we're so accustomed to it, that we don't see it,—but think of the crude, horrid ideas of God that many of the books contain:—anger, revenge, hatred, and or other bad passions are attributed to Him.[40]

Grove's views put him at the extreme liberal end of the theological spectrum, beyond most of those in the Broad Church movement within the Church of England. He became increasingly opposed to Christian dogma and exclusivity, more open to other faiths, and less and less sure in his own beliefs. Yet he retained his membership of and affection for the Church of England, perhaps persuaded partly by his friendship with and deep admiration for Maurice and Stanley. Although increasingly assailed by doubts, and greatly attracted to the writings of that great apostle of Victorian doubt, Arthur Hugh Clough, he continued to believe in the ultimate importance of religion, in terms of its practical value. As he put it, 'I could preach to my heart's content on the theme of nothing being any good without religion, and religion being no good unless it showed itself in the practical shape of faith and unselfishness and good manners

(i.e. grace)'.[41] He commended the prophet Micah 'as the first pro-
moter of the doctrine that practical goodness is better than theology'.[42]

Sullivan's religious position through the 1860s was neither as well
worked out nor anything like as radical. It is more difficult to discern
because of his reticence—as much about his inner beliefs as about his
feelings on other personal matters. He was not a theologian or a
biblical scholar. But it is clear from what he did write that his faith
was much simpler and surer than Grove's, and much less assailed by
doubts and scepticism. He, too, was neither High nor Low Church.
His sympathies, in so far as he expressed them, were those of a Broad
Church Anglican. That was the churchmanship in which he had been
brought up as a youngster in Sandhurst Parish Church and which his
mentor Thomas Helmore had espoused. He shared Grove's view that
practical action, generosity, unselfishness, and good manners were the
true marks of Christianity rather than subscription to a particular set
of beliefs and dogma. His own instincts were naturally inclusive and
liberal. Like Grove, he was devoted to the Church of England,
especially because of its liturgy and its music, but also because of its
breadth, inclusivity, and the strong ties which its established status
gave it with the nation, the Crown, and wider society and culture.

It seems inevitable given their intimacy and the long periods they
spent together that Grove and Sullivan would have talked about
spiritual and theological matters with some candour and depth. As
the one who was much more of a theologian as well as a leading
biblical scholar and who went much deeper into the issues, Grove
almost certainly helped to shape Sullivan's simple boyhood faith into
something more theologically nuanced and biblically informed. It was
to find its fullest expression in his oratorio, *The Light of the World*, and it
is no surprise that he specifically acknowledged Grove's key role in
helping to select texts and frame the overall direction of that work.
Although it is not similarly acknowledged, I suspect that Grove played
a similar role in the earlier oratorio, *The Prodigal Son*, which Sullivan
wrote at the end of the decade when their friendship was at its most
intense.

If Grove contributed to Sullivan's theological and spiritual development in a way that was helpful both personally and professionally,
Sullivan seems to have been able to assuage Grove's growing religious
doubts with the simplicity of his own faith, his hope in the afterlife, and

especially with the soothing and sublime quality of his music. Grove's letters and diary entries through the later 1860s and 1870s constantly bemoan his loss of the simple faith of his youth when 'my religious flame burnt fiercely' and his uncertainty about life beyond death.[43] Sullivan had not lost his childhood faith, particularly in respect of there being another world beyond this one, and he expressed it in his music. That music provided Grove with some balm for his troubled spirit.

Occasionally the growing gloom of doubt which surrounded Grove was relieved, as is clear from this entry in his pocket book in 1866, when his letters suggest that his relationship with Sullivan was at its most intense and intimate:

> I sometimes have a glimpse of religion and such things in this way—as if we were in darkness and cold and misery under a veil on the other side of which was a bright light and great warmth and comfort and happiness and everything good. Then now and then there comes a chink in the veil, and sometimes it comes so that the ray comes right in on one, sometimes only a feint light; sometimes a puff of warm air or sweet smell—sometimes a burst of music.[44]

Grove went on to mention other things that provided chinks in the veil—'the Bible and all the poetry of the world and all the good thoughts and all the sweet lovely ideas that one gets from the women one knows'—but ultimately it was music that he identified as giving him his best glimpses of a religion of warmth and light and 'everything good'. It was the music of two composers in particular that enabled him to penetrate through the veil to the sublime. They were Robert Schumann and Arthur Sullivan. He identified them more than once as his musical heroes, just as he identified Tennyson and Shelley as his literary heroes. In a meditation written towards the end of his life he noted that for all their grandeur, their magnificence, and their tenderness, both Beethoven and Shakespeare remained always somehow earth-bound and fell short of the quality of sublimity which 'involves the highest religious feeling—as it were the presence of God himself . . . sublimity exalts one, brings one near the throne of God'.[45] Sullivan's work did exhibit that quality, and for Grove it was there in his apparently secular pieces, like *The Tempest*, the symphony and the cello concerto as much as in the sacred works. It was the sublime quality that he found in Sullivan's music which perhaps most attracted the middle-aged polymath to the young composer. It brought him the chink of light that penetrated the veil of his troubled faith and gathering doubts.

In Sullivan's presence and personality as well as in his music, George Grove found something rare and very valuable that lifted his spirits and dispelled his demons. Looking back thirty years later on the start of their friendship, he wrote: 'That was the second youth of my life. Everything budded and blossomed to me, and for the first time, though then forty-three, I understood poetry, music—all the world, and Sullivan is bound up with it.'[46] We are, perhaps, given a glimpse of the effect that Sullivan had in a prayer which Grove wrote in his pocket book at the end of the decade when their friendship was at its deepest and most intimate. It ended: 'Soften us and purify us, and make us to love each other and Thee, and bring us to Thy eternal life where there shall be love without misunderstanding and without end, through Jesus Christ our Lord.'[47] This choice of words surely reveals the influence of Sullivan, the one whose music and temperament again and again had a softening effect, who believed in eternal life and whose Gospel was one of understanding and love. George Grove was perhaps the first but by no means the last person to recognize and to benefit from Arthur Sullivan's particular attribute of divine emollient.

First Serious Love Affair

George Grove played a key role in Sullivan's first serious love affair. Among the influential friends to whom he introduced the young composer was John Scott Russell, a near-neighbour in Sydenham and a successful designer and builder of ships who had preceded Grove as secretary of the Society of Arts and was one of the first directors of the Crystal Palace Company. It was almost certainly in Grove's house in 1863 that Arthur first met the second of Russell's three daughters, Rachel, and began a friendship which developed over the next two years into love and a passionate relationship.

Rachel was an accomplished pianist. Realizing that she would never make a career in the male-dominated world of Victorian music, she felt that she would best realize her potential by marrying a musician and becoming his muse and inspiration. 'In every note you write', she told Sullivan early on in their relationship, 'my soul is with yours'.[48] Initially, she was indeed his inspiration. It was largely thanks to her that he completed his symphony and composed other substantial orchestral pieces. For a time at least she seems to have curbed his natural laziness and got him to focus on serious musical composition. There was considerable passion in their relationship, which seems to have been consummated in May 1867. Thereafter she wrote to him once or twice a day, signing herself 'Passion Flower' and calling him 'Dear little bird' or 'Birdie'. He called her 'Fond Dove'. All seemed to be going well, but when in July 1867 Rachel told her parents about her wish to marry Sullivan, her outraged mother banned him from their house and instructed him to cease communicating with her. The couple continued to meet clandestinely, often in Grove's office at the Crystal Palace, but much of their relationship was carried out through letters—over 200 written between 1864 and 1870 survive, the great majority of them from Rachel. Sullivan was a much less frequent and devoted correspondent, and after the affair was over Rachel burned those letters that he did write.

Mrs Scott Russell's objection to Sullivan as a suitor and potential husband for her daughter centred on his impecunious circumstances and lack of financial prospects. This also concerned Rachel who made clear to him on several occasions that she could not contemplate marriage until he was more financially secure. She constantly urged him to write more serious works, beseeching him to compose a second symphony, an oratorio, and an opera based on the Arthurian character of Guinevere in Tennyson's *Idylls of the King*, and to give up the gambling, smoking, and late night carousing in London's clubs to which he had become attached. Her increasingly anguished letters show that although she was very much in love with him, she was also increasingly concerned about his fickleness, flirtatiousness with other women, and overall lack of commitment to their relationship which was becoming ever more tortuous. In a typical letter in May 1867 she wrote: 'May God put some of His infinite love and purity into your heart and make it steadfast and true'.[49]

In the absence of his letters it is difficult to chart the course of Sullivan's feelings through the long years of their tempestuous relationship. In the autumn of 1867 he sent Rachel a gold ring and it is clear that at this point marriage was still very much on the cards. However, it is also clear that she remained keener on him than he did on her. He kept cutting her and proposed a trial separation in the summer of 1868. Rachel went on an extended visit to Switzerland with her father, whereupon Arthur embarked on a close relationship with her older sister, Louise, who described herself as 'his little woman'. She, too, beseeched him not to succumb to temptation with other women and lectured him on purity and constancy. In one of the few letters of his that does survive, he responded petulantly telling her that women do not understand men, that he was indeed seeing other women and that when it came to temptation, 'what's the use of resisting?'[50] Louise broke off their relationship shortly before Rachel's return to Britain.

Rachel still somehow believed that she could redeem Sullivan, clung to her idealized dream of him and took a long time to accept that his feelings towards her had cooled. Although in February 1869 she sent back the ring that he had given her, she still clutched at any straw that suggested he had turned over a new leaf and that they might yet form a lasting union. She was overjoyed when he asked her to copy out the score of his new oratorio *The Prodigal Son* in the later summer of 1869, telling him: 'I should *so* like it, and I will try & do it beautifully & will make as few mistakes as possible'.[51] She asked him if he would conduct the work from the score that she had copied but it is not clear if he did so. It is difficult to avoid the conclusion that, rather as he had used Mary Hamilton to copy out the violin parts of *Cox and Box*, he was using Rachel Scott Russell to help him with his work while toying with her affections. Her continuing expressions of love went largely unrequited and her letters to him became ever more anguished. In one sent on 4 June 1869 and stained with tears she wrote: 'Oh! *Why* did you take all my strength & the best years of my bright young life only to throw them away at the end. The tears come welling up from the agony even as I write'.[52] They met on Christmas Day 1869 when he gave her a camelia, but he failed to show up for a meeting she was expecting with him a week later on New Year's Day. Her last letter to him, written on 9 May 1870, ended: 'God bless you—& send everything that is bright & golden & blessed to you—and watch over you & keep all care & pain & trouble from your dear head'.[53]

It is difficult to know how to assess this protracted and tortuous love affair which went on for six years and involved Sullivan through most of his 20s. The family view, as articulated by his cousin Benjamin Findon, was that it was all the fault of 'the vain mother who thought the young composer not good enough for her daughter to take in marriage.'[54] Findon went on to say that it would perhaps have been better for Sullivan if 'he had had another, and had sacrificed something of the joys of existing *en garçon* for the more tranquil state of matrimony, with its many duties and weightier responsibilities.'[55] In fact, Sullivan had several other women, including during the period of his courtship of Rachel. What this episode showed more clearly than anything else was that he was simply not cut out for marriage. He was too fickle, flirtatious, and unwilling to commit. Although it would be some time before he expressed his own views about his unpreparedness to tie himself down with the yoke of matrimony, two of his best friends spotted this trait in his character at this early stage and warned Rachel about it in 1867. George Grove told her that he did not think that Sullivan knew what 'devotion' meant, while Frederic Clay, a fellow budding young composer, warned her that Sullivan was not given to matrimony. At the time Clay was engaged to Rachel's younger sister Alice. Although he had even less prospect of making substantial earnings from his compositions than Sullivan, his father was a wealthy MP and he himself combined his musical pursuits with a position in the Treasury. As a result, Mrs Scott Russell raised no objection to him as a future son-in-law although in the event, he broke off his engagement to Alice and, like Sullivan, never married.

Rachel herself eventually came to realize that her relationship with Sullivan was doomed and that he ultimately served a higher muse. In a letter which she sent to him in February 1869 returning the gold ring that he had given her and which had suggested to her that he was serious about marriage, she acknowledged 'You have your beautiful genius to work for—& I—nor any other woman on God's earth—is worth wasting one's life for'.[56] In her final letter to him she wrote: 'Spread your wings, my beautiful eagle and show how you can soar!'.[57] She had come to learn the hard way what Sullivan was to say twenty years later, that music was his mistress.

In September 1872, Rachel married William Holmes, an Indian civil servant, and moved to Bengal with him. It is difficult to resist the conclusion that she was seeking to get as far away from Arthur as possible. She died in India in 1882 at the age of 36. Louise never married and died of consumption at the age of 37. Sullivan kept all of Rachel's letters, despite her constant requests that he burn them. According to Benjamin Findon, and once again we can take his words as expressing the wider family view, this was 'the one serious love affair of Sullivan's life.'[58]

Freemasonry

At around the same time that Sullivan was becoming seriously involved with Rachel Scott Russell, he entered the secretive world of Freemasonry. It was to prove a rather more enduring attachment, continuing for more than thirty years and taking him into the higher levels of the Craft. He was initiated in Lodge of Harmony, No. 255, Richmond, Surrey, on the same day (11 April 1865) as his friend Frederic Clay. He went on to progress through the Holy Royal Arch, described as 'the perfection and completion of all Freemasonry', and later joined the Rose Croix Chapter, the eighteenth degree within the Ancient and Accepted Rite for England and Wales, membership of which was open only to master masons of at least one year's standing who professed the Christian faith and went through a series of mystical experiences expressing the figurative passage of humanity through the darkest vale, accompanied and sustained by the three theological virtues, before finally being received into the abode of light. In 1887, he was appointed grand organist by the United Grand Lodge of England although he appears only to have performed once in this capacity at a special Grand Lodge held in the Albert Hall on 13 June 1887 in celebration of Queen Victoria's Golden Jubilee. In 1896, he joined Studholme Lodge, No. 1591, in London.

For the most part Sullivan's biographers have ignored or dismissed this aspect of his life, suggesting that if it had any significance it was simply as a means of improving his social standing. After alluding very briefly to his becoming a Freemason, Arthur Jacobs commented, 'membership of the order may have strengthened his social advancement at a time when the Royal princes and other notables lent their name to it'.[59] It is certainly true that many well-connected and eminent Victorians were Freemasons, not least those involved in music and theatre. However, the record of Sullivan's progression through the higher degrees of the Craft suggests that it was more than just a token or perfunctory matter for him. The three great masonic principles of brotherly love, charity directed both to one's own family and to the community as a whole, and the pursuit of truth were close to his heart. Freemasonry would have had a natural appeal to his warm-hearted and generous personality. Perhaps it also spoke to his deeper spiritual yearnings with its belief in a supreme being (without too much concern about the finer points of interpretation), its strong ethical values, and its romantic and chivalric connotations.

First Family Death and *In Memoriam* Overture

It was while staying with George Grove in Sydenham that Arthur Sullivan heard of the sudden death of his father, Thomas, on 23 September 1866. This unexpected and keenly felt loss directly inspired his most ostensibly religious orchestral composition, the *In Memoriam* overture. He wrote it for the Norwich Festival which had earlier commissioned a work from him. Unable to find a subject, he had informed his father that he was minded to give up the commission, only to be told: 'Don't do that, my boy. Don't give it up. Something will happen that may furnish you with an opportunity'.[60] Three days later Thomas was dead. Arthur wrote the overture immediately after his father's burial on 28 September, having told his mother 'I can't bear it. I must cry out my grief in music'.[61] He appears to have made the first sketch of it on the back of the letter of condolence he had just received from George Grove who told him that he had been thinking of him all day.

In Memoriam is a solemn piece cast in sonata form in C minor and marked *Andante religioso*. It begins and ends with a simple hymn-like tune in C major full of the repeated notes which were such a hallmark of Sullivan's sacred music. His biographers have tended to dismiss it as mawkish, banal, and a classic expression of sentimental Victorian religiosity.[62] In fact, it is wistfully reflective, conveying both a sense of deep affection and profound loss and a calm reassurance and confident faith. The hymn-like tune, played tentatively and quietly at the beginning of the work, is brought back triumphantly at the end with organ, full brass, and percussion in what Benedict Taylor rightly describes as 'an exultant apotheosis' signalling a clear rejection of death's pretended permanence.[63] *In Memoriam* shows Sullivan's faith as much as his Victorian conventionality. For all its raw expression of grief, there is an over-arching sense of dependence on and trust in God. This was picked up by Henry Chorley who noted in his review in the *Athenaeum* 'its mood of lofty hope tempering resigned grief'.[64] A similar theme is evident in the conclusion to a letter that Sullivan wrote to George Smart's widow after her husband died just a few weeks after his own father: 'With *Him*, in whom I sought comfort lately in my own great trouble, You will I know find peace and happiness'.[65]

Sullivan leant heavily on Grove following his loss, just as he seems to have turned to him during his rocky relationship with Rachel Scott Russell, at one stage using him as an intermediary to convey his thoughts to her. Michael Ainger suggests that Grove may have proposed their visit to Tennyson and the project to write a song cycle with him as a way of taking Sullivan's mind off his father's death; and that he may similarly have suggested their Vienna excursion during a particularly tricky period in the protracted affair with Rachel.[66] Grove himself had suffered a family bereavement three years earlier when his daughter, Lucy, died of scarlet fever at the age of 10. It is interesting to observe the different effect that the deaths of close family members had on the two men. While Sullivan poured out his grief and his faith in music, as he was to do again when his brother, Frederic, died, Lucy's death caused Grove, in his own words, to fall madly in love with Mimi von Glehn, one of twelve children of an Estonian merchant who had settled in London. More than twenty years later, in 1886, the loss of another daughter, Millicent, at the age of 24, had the effect of further weakening Grove's already flagging faith. He wrote soon afterwards,

> How am I to pass the remaining years I know not . . . I am not irreligious—but I can't cast my problem on the Lord. It seems to me that all is so vague—years ago I had all that feeling, but the deaths, first of Lucy, and now of Milly, have altered everything.[67]

Sullivan, by contrast, when faced with fatal illness or death in the family, was able to cast his problem on the Lord and to find through music a way of asserting his Christian hope and belief that death was not the end. He did it first with *In Memoriam*, again with 'The Lost Chord', and later with passages in *The Light of the World*.

The Prodigal Son

Sullivan's first oratorio came as the result of a commission from the Three Choirs Festival, a week-long programme of choral and orchestral concerts and cathedral services rotating between the cathedral cities of Worcester, Gloucester, and Hereford. Established in 1715 and still going strong, it is the oldest non-competitive music festival in the world. In accepting the challenge to compose a major sacred choral work he was following in the wake of his heroes Handel and Mendelssohn and also of leading figures in the contemporary British musical establishment. Michael Costa had written *Eli* in 1855 and *Naaman* in 1864, while William Sterndale Bennett (1816–75), Sullivan's piano teacher at the Royal Academy, had written *The Woman of Samaria* in 1867.

With the choice of subject matter left entirely to the composer, Sullivan decided on the well-known biblical story of the Prodigal Son, reflecting how remarkable it was that this parable 'should never before have been chosen as the text for a sacred musical composition'. It had in fact been set both by the French composer Marc-Antoine Charpentier (1643–1704) as a dramatic motet, *Filius Prodigus*, in 1690, and by Samuel Arnold (1740–1802), like Sullivan a chorister in the Chapel Royal, in 1773. Neither of these settings was well-known, however, and Sullivan was effectively breaking new ground in choosing this parable for musical treatment. The preface that he wrote to the work and which appears in published editions of the score explains his reasons for choosing this particular Bible story and also gives a revealing insight into his own religious convictions:

> The story is so natural and pathetic, and forms so complete a whole; its lesson is so thoroughly Christian; the characters, though few, are so perfectly contrasted, and the opportunity for the employment of "local colour" is so obvious, that it is indeed astonishing to find the subject so long overlooked.
>
> The only drawback is the shortness of the narrative, and the consequent necessity for filling it out with material drawn from elsewhere.

In the present case this has been done as sparingly as possible, and entirely from the Scriptures. In so doing the Prodigal himself has been conceived, not as of a naturally brutish and depraved disposition—a view taken by many commentators with apparently little knowledge of human nature, and no recollection of their own youthful impulses; but rather as a buoyant, restless youth, tired of the monotony of home, and anxious to see what lay beyond the narrow confines of his father's farm, going forth in the confidence of his own simplicity and ardour, and led gradually away into follies and sins which, at the outset, would have been as distasteful as they were strange to him.

The episode with which the parable concludes has no dramatic connection with the former and principal portion, and has therefore not been treated.[68]

It is significant that Sullivan described the lesson of the parable of the Prodigal Son as 'so thoroughly Christian'. Perhaps more than any other passage in the Bible it portrays God in an utterly non-judgemental light as a loving parent full of grace and compassion. His conception of the character of the Prodigal Son as 'a buoyant restless youth . . . going forth in the confidence of his own simplicity and ardour' is also highly suggestive, and it is hard to believe that the 27-year-old composer was not either consciously or unconsciously thinking of himself when he wrote those words. It is also significant that he left out the final part of the parable, in which the Prodigal's brother complains to his father about the partiality and favouritism shown to the errant younger son, 'as having no dramatic connection' with the main story. For Sullivan, the dramatic element was the most important in constructing his oratorio. His focus was on the characters of the Prodigal and his father and the relationship between them. The recent death of his own father was surely in his mind and reflected in the way that he portrayed the Prodigal's father in such human and loving terms.

The eclectic selection of texts which make up the libretto for *The Prodigal Son* suggests an extensive, almost encyclopaedic, knowledge of the Bible and an impressive grasp of the theological meaning as well as the dramatic potential of this particular parable. In addition to the story itself as recounted in Luke's Gospel, verses are incorporated from the Book of Revelation, Proverbs, Ecclesiastes, Isaiah, 1 John, Genesis, Hebrews, and especially from the Psalms which are quoted extensively and to particularly strong effect. As Tim Larsen points out in his book, *A People of One Book: The Bible and the Victorians*, many educated Victorians, including those who were not conspicuously Christian, had a good knowledge of the Bible and were able to quote from it extensively. Sullivan's time in the Chapel Royal would have given him a familiarity with many biblical passages but it seems almost inconceivable that he did not lean on Grove's superior expertise in this area. At the very least, the two men, who were still in the early intimate stage of their relationship at this time, must surely have discussed this work during its conception and genesis. I think it highly likely that Grove helped in identifying and selecting suitable Biblical verses for *The Prodigal Son*, as he certainly did subsequently for *The Light of the World*, although I am not sure one can go quite as far as Meirion Hughes does when he writes of 'its libretto by George Grove'.[69]

Structurally, *The Prodigal Son* follows the conventions of oratorio as established by Bach and Handel and is clearly influenced by Mendelssohn's *St Paul* and *Elijah*. A mixture of choruses, solo recitatives, and arias tell the story and also reflect on its wider significance and message, with every word sung being taken directly from the Bible. There are four soloists, tenor (the Prodigal), bass (the father), with soprano and alto used as narrators and to provide theological commentary and moral homily. The themes of repentance, unmerited grace, and forgiveness dominate the work which begins with the chorus singing the words from Luke 15.10 which precede the story of the Prodigal Son and form the conclusion to the parable of the lost coin: 'There is joy in the presence of the angels of God over one sinner that repenteth'. This message is reinforced by a quotation from Psalm 103: 'Like as a father pitieth his own children, even so is the Lord merciful to them that fear him'. These two passages are reprised later in the work, forming a kind of *leitmotif*. Somewhat more surprisingly, though by no means incongruously in the context of the story of the Prodigal, the opening chorus also incorporates words from Revelation 7.16 and 17: 'They shall hunger no more, neither thirst any more; and God shall wipe away all tears from their eyes.' Sullivan was clearly drawn to that text which he was to set again in *The Light of the World*.

While the central section of the oratorio is largely taken up with recounting the story of the Prodigal straight from Luke's Gospel, there are intriguing interpolations, not least a breathless Bacchanalian number for the Prodigal and chorus entitled 'The Revel', which sets words from Isaiah: 'Let us eat and drink, for tomorrow we die. Fetch wine and we will fill ourselves with strong drink'. It expresses the philosophy of '*Carpe diem*' which undoubtedly reflected Sullivan's own attitude to life and is eloquently expounded in the quintet 'Try we lifelong' in *The Gondoliers* (p. 155). Some critics regarded the style and sentiments of this chorus as being not altogether seemly for an oratorio—not for the last time Sullivan seemed to be sympathizing with the sinners more than with the righteous. It is the two powerful male arias, both set in $3/4$ time, that really show his spiritual sympathies, however. The father's 'Trust in the Lord with all thine heart', with words drawn from the Book of Proverbs, has that calm sense of trust that underlined Sullivan's faith. The tenor aria, 'How many hired servants', marks the Prodigal's moment of realization and repentance when, starving and humiliated, he resolves to go back to his father as a penitent confessing his sin. Beginning with the characteristic Sullivan device of eleven repeated notes, it is operatic in its passion and intensity, the angst being conveyed by the pulsating triplets in the accompaniment. There is a real sense of anguish as well as of contrition in the way that Sullivan sets and repeats the line 'Father, father, I have sinned against heaven and before thee'. He was doubtless thinking of his own father and perhaps, too, the words of a recent letter from Rachel were ringing in his ears:

> I want you to live so that at any moment if your father's voice called up
> to you from the sky and you looking up saw his dear face, you could
> meet his eyes boldly and bravely and say, Father, I am leading the life
> you would have me lead.[70]

If Sullivan ever came close to expressing remorse and regret for the way he had treated Rachel, it was perhaps here through his music.

The Prodigal's anguished solo is followed immediately by the chorus calmly and reassuringly repeating the opening refrain, 'There is joy in the presence of the angels of God over one sinner that repenteth', with the added line: 'The sacrifices of God are a broken spirit; a broken and contrite heart, O God, Thou wilt not despise' (Psalm 61.17), a text set by Sullivan with minimal accompaniment and with a particular sensitivity that further reinforces the theological message about genuine repentance and God's reaction to it. The reconciliation of father and son is represented by a poignant duet in which the father is given Jacob's words from the Old Testament story of Joseph: 'My son is yet alive! Now let me die, since I have seen thy face, and thou art yet alive' (Genesis 45.28, 46.30). This is a daring and inspired piece of biblical transposition, which again points to a considerable knowledge of Scripture. There is no suggestion in the parable of the Prodigal Son that the father feels he can now die having seen his son return. By putting into his mouth the words said by Jacob to Joseph, Sullivan enhances the dramatic element in the story without substantially distorting it. An unaccompanied quartet towards the end, which it has been suggested may have been inserted at the suggestion of or for the benefit of Rachel Scott Russell, features words from Psalm 34 about the Lord being nigh those that are of a contrite heart. Did it, too, perhaps express a certain contrition on Sullivan's part about the way he had treated her?[71]

Sullivan took only three weeks to compose *The Prodigal Son*, which had its first performance in Worcester Cathedral on 8 September 1869. George Grove came to hear it and put it on at the Crystal Palace three months later. There were further performances the following year in Hereford Cathedral, Edinburgh, and Manchester. The speed of its composition is evident in some rather over-long and dull choral passages towards the end. The scene in the 1953 film *The Story of Gilbert and Sullivan* in which W.S. Gilbert, having been taken to a performance of *The Prodigal Son* by Richard D'Oyly Carte, nods off near the beginning of the work and remains asleep until the end is fictitious, although it is worth mentioning for the response that Gilbert utters when the anxious impresario asks him what he will say to Sullivan about his oratorio: 'I shall tell him that it has transported me to another world'.[72]

More flattering was the verdict of Rachel Scott Russell who was still on the scene at this time. Unlike Grove, she did not attend the first performance, but after hearing a subsequent one she wrote to Arthur: 'The *divinity* of your gift of God breathes through the whole work and it is a glory to have written a thing which will stir men's souls to their depths, as it does, and make them feel better and nobler.'[73] She went on to say, 'I glory to think that you could not have written this before I knew you', still deluding herself that she was his muse when in fact it was probably Grove.[74] The work confirmed the idealized view of the composer that she was so reluctant to give up despite all his behaviour: 'I am far prouder of The Prodigal than of anything because no man whose soul was not pure and noble could have conceived or executed such music.'[75]

Fellow composers acknowledged the merits of *The Prodigal Son* but felt that Sullivan should put more effort and be more adventurous in future works of this kind. John Goss praised his former pupil but felt that he could do better:

> All you have done is most masterly—your orchestrations superb, and your efforts many of them original and first rate. Some day you will I hope try at another oratorio, putting out all your strength—not the strength of a few weeks or months. Show yourself the best man in Europe! Don't do anything so pretentious as an oratorio or even a symphony without all your power, which seldom comes in one fit. Handel's two or three weeks for the *Messiah* may be a fact, but he was not always successful, and was not so young a chap as you.[76]

John Stainer, now making his name as a church composer, voiced similar concerns:

> I heard the Prodigal Son at Worcester—the instrumentation throughout is charming—but as a whole the work lacks 'bottom'—you understand me. The melodies are graceful but not always original. I do wish dear Sullivan would put his thumb to his nose—to the public and critics,—and write for 'the future'. The later works of Mendelssohn and Beethoven, and all works of poor neglected Schubert and tardily acknowledged Schumann—all point to the future of music. Sullivan ought (I feel that he is a great man and could do so) to begin where they left off—regardless of encores and banknotes.[77]

Despite these candid comments by friends and supporters, the overall critical verdict was overwhelmingly positive. The view of the *Musical Times* was typical:

> *The Prodigal Son* is a thoughtful, conscientious work; and although unequal in merit, there can be no question that it will take rank far above any previous composition of its author. It is deeply sympathetic with the subject, betrays throughout not the slightest sign of haste or carelessness, and may be at once accepted as the latest proof of the development of a mind which has been steadily and diligently trained in that legitimate school of writing which has produced the really great

artists of the world. In constructing the libretto much skill has been shown, the parable itself being accompanied with suitable portions selected from the scriptures, which are woven in so as to form rather an Oratorio than a Sacred Cantata; the composition indeed being of sufficiently ample portion to justify this more important name.[78]

Coming at the end of a decade which had seen him produce a symphony, a cello concerto, several overtures, and other symphonic pieces and settings of Shakespeare, *The Prodigal Son* might seem to have marked Sullivan out as the serious composer that Britain was waiting for. Reviews generally concurred that it elevated him to a whole new level. The *Pall Mall Gazette* reflected that 'Mr Sullivan now occupies a very different position from that in which he stood before the production of his oratorio' and the *Musical Standard* opined that it allowed him to enter the ranks of 'those who have achieved'.[79] The oratorio went into the standard choral repertoire for the next forty years. 'There is joy in the presence of the angels of God' found its way into several church anthem books and the aria 'How many hired servants' was a popular item in church concerts.

Yet discerning friends as well as critics were raising the questions that Goss hinted at with his reference to 'the strength of a few weeks or months' and Stainer with his jibe about 'encores and banknotes'. Was Sullivan really committed to serious music and did he have the application and staying power to put sustained effort into it and forego other easier and more lucrative types of work? There were already signs that his desire to make money to fund his increasing taste for gambling and the high life was leading him to devote his time and talents to producing light popular works at the expense of more serious stuff. He had made his first venture into the world of comic opera in collaboration with Francis Burnand with *Cox and Box*, first performed privately in 1866 and then publicly to considerable acclaim in 1867 and repeated again the following year. It was followed by another comic collaboration with Burnand, *The Contrabandista*. *The Prodigal Son* did suggest a continuing attachment to sacred music and at the same time that he was working on it he was providing additional accompaniments to Handel's *Jephtha*, confirming his interest in oratorio. But there were other ominous signs that his commitment to serious music was flagging. The October 1868 Crystal

Palace programme promised a second Sullivan symphony for the forthcoming Spring season but it never materialized. It was, in Percy Young's words, 'one of the most important non-works in British music—the one which might have turned Sullivan into the symphonic composer expected by the nation.'[80]

Looking back much later, Joseph Bennett, chief music critic for the *Daily Telegraph* from 1870 to 1906 who became both a good friend and staunch supporter of Sullivan, detected as early as 1867 a dangerous change of direction on the part of the 25-year-old prodigy from whom so much was expected:

> The Power which shapes our ends had drawn him very near the line dividing Society (with the large S) from society (with the small s). It would have been better for music, perhaps, if he had never overstepped that line, but the crossing was almost inevitable. 'Society' leading, for the most part, an empty and vapid life, wants to be entertained, and cannot afford to be particular about the entertainers; so it happens that Sullivan, who was already on the side of the angels as far as that position is assured to a church organist, drifted across to the butterflies, became a friend of Royalty, and a darling of the drawing-rooms. He could hardly help himself, poor boy! Was he not under the control of his own fascinating gifts and sunny temperament?[81]

It is not difficult to find evidence to support this theory from incidents in Sullivan's life and remarks in his diary and letters in the late 1860s. There is an increasing emphasis on high society, on hobnobbing with the aristocracy and with royalty, and on frequent late-night visits to London clubs to gamble and party. He was elected to the Garrick Club in March 1869 (the first of several clubs that he would join) and in the same month he was formally presented to Queen Victoria. He soon afterwards began what was to be a close and lasting friendship with her second son, Alfred, Duke of Edinburgh, who had a distinguished career in the Royal Navy and was also a keen amateur musician. Like Sir Joseph Porter in *H.M.S. Pinafore*, Sullivan was keen to rise to the top of the social tree and his combination of consummate musical ability and easy charm enabled him to do so. During the late 1860s and early 1870s, he conducted a choral society which met in grand private houses in London, including William Ewart Gladstone's residence in Carlton House Terrace. He recalled later, 'I had the honour on two occasions of singing bass with him from the same copy'.[82]

A revealing little indication of his priorities comes in a letter of mild reprimand to his mother, who did all his packing for him on his many overseas trips, sent from one of the many Continental watering places which he took to visiting, in this case Baden-Baden, in October 1867: 'You have remembered my Prayer book but forgot my collars which in this world are almost as necessary as the Prayer Book. I shall have to buy one or two over here and charge them to you.'[83] If this suggested that his appearance was becoming more important than his religious observances, another little incident that he recalled from this time seems further to confirm Bennett's thesis that he was drifting across from the angels to the butterflies as he became ever more enmeshed with Society (with the large S). It involved a performance of *The Prodigal Son* by a group of amateur singers whom he was conducting in the house of a well-connected lady in Grosvenor Square: 'Just as the tenor was singing the pathetic solo, "I will arise and go to my father, and will say unto him," he was overpowered by the linkman's voice, who bellowed: "Mrs Johnson's carriage stops the way." It came in so appositely that the interruption proved too much for our gravity, and the performance was very nearly temporarily suspended.'[84] There is just a hint here that the frisson of hi-jinks in high places was coming to mean almost as much as the seriousness and pathos of his sacred music.

Behind all this was a deeper question. Was Sullivan showing himself to be something of a Prodigal? Was the *Wunderkind* of British music, the potential British Brahms, in danger of becoming a playboy, most at home in the casinos of Monte Carlo and the salons and clubs of the West End? Rachel Scott Russell was not the only one of his admirers to beseech him to give up his flirting, gambling, and socializing, and his increasing involvement in comic opera, and to return to serious and sacred music. Nor was it perhaps solely in allusion to his latest work that in the dining club known as 'The Muttonians', set up in the late 1860s by James Davison, music critic of *The Times* from 1846 to 1878, which often met in George Grove's house, he was known as 'the Prodigal Son'. If not quite foraging among the swine, he did seem to be in danger of drifting away from his spiritual home and anchor in the church into a more secular world.

Notes

1. Benjamin Findon, *Sir Arthur Sullivan: His Life and Music* (London: James Nisbet, 1904), p.47.
2. Arthur Sullivan [hereafter AS] to Otto Goldschmidt, 31 May 1861: Pierpont Morgan Library, New York [hereafter PML].
3. *Musical Times*, 1 February 1901, p.101.
4. *Musical Times*, 1 February 1901, p.101.
5. *Musical Times*, 1 January 1901, pp.22–3.
6. *Musical Times*, 1 February 1901, p.101.
7. Herbert Sullivan and Newman Flower, *Sir Arthur Sullivan* (London: Cassell & Co., 1927), p.39.
8. AS to Nina Lehmann, 9 January 1863, quoted in Henry Saxe Wyndham, *Arthur Seymour Sullivan* (London: Kegan, Paul, Trench, Trubner & Co., 1926), p.66; *Musical Times*, 1 February 1901, p.101.
9. *Daily Telegraph*, 26 November 1900.
10. AS to Nina Lehmann, 11 November 1862: PML.
11. *Musical Times*, 1 January 1901, p.22; Chris Brooks and Andrew Saint, *The Victorian Church: Architecture and Society* (Manchester: Manchester University Press, 1995), p.39.
12. Arthur Lawrence, *Sir Arthur Sullivan: Life Story, Letters and Reminiscences* (London: James Bowden, 1899), p.58.
13. *Musical Times*, 1 January 1901, p.23.
14. *Musical Times*, 1 January 1901, p.23.
15. *Musical Times*, 13 December 1867, p.220.
16. AS to his mother, 26 October 1862: PML.
17. Charles Graves, *The Life & Letters of Sir George Grove* (London: Macmillan, 1903), p.95.
18. Graves, *Grove*, p.134.
19. Graves, *Grove*, p.104.
20. Graves, *Grove*, p.95.
21. Graves, *Grove*, pp.133–4.
22. Percy Young, *George Grove* (London: Macmillan, 1980), p.84.
23. Reminiscences of Rev Augustus Legge, Vicar of St Bartholomew's Church, Sydenham, quoted in Graves, *Grove*, p.169.
24. George Grove to AS, 28 September 1866: PML.
25. George Grove to AS, undated: PML.
26. Graves, *Grove*, p.141.

27. Graves, *Grove*, p.146.
28. AS to his mother, 9 October 1867: PML.
29. AS to his mother, 9 October 1867: PML.
30. George Grove to Mary Sullivan, 1 October 1867: PML.
31. Percy Young, *Sir Arthur Sullivan* (London: J.M. Dent, 1971), p.269; see also Young, *Grove*, p.272.
32. Arthur Jacobs, *Arthur Sullivan*, 2nd edn. (Aldershot: Scolar Press, 1992), p.27.
33. Graves, *Grove*, p.92.
34. AS to Helen D'Oyly Carte, 27 October 1900: PML.
35. Graves, *Grove*, p.132.
36. Graves, *Grove*, p.181.
37. Graves, *Grove*, p.360.
38. Graves, *Grove*, p.272.
39. Graves, *Grove*, p.106.
40. Graves, *Grove*, p.127.
41. Graves, *Grove*, p.413.
42. George Grove to Mrs Wodehouse, 11 November 1891, in Graves, *Grove*, p.381.
43. Young, *Grove*, p.156.
44. Graves, *Grove*, p.140.
45. Graves, *Grove*, p.399.
46. Graves, *Grove*, p.392.
47. Graves, *Grove*, p.194.
48. John Wolfson, *Sullivan and the Scott Russells* (Chichester: Packard Publishing, 1984), p.18.
49. Wolfson, *Sullivan*, p.50.
50. Wolfson, *Sullivan*, p.88.
51. Michael Ainger, *Gilbert and Sullivan: A Dual Biography* (Oxford: Oxford University Press, 2002), p.85.
52. Ainger, *Gilbert and Sullivan*, p.42.
53. Ainger, *Gilbert and Sullivan*, p.87.
54. Findon, *Sullivan*, p.186.
55. Findon, *Sullivan*, pp.186–7.
56. Rachel Scott Russell to AS, 3 February 1869: PML.
57. Jacobs, *Sullivan*, p.57.
58. Findon, *Sullivan*, p.186.
59. Jacobs, *Sullivan*, p.40.

60. Young, *Sullivan*, p.42.

61. Young, *Sullivan*, p.43.

62. See, for example, Jacobs, *Sullivan*, p.45; Young, *Grove*, p.87; and, for a particularly damning verdict, Gervase Hughes, *The Music of Arthur Sullivan* (London: Macmillan, 1960), p.66.

63. Benedict Taylor, *Arthur Sullivan: A Musical Reappraisal* (London: Routledge, 2018), p.44.

64. *Athenaeum*, 3 November 1866.

65. Young, *Sullivan*, p.52.

66. Ainger, *Gilbert and Sullivan*, pp.62, 71.

67. Young, *Grove*, p.190.

68. AS, *The Prodigal Son*, Vocal Score (London: Amber Ring, 2003), p.vii.

69. Meirion Hughes, *The English Musical Renaissance and the Press 1850–1914*, paperback edn., (London: Routledge, 2017), p.123.

70. Wolfson, *Sullivan*, p.123.

71. The suggestion that the quartet may have been either suggested by or intended for Rachel Scott Russell comes in a letter to her from George Grove which is quoted in Ainger, *Gilbert and Sullivan*, p.85. Ainger states that it includes 'the aptly chosen words "They went astray".' In fact, these words come in an earlier chorus 'O that men would praise the Lord'.

72. Ian Bradley, *Lost Chords and Christian Soldiers* (London: SCM Press, 2013), p.118.

73. Leslie Baily, *The Gilbert & Sullivan Book* (London: Cassell & Co., 1956), p.94.

74. Wolfson, *Sullivan*, p.109.

75. Wolfson, *Sullivan*, p.110.

76. John Goss to AS, 22 December 1869: PML.

77. Jeremy Dibble, *John Stainer: A Life in Music* (Woodbridge: Boydell Press, 2007), p.114.

78. *Musical Times*, 1 October 1869.

79. Quoted in sleeve notes to CD recording of *The Prodigal Son* (Hyperion, 2003).

80. Young, *Sullivan*, p.103.

81. Joseph Bennett, *Forty Years of Music* (London: Methuen, 1908), p.65.

82. Lawrence, *Sullivan*, p.242.

83. AS to his mother, 1 October 1867: PML.

84. Lawrence, *Sullivan*, p.242.

4

1871–1877

A Spiritual Spell

Arthur Sullivan entered the 1870s widely recognized as England's leading composer, lauded by many critics and lionized by aristocratic patrons while still in his late 20s. Confounding the fears of those who felt that he was in danger of dissipating and prostituting his considerable talents in lightweight theatrical work and not fulfilling his early promise, he devoted the first half of the decade very largely to sacred works, which included a massive *Te Deum*, his most significant biblical oratorio, numerous hymn tunes, and sacred songs. Indeed, it was the period of his life when he was perhaps most intensely committed to religious music.

The opening year of the decade brought him into contact with the man with whose name he would be forever partnered and in collaboration with whom he would achieve lasting fame. W.S. Gilbert and Arthur Sullivan first seem to have met, or at least to have been first formally introduced, in July 1870 at the Gallery of Illustrations, a 500-seat theatre in Regent Street, London, specializing in small scale entertainments with music which was run by Priscilla and Thomas German Reed. Sullivan and Burnand's *Cox and Box* had been playing at the Gallery through much of the previous fifteen months in a double bill with one of Gilbert's plays, initially *No Cards* and subsequently, from November 1869, *Ages Ago*, which was the dramatist's first real popular success. Following the completion of its run in June 1870, *Ages Ago* was revived in a shortened form with music by Frederic Clay. Clay invited Sullivan to a rehearsal the following month and introduced him to Gilbert who promptly posed an abstruse and absurd musical question about tetrachords and disdiapason. This appropriately quirky introduction to the master of topsy-turvy would lead to the two men's first collaboration the following year, although it was some time before they settled into their regular partnership. For the time being, Sullivan's sights were set elsewhere than on the theatre.

In 1871, the year in which he reached his 29th birthday, and the mid-way point in his life, Sullivan signalled his increasing wealth and status by moving house with his mother, a cook, and four servants to Albert Mansions in Victoria Street in the heart of London. At one end of the street stood those pillars of the establishment in church and state, Westminster Abbey and the Houses of Parliament, and at the other end Victoria Station, allowing him rapid access to the boat trains which took him on the first leg of his increasingly frequent journeys to the Continent. Also nearby was Buckingham Palace, the seat of the royal family, with one of whose members Sullivan was becoming increasingly friendly. Alfred, Duke of Edinburgh, regularly came round informally to Albert Mansions to play the violin, accompanied by Sullivan on the piano. Following the opening of the Royal Albert Hall by Queen Victoria in memory of her much missed consort in March 1871, an orchestra was formed to play there, with Sullivan as conductor and the Duke as leader.

For the first major concert in the Royal Albert Hall, on 1 May 1871, four new works were commissioned from British, French, German, and Italian composers. Charles Gounod was responsible for the French contribution and Arthur Sullivan was chosen to represent Britain. His cantata *On Shore and Sea*, with a libretto by Thomas Taylor, a future editor of *Punch*, tells of sea battles between Italian Christians and North African Moors in the sixteenth century. The Christian hero, Il Marinajo, a Genoese sailor, has arias invoking the protection of the Virgin Mary, Star of the Sea, and asserting that 'They chain not Christian souls that chain their limbs', for both of which Sullivan supplied suitably soaring melodies. Rather more daringly, he deployed Arabian musical motifs and instruments, including Turkish bells, for a processional dance entitled 'Moresque' and a powerfully percussive Muslim call to prayer. A more subdued melody accompanies the pious response of the Genoese sailors as they find themselves chained in slave galleys:

Hold to Christian manhood, firm in Christian faith.
Faithful hearts make fearless hands, and faithful hearts have we,
The Christians 'gainst the infidel, chained though we be.

On Shore and Sea, which Sullivan dedicated to George Grove, ends with a stirring chorus, 'Sink and Scatter, Clouds of War' invoking Britain as the home of 'peaceful progress'. Later detached from the cantata and inserted into the concert repertoire as 'The song of peace', its tune is a touch too martial and bombastic to carry comfortably the message of the blessings and benefits of peace proclaimed in the text. Not for the first or last time Sullivan allowed himself to be somewhat carried away with patriotic sentiment.

The end of 1871 saw Sullivan's first collaboration with Gilbert, *Thespis*, variously described as an 'operatic extravaganza' and 'an original grotesque opera' and designed for the Christmas season, which opened on Boxing Day at the Gaiety Theatre on Aldwych at the eastern end of the Strand. Framed in the burlesque tradition and in the style of the *opéra bouffe* pioneered by Jacques Offenbach, it involves a travelling theatrical troupe swopping places and roles with the Greek gods on Mount Olympus. It had a moderately successful run of sixty-three performances but was never revived and the score was lost or perhaps even destroyed. Both librettist and composer were subsequently inclined to disown their first joint production and it was to be another four years before they collaborated again in the rather different genre of comic opera.

Just two months after the opening of *Thespis*, in February 1872, Sullivan resigned from his post as organist of St Peter's Church, Cranley Gardens, ending his time as a musician working in a church context. It is tempting to see this action, as some of his biographers have, as signalling a decisive turning away from the world of sacred music which had so gripped and enthralled him in the early part of his life. Did his departure from the organ loft on the eve of his fourth decade also signal a move away from his early faith towards a more agnostic outlook? I am not sure that we can draw either of these conclusions. He clearly enjoyed his ten years as a church organist— he was earning enough from his songs by the mid-1860s to have quitted earlier if his motives for doing the job were purely financial—but he was becoming increasingly busy on the conducting circuit as well as being more immersed in social and other distractions. He was also receiving numerous invitations to spend weekends at the country homes of his growing circle of wealthy and aristocratic friends. The decision to give up the duties of a London church organist and choir master, with the regular weekend commitments that they entailed, was almost certainly prompted by these changes in lifestyle rather than by waning religious commitment. It may also have been a consequence of the debilitating kidney disease which was possibly beginning to afflict him around this time and was to be his constant companion and curse for the rest of his life, often bringing bouts of excruciating pain, confining him to bed and necessitating strong medication in the form of morphine.

Although he stopped being in church every Sunday, Sullivan did not give up the practice of churchgoing after leaving his post at St Peter's. His diary records that although he seldom seems to have attended a Sunday service while on his own in London or in one of the out-of-town retreats where he escaped to work, he generally worshipped at the local parish church or private chapel when staying as a weekend country house guest. He was often prevailed on to play the organ or harmonium at such services, an activity which he always enjoyed. It was while on one of these weekend visits in 1871 that he composed his most famous hymn tune, ST GERTRUDE, which has become the standard tune for 'Onward, Christian soldiers'. It came to him while he was playing the piano in the drawing room of Hanford House in the hamlet of Childe Okeford, Dorset, the home of Ernest Clay Key Seymer, a distinguished diplomat and brother of the composer, Fred Clay, and his wife Gertrude, after whom Sullivan named his characteristically stirring march-like melody. 'We sang it in the private chapel', she later recalled, 'Sir Arthur playing the harmonium, and having taught us the tune.' [1]

These sojourns with his aristocratic friends and patrons were not without their spiritual moments. While staying at Costessey Hall near Norwich, the home of Lord and Lady Stafford, who were both staunch Roman Catholics, in 1872, he was much taken with the altar light burning in the private chapel. He also reported to his mother that on his arrival the household were dancing 'and a priest was playing a choice selection of waltzes'.[2] He particularly enjoyed hearty hymn singing. An entry in his diary for 9 September 1874, while staying at Balcarres in Fife, the Scottish home of Sir Coutts and Lady Lindsay, is typical: 'We had a heavenly day yesterday and drove in the morning to the English Church, six miles distant. There was a very nice service, and we all sang the hymn lustily, to the accompaniment of a small organ, played by one young lady and blown by another.'[3] The journey to the 'English' (i.e. Episcopal) church, rather than the nearer Presbyterian parish church (the Kirk), where the musical diet would have been restricted to unaccompanied metrical psalms, met with his approval. On another visit to Balcarres he told his mother, 'Today they have all been to the Kirk—but I stayed at home to work' and he later complained to her from Glasgow, 'A Scotch "Sawbath" is a ghastly thing. I tried to find a good Anglican church, but they are all dull or else Kirks. Cabs are double fares on Sundays, all locomotion and recreation are discouraged, and whisky-drinking encouraged.'[4] The youthful Sabbatarianism which had led him to boycott the *Gewandhaus* concerts at Leipzig had long since disappeared.

Although Sullivan ended his regular weekly active involvement in making church music in 1872, he did not stop composing in this area. On the contrary, in the two years following his resignation from St Peter's he wrote relatively few secular works and devoted himself very largely to sacred compositions. They include the *Te Deum* of 1872, the oratorio *The Light of the World* (1873), and the great majority of his hymn tunes.

The *Festival Te Deum*

Towards the end of 1871, Queen Victoria's eldest son, Albert Edward, the Prince of Wales, fell ill with typhoid fever, the disease which had killed his father, Prince Albert, ten years earlier, leading his mother to withdraw almost completely from public life. Daily reports of his condition were carried in the press and more than once the end was thought to be near. However, he rallied and recovered in the New Year and, following a Thanksgiving Service in St Paul's Cathedral, the directors of the Crystal Palace Company decided to mount a large fête to reflect the mood of deliverance and thanksgiving felt across the nation. They commissioned Sullivan to provide a grand *Festival Te Deum* which would be performed in the presence of the Queen at the Crystal Palace on 1 May 1872.

This commission confirmed Sullivan's position as composer laureate to both Crown and nation. In accepting it, he was standing in the tradition of Handel who had composed similar celebratory *Te Deum*s to mark the end of the War of Spanish Succession with the signing of the Treaty of Utrecht in 1713 and the British victory over the French at the battle of Dettingen in 1743. These works established a precedent for using this particular liturgical text for what were effectively secular purposes, extolling the United Kingdom and its monarchy and expressing national pride.

As a strong monarchist and patriot, Sullivan warmed to his task and resolved to set the *Te Deum* for soprano soloist, massed choirs—the chorus numbered around 2,000 at the first performance—orchestra, organ, and military band. He obtained Queen Victoria's permission to dedicate the work to her and for the opening performance, one of the first occasions in which she appeared in public following her long period of seclusion after her husband's death, he changed the penultimate line from 'O Lord, have mercy upon us' to 'O Lord, save the Queen'.

The *Festival Te Deum*, which lasts for around thirty-three minutes, is characterized by a juxtaposition of sacred and secular musical themes. There are suitably 'churchy' passages for organ and choir, including some plainchant, and much use is made of the hymn tune ST ANN, probably composed in the early eighteenth century by William Croft, organist at the Chapel Royal, and indissolubly linked in the public mind with Isaac Watts' paraphrase of Psalm 90, 'O God our help in ages past'. There is also a lilting waltz and towards the end a military band enters with a jaunty march tune which sounds as though it belongs to *The Marriage of Figaro*, if not even *H.M.S. Pinafore*. Two modern musicologists, Roderick Swanston and Benedict Taylor, have argued that Sullivan's combination of the sacred and secular was deliberate. In Taylor's words: 'Sullivan is fusing two opposing worlds—the "high", sacred, official style suitable for the national celebration of the recovery of the Prince of Wales, and the everyday, common, secular, style of the people who were the subjects of their Prince, and after all, Sullivan's public.'[5] It was an early indication of his lifelong concern to make his settings of religious texts as accessible and popular as his music for the stage and drawing room.

The composer was 'uproariously cheered' by the audience of 26,000 in the Crystal Palace. Music critics were in agreement with the public in their enthusiasm for the work. A positive review of the published score in the *Musical Times* drew comparisons with Handel's *Dettingen Te Deum* and concluded:

> With much of the breadth of Handel, some of the grace of Mozart, and an orchestral colouring almost unique in its masterly handling, this Te Deum ought to serve as a gratifying promise that English music is blossoming into a Spring to be succeeded by a Summer, such as this land has not experienced since the death of Purcell.[6]

Like so much of Sullivan's religious work, the *Festival Te Deum* is vulgar in the best sense of the word, in being accessible, stirring, and written for the people rather than the critics. As the cultural historian Jeffrey Richards has observed, 'It somehow encapsulates the Victorian age musically: the devotion of a Protestant church interwoven with the military swagger of imperial pomp, all in a work dedicated to the recovery of the Prince of Wales'.[7] The *Te Deum* perfectly expressed public relief at the recovery of the heir to the throne from a near-fatal illness but perhaps even more it expressed public joy at the emergence of a beloved Queen out of purdah, and a broader sense of national thanksgiving and well-being. Sullivan did not just catch the national mood; he felt it deeply himself. Like all his work, it is sincere and from the heart. He was genuinely full of gratitude to God for giving Britain such a wonderful Queen, to whom he was devoted, as well as for sparing her somewhat dissolute and prodigal son.

The Light of the World, 1873

Sullivan's second biblically based oratorio was the result of a commission from the Birmingham Musical Festival which had an impressive record in this sphere, having hosted the first performances of Mendelssohn's *Elijah*, Costa's *Eli* and *Naaman*, and, more recently, Julius Benedict's *St Peter* in 1870.

There have been various suggestions as to where Sullivan got the inspiration for *The Light of the World*. Herbert Sullivan and Newman Flower stated with some conviction that it was from an Irish lady with whom he was in love.[8] Michael Ainger has speculated that it might have come from the altar lamp that had impressed him during his visit to Costessy Hall.[9] It is more commonly suggested that the inspiration for the oratorio came from the painting of the same name by William Holman Hunt showing Jesus with a lantern in his hand knocking at a door overgrown with brambles. The Pre-Raphaelite artist produced the original version of the painting between 1851 and 1853 following a religious conversion. A smaller version, probably painted by a friend of Hunt's, was exhibited around the United Kingdom and the United States, and an engraving made in 1860 sold widely, boosting the painting's iconic status. Its popularity may have been a factor in determining the title and theme of Sullivan's work, although there is no mention of it in his letters or diary. Neither Jesus' description of himself as the Light of the World (John 8.12, 12.46) nor the specific verse which inspired Holman Hunt's painting, 'Behold, I stand at the door and knock' (Revelation 3.20) appear in the libretto. The painting may possibly have been in Sullivan's mind when he selected the title of his work but it was certainly not a major influence in terms of its theme.

It would not be at all surprising if the idea and broad outline of the oratorio came from George Grove. He certainly played a major role in selecting the eclectic and diverse range of biblical texts that make up the libretto. In a letter to James Davison in May 1873, Sullivan wrote 'The words are all compiled from the Bible by Grove and myself. I think the book is really beautiful thanks to dear old "G".' He went on to say, 'I never go out in the world as my oratorio takes all my time and thought . . . I have stuck to my work since last Michaelmas without faltering.'[10] If this was, indeed, the case then he worked on it for longer than he did on most of his sacred works.

As well as helping to select the text, Grove wrote a forty-six-page analysis of the oratorio, published by J.B. Cramer & Co. to coincide with its first performance. It begins with an opening statement which also appears as a preface entitled 'Argument' on the first page of the published vocal score. I suspect that Grove may well have been responsible for this, or at the very least have had a significant role in its drafting. It begins with a short single paragraph introduction setting out the purpose of the work:

In this oratorio the intention has not been to convey the spiritual idea of the Saviour, as in the *Messiah*, or to recount the sufferings of Christ, as in the '*Passionsmusik*,' but to set forth the human aspect of the life of our Lord on earth, exemplifying it by some of the actual incidents in His career, which bear specially upon His attributes of Preacher, Healer, and Prophet.[11]

Several prominent themes in Grove's own liberal theological outlook are evident here, notably the emphasis on the human rather than the supernatural Jesus, and the downplaying of his suffering and death with their soteriological atoning significance in favour of a more incarnational focus on his life and activities as preacher, healer, and prophet. As we have already noted, probably largely because of Grove's influence, Sullivan broadly shared this liberal perspective. His setting of Jesus' words is simple and restrained, set within a relatively limited vocal range suggestive of plainchant, and always accompanied by a small inner orchestra with the *cor anglais* having an especially prominent role. This establishes Jesus as both calm and authoritative as well as very human. It also establishes him as someone who is open and accessible, interacting with other people while preserving a degree of detachment. In addition to what he took from Grove, Sullivan also brought to the oratorio the particular emphasis in his own faith on consolation, forgiveness, and assurance.

The Light of the World, which runs in its original version to two and three-quarter hours, is divided into two parts. It begins with the chorus singing a prologue made up of verses from Isaiah about the coming Messiah, beginning with the words 'There shall come forth a rod out of the stem of Jesse' and continuing with the more specific prophecy of the coming of one sent by the Lord not to judge or reprove but to preach good tidings unto the meek, bind up the broken-hearted, proclaim liberty to the captives, and open the prison to those who are bound. Sullivan sets this chorus so that the phrases 'good tidings', 'liberty', and 'the opening of the prison' are repeated and emphasized, reinforcing the portrayal of Jesus as liberator and enabler. The opening chorus ends with a vigorous and affirmative setting of Isaiah's further promise: 'He will swallow up death in victory, and the Lord God will wipe away tears from off all faces'. This is a theme that recurs again and again in the oratorio—four of its arias (three of them given to an angel to sing) directly repeat its message that God will wipe away all tears, and counsel against weeping for the dead. Here we see a clear reflection of Sullivan's own faith with its strong element of consolation and reassurance in the face of death, and his own lack of fear of dying and what lies beyond it.

Despite Grove's unease about taking the Bible too literally, considerable reverence is accorded to Scripture in the oratorio and it does include several traditional and well-loved texts that biblical scholars might question in terms of their authenticity and provenance. The first scene, set in Bethlehem and telling the story of the Nativity, is replete with angels and a very sprightly chorus of shepherds, although it avoids any mention of the Virgin birth. The following scene, which in Grove's words, 'alludes to rather than actually describes the Murder of the Innocents, the Flight of the Holy Family into Egypt, and their Return thence to Palestine', focuses on Rachel's lamentation over her children in Rama with her wailing voice plaintively floating over the chorus' quiet lament.[12] It is answered by the first two of the four arias of consolation mentioned above, the gentle tenor and contralto solos 'Refrain thy voice from weeping' and 'The voice of weeping shall be no more heard'.

It is in the next scene set in the synagogue, and identified by Grove as focusing on Jesus as preacher, that the daring break with tradition that Sullivan made in *The Light of the World* is introduced and revealed. Instead of there being a narrator as in all previous English oratorios, Jesus introduces himself directly in the first person as the liberator and emancipator promised in the passage from Isaiah 61 used in the opening chorus and taken up in Luke 4.18–19. Here is the Christ of Christian socialism, a movement to which Grove was sympathetic. Jesus sings of preaching the Gospel to the poor rather than, as in the opening chorus, of bringing good news to the meek. His radical inclusivity is further emphasized in his subsequent exchange with the increasingly angry crowd whom he outrages by pointing out how previous prophets, Elias (Elijah) and Eliseus (Elisha), deliberately reached out to and healed those like Sarepta and Naaman the Syrian who, in Jewish eyes, were heathens and outcasts. Throughout this exchange, Sullivan maintains his portrayal of Jesus as the voice of calm assurance, firm but not hectoring, and never losing his cool or his measured detachment in the face of the growing fury and discord on the part of his hearers. The synagogue scene closes with Jesus, expelled by the angry crowd and left alone with his disciples, chanting an extract from the Sermon on the Mount, accompanied by his distinctive inner orchestra and pointedly focusing on the passage: 'Judge not, that ye be not judged; condemn not, and ye shall not be condemned; forgive, and ye shall be forgiven'. His solo ends with those enigmatic and challenging words about God intended to reinforce the teaching that we should love our enemies and pray for our persecutors, 'He maketh the sun to rise on the evil and on the good, and sendeth rain on the just and on the unjust' which are taken up by the chorus in a sprightly semi-fugal setting which brings out the playfulness as well as the inscrutability of divine providence.

The third scene, which Grove in his analysis headlines 'The Healer', recounts the story of Lazarus. As one might expect given Grove's unease about miracles, it actually leaves out the central element in the biblical narrative, the raising of Lazarus from his tomb. Grove justifies this omission by saying that 'the actual resurrection of Lazarus is too solemn for any music'.[13] So there is, in fact, almost no miraculous element in this scene. It portrays Jesus as a healer, not as a miracle worker. The accent once again is overwhelmingly on the themes of reassurance and consolation, with the contralto aria 'Weep ye not for the dead', the oratorio's third song of consolation, which is preceded by an orchestral passage entitle 'In Bethany' of almost unbearable poignancy, being picked up by the chorus, who return to a passage from Isaiah to celebrate and affirm the defeat of death by life.

Having demonstrated Christ's character as preacher and healer, the fourth and final scene of the first part, 'The way to Jerusalem', presents him as prophet. Grove's commentary on this scene has a distinctly liberal Protestant and indeed political emphasis. Arguing that what Jesus accomplished as a prophet was more significant than his work as either a preacher or a healer, he portrays him as

> the successor and Chief of those great men, peculiar to the Jewish people, who throughout their history were successively raised up to bring the nation back to its allegiance to Jehovah its King, to fight the cause of the poor and oppressed against the rich and powerful, to expose the hollowness and evil of priestcraft, to teach the true politics

of the day—in a word, to restore the nation to the high ideal with which it had started.[14]

In fact, Jesus' utterances are sparing in this section, being confined to brief and enigmatic predictions about his own fate and that of the city of Jerusalem, and are almost lost amidst the joyful Hosanna choruses acclaiming him as the Son of David.

It is in the opening scene of the second part of the oratorio, set now in Jerusalem itself, that Jesus has his longest and most sustained solo passage, expounding in full the parable of the sheep and the goats. Here there is an undeniable and uncomfortable emphasis on judgement. Indeed, Grove comments in his analysis that this passage was selected 'amongst other reasons, because in it our Lord, as the Son of Man, assumes the office of Judge of the World'.[15] But if this note of judgement marks a departure from the generally liberal theology of Grove and Sullivan, the overall message of this parable, the only one to feature in the text of *The Light of the World*, is, of course, highly consistent with it, being among the most powerful expressions in the New Testament of the social gospel and the command to Christians to engage in practical action to feed the hungry, tend the sick, and visit those in prison.

The second part continues with the build-up to Jesus' passion and death. Once again, the prevailing message is one of reassurance and consolation. Jesus, in more lyrical mood and accompanied for the first time by violins as well as the lower strings, tells the daughters of Jerusalem that he has overcome the world and this is followed by an unaccompanied quartet singing the fourth verse of Psalm 23 'Yea, though I walk through the valley of the shadow of death, I will fear no evil'. Of the actual crucifixion there is virtually nothing other than a brief allusion to it from the Book of Acts—in Grove's words, 'That catastrophe forms no part of this Oratorio, except in so far as it can be conveyed by implication'.[16] Rather, the action moves straight to the sepulchre in the garden where an angel reassures Mary Magdalene that the Lord has risen and, in the oratorio's fourth and most substantial aria of consolation, that 'God shall wipe away all tears from their eyes. There shall be no more death, neither sorrow nor crying, neither shall there be any more pain'. A thrilling a cappella six-part chorus confirms that the Lord is risen and, following the call by a disciple to fight the good fight of faith, the closing chorus, drawing on verses from Acts, Revelation, and Galatians, finally introduces the theme of salvation from sin and deliverance from evil.

Despite this last-minute expression of soteriology, the clear and abiding impression given of Jesus in *The Light of the World* is of a preacher, healer, and prophet, and indeed a liberator, enabler, and agitator, rather than a saviour who dies on the Cross to atone for human sin. The theme of resurrection is prominent in the Lazarus scene in the first part and the risen Lord is enthusiastically affirmed in the second part but the figure of the suffering and crucified Saviour is almost completely absent throughout. Overall, there is little or no expression of the doctrine of atonement as there is so clearly, for example, in John Stainer's later oratorio *The Crucifixion* (1887). The emphasis is rather on the social gospel and on a political as well as a spiritual message. That may well have come in large part from Grove's sympathy with Christian socialism. Sullivan's softer, simpler, and less political brand of liberal Christianity finds its expression in the calm and reassuring authority with which he invests the character of Jesus and in the tender and emotional way in which he sets those repeated passages which promise an end to sorrow and pain, and a victory over death. This is not to say that the mood of the oratorio is consistently comfortable and undemanding. There is enough dissonance and agitation in the scoring to disturb and unsettle. But overall, just as in *The Prodigal Son*, God is revealed through his Son as full of mercy, compassion, forgiveness, consolation, and reassurance, and above all as the One who will wipe away all tears and comfort the sorrowful. It is a work shot through with a sense of divine emollient.

The Light of the World was given its first performance in Birmingham on 27 August 1873 in the presence of Sullivan's close friend, the Duke of Edinburgh, to whose Russian bride, Grand Duchess Maria Alexandrovna of Russia, the work was dedicated. It was received with enormous enthusiasm by the audience—three pieces were encored and there were requests for more. The Duke of Edinburgh, to whom the composer left the score in his will 'in remembrance of the many happy hours which he spent with his Royal Highness while he was writing it', contented himself by repeating again and again to the composer, 'a triumph'.[17] Music critics were divided in their opinion of the work, although they were generally agreed in finding the libretto weak and badly arranged. The *Observer* was enthusiastic, concluding that 'the oratorio is one of imagination, of not only clever ideas but of really devotional religious thought . . . we may safely look now to Mr Sullivan for sacred works of the highest class'.[18] James Davison was similarly positive in *The Times*, expressing the view that 'To the profound feeling of reverence with which Mr Sullivan has musically illustrated all the passages relating to the Saviour, and in which the Saviour is supposed to hold forth, no intelligent listener can be insensible' and rating the work as 'the best oratorio for which we are indebted to an English musician'.[19]

The oratorio was performed in an abridged version in London, Liverpool, Bootle, Norwich, and Manchester in 1874, and in Glasgow in 1876. Gounod came specially to hear it in London and declared it 'a masterpiece' and Queen Victoria said that it was 'destined to uplift British music'.[20] 'Yea, though I walk through the valley of the shadow of death' was taken up as an anthem in churches and the contralto aria 'The Lord is risen' from the final scene was issued by J.B. Cramer as a sacred parlour ballad under the title 'God shall wipe away all tears' and recorded by the hugely popular British singer Clara Butt who described *The Light of the World* as her favourite oratorio, and noted approvingly that its performance almost always led to much weeping in the audience. Her comment underlines the work's unashamed sentimentality and emotional pull. Like much of Sullivan's sacred output it has a distinctly theatrical and operatic flavour and could perhaps have applied to it Hans von Bülow's famous description of Verdi's *Requiem* as 'opera dressed up in ecclesiastical robes'. Not that it is secular in style. The influence of Mendelssohn's sacred oratorios is very clear and there are several appropriations of church music, including Russian Orthodox chant in the chorus 'The Lord is risen', suggestions of Byrd and Tallis, and a direct quotation of Orlando Gibbons. Its lyrical accessibility make it very different in feel from the heavy, self-conscious religiosity of most nineteenth-century British oratorios, while still clearly being the product of a clear and sincerely held faith.

The Light of the World further cemented Sullivan's unassailable position as the leading English composer of his day, if not of his century. It also persuaded some of those who had accused him of squandering his talents that for all his backsliding into parlour ballads and theatrical extravaganzas, he was still committed to serious sacred work. One such, the critic of *The Academy*, after somewhat begrudgingly noting 'We should by no means have selected him as the man best fitted to carry out so serious an undertaking' went on to express delight that 'Mr Sullivan, who possesses undoubted talent as a composer, after frittering away much valuable time on the production of ballads for the music shops, has again turned his attention to a work of serious import'.[21]

Church Hymns, 1874

Arthur Sullivan wrote forty-two of his sixty-one original hymn tunes and seventy of his seventy-five hymn tune arrangements between 1871 and 1874. It may seem strange at first sight that this activity largely occupied him in the years after he had ceased playing the organ and being a regular church musician. The reason for this great outburst of productivity was that the great majority of his tunes were specifically written for two Anglican hymn books which came out during this period, *The Hymnary*, published in 1872, and *Church Hymns with Tunes*, of which he was musical editor, which appeared in 1874.

The early 1870s marked the height of the Victorian hymn boom which had begun twenty or so years earlier when the Church of England fully embraced hymn singing and allowed its congregations to extend their repertoire beyond the narrow confines of metrical psalmody that had prevailed since the Reformation. With new hymn books selling in their thousands and undergoing regular reprints, commissions and royalty payments for tunes provided a lucrative source of income for both up-and-coming and established composers. Some of Sullivan's biographers have suggested that for him the composition of hymn tunes was essentially hack work undertaken purely to make money. Such was David Eden's view: 'I think it is safe to conclude that Sullivan's considerable output in this area came into existence simply because he needed the money . . . His reason for writing had nothing to do with religious conviction as such'.[22] In fact, there is evidence that this was work that he took seriously and regarded as a service to the church as well as a favour to his friends among the clergy and church musicians. Some of his earliest efforts in this area, including an arrangement of the hymn tune ST ANN, were written at the request of Robert Brown-Borthwick, whose *Supplemental Hymn and Tune Book* appeared in 1869. He wrote a further batch of tunes, including ST GERTRUDE for 'Onward, Christian soldiers', for Joseph Barnby, musical editor of *The Hymnary*, published by Novello in 1872, and two years later produced thirty-six original tunes and sixty-nine arrangements for *Church Hymns with Tunes*.

Most of Sullivan's hymn tunes were specially written to accompany new texts written by his contemporaries. He set the words of several of the great Victorian religious poets and hymn writers, including John Ellerton, John Henry Newman, John Mason Neale, Horatius Bonar, and William Walsham How. In terms of his popularity and impact, a tally of between twenty-five and thirty original tunes in virtually every hymnal published in the late nineteenth century puts him firmly among the top ten Victorian hymn tune composers alongside John Bacchus Dykes, Joseph Barnby, Henry Gauntlett, Edward John Hopkins, Henry Smart, John Stainer, Samuel Sebastian Wesley, William Henry Monk, and Richard Redhead. All of these others were first and foremost church musicians, who for the most part composed nothing other than sacred pieces. They were also predominantly Anglo-Catholic in their churchmanship and theological outlook. In both respects, Sullivan was out of step with his fellow practitioners in this genre.[23]

Sullivan is usually ranked alongside Barnby and Stainer as a leading exponent of the high Victorian hymn tune, distinguished by an emotional and sentimental style achieved through intricate part writing, chromatic progressions, and other devices designed to enhance the impact of the text. The three composers were good friends and much of an age—Barnby was four years older and Stainer two years older than Sullivan. They are often seen as following the lead of their seniors Dykes and Monk, both of whom were born in 1823, in eschewing the restraint, austerity, and classical harmony of an earlier generation of nineteenth-century composers, led by Sullivan's old teachers, John Goss (born in 1810) and Henry Smart (born in 1813). Sullivan did, in fact, have considerable respect for the work of older composers like Goss and retained a fondness for the plainchant in which he had been schooled by Thomas Helmore. Some of his own hymn tunes use Anglican chant, notably VENI CREATOR, LITANY No.2, and HOLY CITY. The great majority, however, are distinctively high

Victorian in being lyrical and flowing, written and harmonized like part songs, and carefully crafted to heighten the emotional impact of the text. They are more sentimental and less austere and restrained than what had gone before and what would come after in the tunes of Vaughan Williams, Stanford, and Parry. Sullivan stands very clearly alongside Dykes, Stainer, and other leading exponents of the high Victorian hymn tune in his almost evangelistic determination to enhance the meaning of the texts that he set, pointing up their poignancy and drama, and eliciting the maximum response from those singing them.

Sullivan's hymn tunes encompass a huge range of styles and moods, reflecting the very different themes of the texts to which they were set. Some, like ST GERTRUDE and LUX EOI, come straight off the parade ground and could have been written for the chorus of heavy dragoons in *Patience*. In this, they are entirely in keeping with the triumphant words to which they are set. ST GERTRUDE perfectly fits the mood and purpose of 'Onward, Christian Soldiers', which had been written by Sabine Baring Gould while a curate in Horbury, West Yorkshire, as a 'Hymn for Procession with Cross and Banners' to be sung by children processing on Whit Monday from one village to another. It is not surprising that it rapidly supplanted the sluggish ST ALBAN, based on the slow movement in a Haydn symphony, to which the hymn was initially set. LUX EOI was written for a triumphalist hymn by Christopher Wordsworth, Bishop of Lincoln, about the second coming of Christ, 'Hark a thrilling voice is sounding: "Christ is nigh!" it seems to say'.

Other similarly bouncy and affirmative tunes express Sullivan's own simple, trusting faith, perhaps none more so than COURAGE BROTHER for Norman MacLeod's hymn 'Courage, brother, do not stumble', itself a great statement of straightforward, manly, muscular faith by the Church of Scotland minister who was Queen Victoria's favourite chaplain. Sullivan's tune reinforces the hymn's central message by repeating the phrase 'Trust in God' so that it rings out three times as a stirring clarion call above the steady march-like rhythm of the verses. A similar affinity with the text informs CONSTANCE, written for the hymn 'Who trusts in God a strong abode in heaven and earth possesses'. Sullivan's intrinsic optimism and love of life come across in other tunes which are not so obviously bouncy and 'rumpty-tumpty'. The lyrical but gentle GOLDEN SHEAVES perfectly fits William Chatterton Dix's harvest hymn 'To Thee, O Lord, our hearts we raise in hymns of adoration' with its rich imagery of bright robes of gold adorning the fields and the valleys standing so rich with corn that they are singing. Sullivan provides this pastoral hymn of thanksgiving with a melody so appropriate and vivid that you can almost smell the newly mown hay and hear the threshing machines as you sing it. In its way it is as evocative of the English landscape as the music of Delius or Vaughan Williams, but in a lusher, more comfortable, and more Victorian way. There is a similarly gentle but affirmative quality in Sullivan's setting of Sarah Flowers Adams' 'Nearer, my God, to Thee', a highly sentimental hymn of personal faith that was immensely popular with the Victorians. His tune, PROPIOR DEO, which was almost certainly the one used by the musicians on board the *R.M.S. Titanic* when they played the hymn shortly before the liner went down on the night of 15 April 1912, manages to be affirmative and filled with hope while acknowledging the poignancy and yearning conveyed in the words.

There are other Sullivan tunes which are similarly touched with pathos and poignancy. Perhaps the most nuanced and sensitive is LUX IN TENEBRIS, written for John Henry Newman's 'Lead, kindly light', another favourite which was regularly at the top of the Victorian hymnological hit parade. It is essentially an expression of doubt-tinged faith, penned by Newman when he was at the height of the spiritual crisis which was to find its resolution in his reception into the Roman Catholic church. Many composers tried their hand at setting it. Probably its best known accompaniment is Dykes' LUX BENIGNA, which although commended by Newman himself, hardly reflects the hesitant, tentative nature of his text, being altogether too positive, with a strong forward movement in its steady, reassuring repeated minims. Sullivan's tune, which first appeared in a selection of sacred part songs and is perhaps better suited to choirs than to congregations, provides a more sensitive and honest reflection of Newman's ambiguity and expressions of doubt. The supposedly worldly Sullivan understood and captured the mood of this classic spiritual text better than the pious Dykes. He also excelled in setting hymns telling a strong human story and eliciting a moral and emotional response. A good example is James Drummond Burns' dramatic retelling of the story of God's appearance to the young Samuel, 'Hushed was the evening hymn', which is full of descriptive writing and dramatic narrative and is perfectly served by SAMUEL with its evocation of simple, innocent faith.

Sullivan's contribution to Victorian hymnody was not limited to supplying tunes. He acted as musical editor for a major mid-Victorian hymn book, *Church Hymns with Tunes*, published by the Society for Promoting Christian Knowledge in 1874. Originally published in a words-only format with 592 hymns under the title *Church Hymns* in 1871, it was intended to provide a middle-of-the-road alternative to High Church hymnals like Helmore's *The Hymnal Noted* and Barnby's *The Hymnary*. Less sacramental in ethos than *Hymns Ancient and Modern*, the book which really triggered the Victorian hymn explosion when it came out in 1861, *Church Hymns* was at the same time markedly less Evangelical than the other widely used Victorian Anglican hymn book, *The Hymnal Companion to the Book of Common Prayer*. The editors of the original words-only edition were William Walsham How, the pastorally minded rector of Whittington, Shropshire, who stood in the liberal Catholic tradition, John Ellerton, vicar of Crewe Green in Staffordshire and a committed Broad Churchman, and Sullivan's good friend, Robert Brown-Borthwick.

Musical editorship of such a large and complex volume brought financial reward but also a great deal of hard work in commissioning, selecting, and arranging tunes. Describing his own travails, Sullivan confessed to Brown-Borthwick, 'Had I known the wearisome labours of it, I would not have undertaken it for a <u>thousand pounds</u>' and told his mother, 'I hope that the hymn-book will be a blessing to the Church. It's a curse to me'.[24] Most of his biographers have tended to emphasize the negative aspect of these remarks and suggest that they showed that the project was a tiresome chore which he only undertook for the money. However, we should perhaps take the remark to his mother expressing his hope that the book would be a blessing for the church at face value. A similar sentiment is expressed at the end of his preface to the hymnal: 'the Editor trusts that this book may prove one more step towards the advancement of good and worthy music in the service of God'.[25]

Sullivan worked particularly closely on *Church Hymns with Tunes* with William Walsham How, who went on to become the first bishop of

Wakefield and is remembered today for his fine hymn 'For all Thy saints, who from their labours rest'. How undertook the task of inserting expression marks indicating appropriate levels of volume and points for crescendo and diminuendo in each of the 592 hymns in the book. He and Sullivan became good friends and were to collaborate later on the hymn to celebrate Queen Victoria's Diamond Jubilee. Their hymn book enjoyed substantial sales and influence within the Church of England. By 1890, it had sold over 85,000 copies and established itself as the second most used hymn book in Anglican churches after *Hymns Ancient and Modern*. Sullivan was at least partially responsible for its two most enduring contributions to English hymnody, the tunes NOEL and ST CLEMENT which it introduced as the accompaniments for 'It came upon the midnight clear' and 'The day, Thou gavest, Lord, is ended', respectively. Edmund Sears' wistful Christmas hymn had first appeared in Britain in 1870 set to FLENSBURG, an uninspiring melody derived from a tune by Ludwig Spohr. For its appearance in *Church Hymns*, Sullivan reworked a traditional Herefordshire carol tune which had been sent to him by a friend. The eight opening bars which constitute the first half of NOEL are made up of Sullivan's arrangement of this tune and the last nine bars which make up the second half are his own original composition. Although more than half of NOEL is an original Sullivan composition, with characteristic modesty he published it with the attribution 'Traditional Air arranged'. ST CLEMENT, set to John Ellerton's beautiful evening hymn and destined to be one of the most enduring and popular of all Victorian hymn tunes, is credited in *Church Hymns With Tunes* to Clement Scholefield, who had served as curate at St Peter's, Cranley Gardens, when Sullivan was organist there and had become a good friend. Sullivan commissioned six tunes from Scholefield, none of which displays anything approaching the merit or originality of ST CLEMENT. I and others have suggested that there is strong musical evidence to suggest that Sullivan perhaps had a rather greater hand in this tune than the attribution suggests, but that with characteristic generosity he let his friend take the full credit and named it ST CLEMENT in his honour, just as he had named ST GERTRUDE after another friend.[26]

Sullivan's hymn tunes were generally held in high regard by his contemporaries. Those fellow composers who devoted themselves almost entirely to church music were largely enthusiastic about the efforts of one who might be regarded as something of an interloper in the field, none more so than John Stainer who used twenty-eight of Sullivan's tunes in the first edition of the 1898 Presbyterian *Church Hymnary* of which he was musical editor. The views of the writers of hymn texts were more varied. The ultra-Tractarian Francis Pott was not a fan of the tune Sullivan composed for his 'Angel voices, ever singing', which he dismissed as 'a trivial, pretty but altogether unfit tune . . . which caught the ear of people who did not trouble themselves to see that the hymn was of quite another character.'[27] Doubtless it was the waltz-like lilt and chromatic swoops of ANGEL VOICES that made Pott feel that Sullivan's tune was trivial and inappropriate for his angelic meditations. Other leading hymn writers of a more liberal and pastoral persuasion did not share such misgivings about their hymns being made more popular by a rousing if slightly vulgar tune. John Ellerton commended Sullivan's tunes for so sensitively interpreting the words; and William Walsham How, who also expressed admiration for them, strongly protested when the editors of *Hymns Ancient and Modern* threatened to drop ST CLEMENT on the grounds that it was vulgar and populist.[28] It is significant that these two deeply pastoral and theologically liberal clergymen, both committed to ministering among ordinary working people, and perhaps of all clerical Victorian hymn writers the most attuned to popular taste, should have backed Sullivan, the least 'churchy' of the major Victorian hymn tune composers. They recognized the value of his great gifts of accessibility and consummate word setting to the church as much as to the other more secular areas in which he exercised them.

Trial and Travel, 1875–6

It was almost certainly with some relief that Sullivan turned from the demanding work on his hymn book to another theatrical commission. On 25 March 1875, the curtain went up on his second collaboration with W.S. Gilbert, *Trial by Jury*. The two men had been brought together again by Richard D'Oyly Carte, impresario and manager of the Royalty Theatre, Dean Street, Soho. Their one-act, sung-through, 'novel and original dramatic cantata', based around a trial for breach of promise of marriage, was a considerable success. It played at the Royalty until December, transferred to the Opera Comique Theatre just off the Strand in January 1876, and had a further run at the Royal Strand Theatre in the Spring of 1877. Although much shorter than Gilbert and Sullivan's later works, and differing from its successors in having only one act and lacking any spoken dialogue, it otherwise has all the distinctive characteristics of the operas which were to follow it. There is the gentle mockery of British institutions—in this case, the legal system—the central role for the chorus and the juxtaposition of rollicking patter song and tender romantic aria. There is also the extraordinary creative rapport between librettist and composer. As *The Times* critic observed in his review of the first night, 'it seems, as in the great Wagnerian operas, as though poem and music had proceeded simultaneously from one and the same brain.'[29]

Despite its great success, it was to be another two years before Gilbert and Sullivan came together again at D'Oyly Carte's behest to begin their partnership in earnest. Sullivan focused rather on building his conducting career, initially with the Glasgow Choral and Orchestral Union for the winter seasons of 1875 and 1876 when he laid the foundations of the Royal Scottish National Orchestra, which still exists today. This allowed him to showcase several of his own orchestral works in Scotland, alongside Beethoven symphonies and other mainstays of the classical repertoire. It also reinforced his views about the awfulness of the Scottish Sabbath and the perils of living in lodgings:

> There is a wretched creature on the floor above who plays the piano a little. He or she has been playing *my* hymn tunes all this afternoon. I hope they don't do it out of compliment to me, for they put their own harmony, which to say the least isn't as good as mine.[30]

Visits to the Continent became more frequent and of longer duration. Arthur delighted in sending his mother long letters about his travels and reporting on the characters whom he encountered, including 'a venerable-looking' Catholic priest in the spa town of Franzensbad in Bohemia which he visited in August 1874: 'I believe he is a gay old dog. But that's between ourselves.'[31] Although he gravitated increasingly towards the French Riviera and the gaming tables and salons of Monte Carlo, there were also more cultural and spiritual interests to pursue while abroad. A visit to Cologne Cathedral made with an American friend, Mrs David Beach Grant and her two children in the summer of 1875 left him deeply moved.

> We went into the cathedral and heard a pretty children's service. It is a blazing hot day, the first they have had here, and the cathedral was so peaceful and cool it did one good and took me out of this world for a time. When the service began, the organ struck up, and then in the far distance the boys' voices were heard singing a little motet, and they came nearer and nearer singing all the while. The result was I burst out crying, as I always do at children's voices. I have no doubt the music was weak, and the boys' voices execrable, but the whole thing moved me and did me good. The priest, after the service, which was a sort of little litany, gave a short address. It seemed earnest and simple, but as the very young folks didn't understand a word I brought them out.[32]

This passage underlines the importance of music to Arthur Sullivan's faith and also points to its simplicity and sentimentality. He was moved to tears by the sound of children singing church music of the kind that he himself had sung and loved as a child. He also appreciated the earnestness and simplicity of the priest's homily. Typically, although he would like to have stayed to hear it all, he thought of others and brought the children out. Indeed, the whole trip of which this day was a part underlined his generosity and kindness. He had originally been due to accompany the Grants only as far as Cologne, but Mrs Grant had fainted on the journey and, as none of the party spoke German, he rerouted his ticket and baggage, and accompanied her and the children to their destination, the spa town of Kissingen where she was to take the waters.

In 1876, after briefly serving as musical director of the newly opened Royal Aquarium in Regent's Park, he was appointed principal and professor of composition at the new National Training School for Music in South Kensington, a post that he held for five years. This was a significant position in an institution which was established to raise the whole level of musical education in Britain and which later morphed into the Royal College of Music. In the same year he was awarded an honorary doctorate in music by Cambridge University.

Oxford followed suit in 1879. More and more, he was becoming both an established and an establishment figure.

Second Family Death, 'The Lost Chord', and Fanny Ronalds

We have already noted the way in which the serious illness and death of family members brought out the faith that Sullivan was otherwise often reticent about expressing and inspired some of his most obviously spiritual compositions. This was pre-eminently true in the case of his most famous sacred parlour ballad, 'The Lost Chord', which took on an iconic status in the later nineteenth century, becoming one of the best-selling songs of all time.

Fred Sullivan died on 18 January 1877, aged just 39. Like his younger brother, he had suffered for some time with liver disease, although his death certificate recorded that he died of phthisis, or pulmonary tuberculosis. According to an account by Charles Willeby, apparently based on Arthur Sullivan's own recollections, and corroborated by Arthur Lawrence and by Herbert Sullivan and Newman Flower in their biographies, the inspiration for 'The Lost Chord' came as Arthur sat at his dying brother's bedside.

> One night—the end was not very far off then—while his sick brother had for a time fallen into a peaceful sleep, and he was sitting as usual by the bed-side, he chanced to come across some verses of Adelaide Procter's with which he had some five years previously been much struck. He had then tried to set them to music, but without satisfaction to himself. Now in the stillness of the night he read them over again, and almost as he did so, he conceived their musical equivalent. A stray sheet of music paper was at hand, and he began to write. Slowly the music grew and took shape, until, becoming quite absorbed in it, he determined to finish the song. Even if in the cold light of day it were to prove worthless, it would at least have helped to while away the hours of watching. So he worked on at it. As he progressed, he felt sure this was what he had sought for and failed to find on the occasion of his first attempt to set the words. In a short time it was complete.[33]

A convert to Roman Catholicism, Adelaide Ann Procter was a pious and sickly spinster who died of tuberculosis in 1864 at the age of 38. She devoted her short life to religious poetry, feminist causes, and charitable work among the poor. Her verse was greatly admired by Queen Victoria and Charles Dickens (who published many of her poems in his magazine, *Household Words*), and according to Coventry Patmore she was second only to Tennyson as the most popular poet of the age. Sullivan set five of her religious poems as sacred ballads or part songs and composed a tune for her hymn 'My God, I thank Thee, who hast made the earth so bright'. Her poem 'A Lost Chord' first appeared in 1858 in *The English Woman's Journal* which she and a number of feminist friends had founded to encourage women's involvement in the management of philanthropic activities such as temperance campaigns, industrial and ragged schools, cottage hospitals, and local refuges. It tells of a troubled organist, 'weary and ill and ease' whose fingers 'wandered idly over the noisy keys' before striking one particular chord, 'like the sound of a great Amen' which had the effect of flooding 'the crimson twilight', calming the fevered spirit, and linking 'all perplexed meanings into one perfect peace'. Despite desperately seeking it, the organist could not find the chord again and concluded:

> It may be that Death's bright angel
> Will speak in that chord again,—
> It may be that only in Heaven
> I shall hear that grand Amen.

Procter's poem is a powerful religious text at a number of levels. As David Eden has pointed out, it provides an almost classic account of a mystical experience—the initial agitation, the sudden sense of being flooded with inward light, the intense feeling of well-being and harmony, the fading of the experience, and the desperate desire to repeat and recover it with the final realization that it will only come again with death.[34] There are other clear theological resonances in its glimpses of glory and intimations of eternity. It describes one of those moments when we experience heaven on earth.

With its strong assertion that music is the messenger of transcendent calm and harmony, providing a gateway to the eternal, it is not surprising that 'A Lost Chord' should have appealed to Victorian composers. It first appears to have been set as a song by George Macfarren in 1866. Sullivan, who had first come across it in *Household Words*, made an attempt to set it in 1872 but was dissatisfied with the result. It was only while sitting with his dying brother that he came up with a melody which he felt was worthy of the intensity of the text. When his version was published a few months after Fred's death, Procter's mother objected to the use of the original title and so it was changed to 'The Lost Chord'. The song was first performed at a ballad concert by the popular American-born soprano Antoinette Sterling, who had already made a success of some of Sullivan's other sacred ballads, with the composer at the piano and Sydney Naylor on the organ. Its success was both immediate and lasting. Greeted with thunderous and prolonged applause at its first performance, it went on to sell half a million copies over the next twenty-five years, making it easily the best-selling ballad of the later nineteenth century.

Although Sterling premiered 'The Lost Chord', the singer who became most associated with it during Sullivan's lifetime was Fanny Ronalds (1839–1916). Born and brought up in Boston in the United States, she entered into an unhappy marriage and separated from her husband in 1865 although she never divorced and always kept her married name. A noted society beauty and talented amateur singer, she moved to London in 1871 and subsequently became Sullivan's constant companion and lover, their relationship deepening after 1877, helped by the fact that his mother moved to Fulham to help Fred's widow, Charlotte, look after her seven young children. Arthur and Fanny kept their public and private lives discreetly separate. In his diaries he referred to her as Mrs Ronalds when they met in a public setting and L.W. (Little Woman) when they were alone together. The mores of the time made marriage out of the question, a situation which almost certainly suited Sullivan because of his reluctance to commit himself to the matrimonial state. Their relationship, which lasted until his death in 1900, was the longest and the most satisfying of his rather troubled love life.

Fanny Ronalds sang 'The Lost Chord' regularly at Sunday evening musical soirées at her house at 7 Cadogan Place, Belgravia. The Prince of Wales, later King Edward VII, famously said that he would happily travel the length of his future kingdom to hear her sing it and it was also said to be the favourite song of his consort, Queen Alexandra. For Sullivan, Fanny Ronalds was the song's supreme exponent. According to Herbert Sullivan and Newman Flower,

She sang the song to his liking as no one else ever sang it, and of all those who rendered it during the many years when it was the most widely sung melody in the world, put into it that sorrow he knew when he composed it. He openly said that she alone brought tears to his eyes with his own notes.[35]

He gave her the original manuscript of the song which she in turn left in her will to the English contralto Clara Butt (1872–1936), who made the song her signature piece, recording it and singing it to an audience of 10,000 in the Albert Hall to support British troops fighting in the Boer War in January 1900 and again in the same venue in August 1902 at the request of Queen Alexandra on the occasion of the postponed coronation of Edward VII. During the First World War, Clara Butt declared, 'What we need now is more songs like "The Lost Chord". There is something of the grandeur of Beethoven in it'.[36] In 1950, her widower, Kennerley Rumford, gave the manuscript to the Worshipful Company of Musicians and it remains in their possession today.[37]

'The Lost Chord' has an important place in musical history. It featured on the first phonographic recording ever made in Britain. Newman Flower and Herbert Sullivan assert erroneously that this was a vocal rendition made by Fanny Ronalds in Sullivan's drawing room but in fact it was an instrumental performance on cornet and piano, recorded in August 1888.[38] Inevitably, as the most popular of all Victorian parlour ballads, it became the subject of numerous parodies. Sullivan responded to one of the earliest, by the operetta composer, Edward Solomon, with the rebuke 'I wrote The Lost Chord in sorrow at my brother Fred's death, don't burlesque it'.[39] It inspired at least three early-twentieth-century films, which took its title, and appeared on numerous postcards sent with messages of condolence to the bereaved.

Critics have long mocked the song's excessive emotionalism. The late Victorian and early-twentieth-century novelist Edward Benson described it as 'a test piece for tears' in which every female singer tried her strength as if with a punching machine at a fair which registered muscular force: 'If there were not a dry eye in the room when she had delivered her blow she was a champion'.[40] Several more recent writers have castigated its dull and contrived religiosity and maudlin sentimentality, although others have defended it and recognized its authenticity and spiritual power.[41] Nicholas Temperley has described it as 'Sullivan's maligned masterpiece' and Maurice Disher commented that Adelaide Procter 'endowed it with devotion' and 'Sullivan, in a mood of mourning, matched it with strains suited to church organs', effectively creating an anthem rather than a song.[42] The intense chromaticism gives it the feel of a high Victorian hymn tune while the scoring for harmonium as well as piano accompaniment and the use of the traditional contrapuntal texture associated with Anglican organ music further enhances its ecclesiastical atmosphere. So does the influence of plainchant which pervades it from the string of repeated notes at the beginning, a favourite Sullivan device found also in 'How many hired servants' in *The Prodigal Son*, 'I hear the soft note' in *Patience*, 'Now to the sunset' in *The Golden Legend*, and in the opening bars of the hymn tune ST GERTRUDE. Arthur Jacobs suggested that they are there to convey 'solemn intensity' but maybe they are rather the almost sub-conscious echoes of that style of church music instilled into Sullivan in his Chapel Royal days by Helmore.[43] The opening bars, setting the words 'Seated one day at the organ, I was weary and ill at ease', are uncannily similar to the versicle and response found in Anglican Morning Prayer and Evensong: 'Oh Lord, open thou our lips, and our mouths shall show forth thy praise'. There is also a striking similarity between the notes for 'I struck one chord of music' and the opening phrase of 'The day, Thou gavest' set to ST CLEMENT.

The way that Sullivan set 'The Lost Chord' tells us something about his religious leanings as a composer and perhaps a little, too, about his own faith. The almost unbearably affecting melody which was wrung out of his grief for his dying brother is infused with a sense of restlessness and yearning which seems to go beyond the expression of these feelings in the text. Was this song, destined to be so popular, so parodied and so pilloried, not just playing to the gallery of Victorian sentiment but also reflecting the spiritual state of its composer, seeking to link all perplexed meaning into one perfect peace and yearning in a life that was increasingly restless and ever more bent on pleasure and distraction for a sense of infinite calm?

There is undoubtedly a sense of anguished yearning in 'The Lost Chord', but there is also a very clear faith in death as the final comforter and the solver of all mysteries. We are drawn back yet again to Sullivan's own lack of fear of death and his strong belief in a life beyond it. The way that he sets the two final lines, 'It may be that only in heaven I shall hear that Great Amen', to be sung '*con gran forza*' takes us perhaps as near to the heart of his own faith as anything that he wrote. There is no hint of the text's conditional 'may' in the triumphal closing chords but rather a ringing sense of certainty and expectancy about heaven and the life to come.

The year 1877 had been a traumatic one for Sullivan and it was also something of a turning point in the direction of his work. Undoubtedly Fred's death was a major blow, both in personal and in financial terms. From now on he took over responsibility for providing for seven nephews and nieces, which he did with enormous generosity. This may well have been a major factor in turning him increasingly away from sacred works to the more lucrative theatrical commissions. The year 1877 was also that of his first full-length collaboration with Gilbert, *The Sorcerer*. Its music, which as he rightly said was 'thought to be so merry and spontaneous', was actually produced in the midst of the intense pain from his kidney complaint that would dog him increasingly for the rest of his life: 'I would compose a few bars, and then lie insensible from pain. When the paroxysm had passed, I would write a little more.'[44] For the next twelve years he would be largely engaged in composing a string of highly successful comic operas, although not completely to the detriment of more serious work of which there was still some more to come. He would also be increasingly bent on pleasure, whether in the company of Fanny Ronalds, at the gaming tables of Monte Carlo, or at London parties and country house weekends.

Sullivan spent that Christmas and New Year in France. His letters home to his mother reveal something of the juxtaposition in his own personality between the spiritual and the worldly, his love of church music and of the gaming table, his continuing sense of loss at his brother's passing, and his desire to move on from mourning and get on with living. He went to the Christmas Eve Midnight Mass at St Sulpice Church in Paris 'where my friend Widor is organist'. Although the church was absolutely packed he managed to get in 'by the help of a stalwart gendarme' and went up to the organ loft: 'When the mass was over—that is the communion—judge my surprise and pleasure when they struck up the *Adeste Fideles*'. The letter describing the service went on to say that he was coming out of mourning for Christmas Day:

> I don't see why I should wear black on dear old Fred's birthday [he was born on 25 December 1837]. I shall drink a glass of wine into his memory, bless him . . . It is of no use grieving and repining. Those who are left have cares and responsibilities and must brace themselves up and face them courageously.[45]

A few days later, writing from Nice, he reported that he had been to Monaco 'to have a look at the gaming tables. I staked a few five franc pieces and came away the winner of 100 francs . . . Tomorrow I shall make a colossal effort and go to church to counterbalance the wickedness of gambling'.[46] If he did, indeed, go to church, it did not lead him to give up his 'wicked' weakness. Less than a month after telling his mother in that same letter that 'the gambling table has no attraction for me', he was reporting to Richard D'Oyly Carte, 'I have lost all my money gambling—a regular facer'.[47]

At the age of 25, the Prodigal Son was still prodigal but also a touch repentant. He was very much in love with life, not least its more racy aspects, but he also felt the power of the spiritual, especially as expressed through music, the call of duty, and the pull of family affection and filial love.

Notes

1. *Musical Times*, 43:71 (1 July 1902), p.477.
2. Arthur Jacobs, *Arthur Sullivan*, 2nd edn. (Aldershot: Scolar Press, 1992) p.80.
3. Arthur Lawrence, *Sir Arthur Sullivan: Life Story, Letters and Reminiscences* (London: James Bowden, 1899), p.98.
4. Letters from Arthur Sullivan [hereafter AS] to his mother, 23 January 1870, 13 November 1875: Pierpont Morgan Library, New York [hereafter PML].
5. Benedict Taylor, 'Features of Sullivan's Religious Style found in the Festival Te Deum', *SASS Magazine* 58 (Summer 2004), p.13. See also Roderick Swanston's sleeve notes to recording of the *Te Deum* by BBC Symphony Orchestra (BBC, 2001).

6. *Musical Times* 15:352 (1 June 1872), p.502.

7. Jeffrey Richards, *Imperialism and Music: Britain 1876–1953* (Manchester: Manchester University Press, 2001), p.23.

8. Herbert Sullivan and Newman Flower, *Sir Arthur Sullivan* (London: Cassell & Co., 1927), p.72.

9. Michael Ainger, *Gilbert and Sullivan: A Dual Biography* (Oxford: Oxford University Press, 2002), p.102.

10. Letter from AS to James Davison, 16 May 1873: PML.

11. George Grove, *The Light of the World: Analysis* (London: J.BCramer & Co., 1873), p.1.

12. Grove, *The Light of the World*, p.8.

13. Grove, *The Light of the World*, p.27.

14. Grove, *The Light of the World*, p.30.

15. Grove, *The Light of the World*, p.39.

16. Grove, *The Light of the World*, p.47.

17. Percy Young, *Sir Arthur Sullivan* (London: J.M. Dent, 1971), p.96.

18. *Observer*, 31 August 1873.

19. *The Times*, 3 September 1873.

20. Harold Orel, *Gilbert & Sullivan: Interviews and Recollections* (Iowa City: University of Iowa Press, 1994), p.73.

21. *The Academy*, 28 March 1874.

22. *SASS Magazine* 41 (Autumn 1995), p.23.

23. For statistical details and analysis of the church affiliations of these hymn tune writers, see Ian Bradley, *Abide With Me: The World of Victorian Hymns* (London: SCM Press, 1997), pp.140–68.

24. Jacobs, *Sullivan*, pp.74–5.

25. *Church Hymns with Tunes* (London, SPCK, 1881), p.iv.

26. For a fuller discussion of this, see 'Sullivan's Possible Involvement in ST CLEMENT', Appendix 3, in Ian Bradley, *Lost Chords and Christian Soldiers* (London: SCM Press, 2013), pp.201–4.

27. Francis Pott to Mr Murray, November 1887: HAM Archives.

28. John Ellerton to Henry Baker, 8 June 1874; William How to W.H. Frere, 12 June 1897: HAM Archives.

29. *The Times*, 29 March 1875.

30. AS to his mother, Sunday (? 5 December 1875): PML.

31. AS to his mother, 8 August 1874: PML.

32. AS to his mother, Sunday 1875: PML.

33. Charles Willeby, *Masters of English Music* (London: James Osgood, 1893), pp.41–2. There is another account of the writing of the tune, by Fred's daughter, Amy, which suggests that Fred had some involvement in its construction. See Bradley, *Lost Chords and Christian Soldiers*, p.107.

34. David Eden, 'Sullivan's Christianity' in *SASS Magazine* 41 (Autumn 1995), pp.25–6.

35. Sullivan and Flower, *Sullivan*, p.85.

36. Maurice Leonard, *Hope and Glory: A Life of Dame Clara Butt* (Brighton: Victorian Secrets, 2012), p.53.

37. The history of the original manuscript of 'The Lost Chord', which is often mistakenly described as having been buried with Fanny Ronalds, is described by David Mackie in 'The Manuscript of "The Lost Chord"', *SASS Magazine* 83 (Winter 2013), pp.24–6.

38. Sullivan and Flower, *Sullivan*, p.84.

39. Sullivan and Flower, *Sullivan*, p.83

40. Edward Benson, *As We Were* (London: Hogarth Press, 1985), p.20.

41. See, for, example, Erik Routley in *The Hymn Society Bulletin*, 2:7 (July 1948), p.108; and John Caldwell in *The Oxford History of Music*, Vol.II (Oxford: Oxford University Press, 1999), p.276.

42. Nicholas Temperley (ed.), *Music in Britain: The Romantic Age 1800–1914* (London: Athlone Press, 1988), p.129; Maurice Disher, *Victorian Song: From Dive to Drawing Room* (London: Phoenix House, 1955), p.141.

43. Jacobs, *Sullivan*, p.110.

44. Jacobs, *Sullivan*, p.121.

45. AS to his mother, 25 December 1877: PML.

46. AS to his mother, 5 January 1878: PML.

47. AS to Richard D'Oyly Carte, 5 February 1878: PML.

5

1877–1889

The Gilbert and Sullivan Years

The Sorcerer was the first of a string of ten highly successful comic operas that Sullivan wrote with Gilbert on an almost annual basis between 1877 and 1889. The others were *H.M.S. Pinafore* (1878), *The Pirates of Penzance* (1879), *Patience* (1881), *Iolanthe* (1882), *Princess Ida* (1884), *The Mikado* (1885), *Ruddigore* (1887), *The Yeomen of the Guard* (1888), and *The Gondoliers* (1889). They brought him further fame and fortune, and although he kept threatening to end his partnership with Gilbert, whom he found increasingly frustrating, and return to more serious work, he never did so, largely because the money was so good. He calculated his annual earnings for 1880 at just under £10,000 (equivalent to around £1.2 million today), considerably more than W.E. Gladstone's salary of £7,500 as prime minister. Over the following decade he made over £90,000 from his partnership with Gilbert and Richard D'Oyly Carte.

Sullivan needed the money to support his increasingly luxurious and hedonistic lifestyle. He moved in 1881 to a more spacious home in Queen's Mansions in Victoria Street, where he remained for the rest of his life with a household of four live-in servants; he took long foreign holidays, often spending several months abroad through the winter; and his penchant for gambling expanded to embrace betting on horse races as well as card games in London clubs and roulette on the Riviera. He had an active sex life, mostly though not exclusively with Mrs Ronalds, whom he supported financially, and he also gave large amounts of money to his mother, his uncle John, and his brother Fred's widow and children. Prodigal and profligate as he may have been, he was also extremely generous and ever ready to help a good cause. In August 1879, for example, he put on a charity performance of *Cox and Box* to raise funds for the English church in Pontresina in the Engadine region of Switzerland where he was recuperating from an operation to crush his kidney stones. Although overall he seems to have balanced out his gains and losses through gambling, there were occasions when he lost heavily and he was also unlucky in his investments. His broker went bankrupt in 25 July 1882, leading him to lose £7,000 on the same day that *Iolanthe* opened, a misfortune which he faced with equanimity and without apportioning any blame to his rather reckless financial adviser.

Although they became something of a millstone round his neck, his collaborations with Gilbert brought him further into the establishment and reinforced the patriotic English credentials that meant so much to him. Richard D'Oyly Carte established his Comedy Opera Company in 1877 very consciously as an English equivalent to the French Opéra Comique. In 1881, he built the Savoy Theatre in the Strand as the home for Gilbert and Sullivan's operas, confirming their status as a national institution. Sullivan was knighted in 1883 for his services to music (Gilbert had to wait until 1907) at the same ceremony in Windsor Castle as George Grove, and developed ever closer links with members of the royal family. Both the Prince of Wales and the Duke of Edinburgh were regular guests at his dinner parties and soirées.

For some commentators, Sullivan's highly successful collaborations with Gilbert constituted a happy release which allowed his true talents to flourish. Writing some years after his death, Augustine Godwin argued that Sullivan was in danger of 'drooping into a sentimental ecclesiastical composer, a pot-boiler of anthems and syrupy hymns' until Gilbert rescued him and 'focused his vision on the brighter, if not precisely the higher, things'.[1] But most contemporary critics took a rather different view of the composer's change of direction. Their views were made plain in reviews of the first night of *The Sorcerer*, with *The World* remarking 'It was hoped that he would soar with Mendelssohn, whereas he is, it seems, content to sink with Offenbach', and the London weekly *Figaro* expressing disappointment 'at the downward art course that Sullivan appears to be drifting into. He has the ability to make him a great composer, but he wilfully throws his opportunity away. A giant may play at times, but Mr Sullivan is always playing'.[2] The knighthood elicited a further caustic comment from the *Musical Review*: 'some things that Mr Arthur Sullivan may do, Sir Arthur Sullivan ought not to do'. Those things included writing any more comic operas with Gilbert, or any more 'shop ballads'. Indeed, 'a musical knight must not dare to soil his hands with anything less than an anthem or a madrigal; oratorio, in which he has so conspicuously shone, and symphony must now be his line'.[3]

In fact, while collaboration with Gilbert dominated the years between 1877 and 1889, Sullivan did compose two substantial, serious works during this period, *The Martyr of Antioch* and *The Golden Legend*, although it is true that he also failed to deliver several other promised pieces, including a *Magnificat* which had been commissioned for the Sons of the Clergy Festival in May 1887. He told Stainer that he found it impossible to set, just as he had when he had tried before in 1866: 'I have covered pages with sketches but I hate them all . . . My endeavours are fruitless. Pray forgive me. I can't help it'.[4] Why he should have had a block with the *Magnificat* when he found no difficulty in setting the *Te Deum* is something of a mystery. He continued to conduct serious and sacred music. The fifty concerts that he conducted for the 1878 Covent Garden summer Promenade season included the first complete cycle of Beethoven symphonies under the baton of a British conductor. He returned to conduct the Covent Garden Proms the following year, but because of illness only managed twenty-four out of the forty-eight scheduled concerts. In 1880, he took over as conductor of the prestigious Leeds Musical Festival and for three seasons from 1885 to 1887 he conducted the Philharmonic Society in London. His distinctive style of conducting, which involved often remaining seated and apparently burying his head in the score, was criticized for being lazy and lethargic but appreciated by more discerning critics for its attention to detail and lack of ostentation. Writing about his handling of the Covent Garden Proms, the *Globe* critic commended 'his unobtrusive but earnest and masterly mode of conducting' and noted that 'Mr Sullivan showed that' he rightly regarded the post of conductor as one in which conscientious work is of more importance than self-display.'[5]

It was, indeed, through conducting as much as through composing that Sullivan showed his continuing commitment to serious and sacred music. He went on making time to conduct his own oratorios and cantatas even when he became frantically busy with other things.

On several occasions he broke off work on the Savoy operas to conduct a sacred piece. Soon after arriving in the United States in November 1879 to supervise the first authorized performance there of *H.M.S. Pinafore* and to premiere *The Pirates of Penzance*, he took off for Boston to conduct *The Prodigal Son*. In September 1889, he took a break from composing *The Gondoliers* for two days to rehearse and conduct *The Prodigal Son* and *The Golden Legend* at Gloucester Cathedral. His frenetic schedule over two days in October 1881 provides a dramatic demonstration of the way that he managed to combine conducting sacred music with the increasing demands of the Savoy operas. After an all-day rehearsal on the 10th, he conducted the first performance of *Patience* in the newly opened Savoy Theatre in the evening, attended a reception afterwards, and then went on to supper with Gilbert. His diary notes: 'returned home at 3 am, changed my clothes, had coffee and then drove to Liverpool Street station to take the 5.10am train to Norwich'.[6] He arrived in Norwich at 9am on the 11th and, after a quick breakfast, went straight into an all-day rehearsal of *The Martyr of Antioch* for a performance the following evening. This not untypical way of working underlines his tendency to cram far too much into each day and night for his own well-being, habitually leaving things to the last minute, staying up much of the night and burning the candle at both ends to the detriment of his health. It also shows that the former Chapel Royal choirboy could not break his abiding attachment to sacred music even though he was now primarily engaged in a lighter and much more lucrative sphere of composition.

The Martyr of Antioch

In January 1878, Sullivan was approached by the committee of the Leeds Musical Festival for an oratorio for the 1880 Festival. He received the invitation when he was ill in Nice and turned the offer down but on his return to London and to better health he reconsidered it and told the committee that while unable to 'undertake the composition of an oratorio which should occupy the whole of the concert . . . I should not be unwilling to write a work of the same length and character as the "Prodigal Son"—a work of about an hour or an hour and a half, and forming one part of a concert'.[7] He was duly commissioned to write a piece of the kind he proposed.

His initial idea was to base this new work around the Biblical story of David and Jonathan. He had been commissioned to write an oratorio on this theme for the Norwich Musical Festival in 1875 but had abandoned the project at a very early stage because of ill health. It may well be that George Grove's influence inspired this choice of subject. Grove had a lifelong interest in the figure of David and started writing a book about him which was published posthumously. Returning to this particular biblical story after a four-year gap, Sullivan decided to prepare the libretto himself and told the Leeds Festival secretary Fred Spark, 'I search the Scriptures daily only to find that the best verses for filling up in the orthodox fashion have been used by oratorio writers before me. If I take these, there will be always comparisons drawn as to the setting. One will say, "Oh, Handel's music to those words is much better," or "Mendelssohn's ideas are far superior to Sullivan's".'[8] In fact, although Handel had incorporated the figures of David and Jonathan in *Saul*, Mendelssohn had not set this particular story. A rather different explanation as to why Sullivan went off this subject was given in a report in the *Leeds Express* in June 1880 which noted that after wrestling with the story of David and Jonathan for some time, he had abandoned it as the basis for a libretto because of his realization 'that words from the Sacred Book required a certain amount of conventional treatment, somewhat limiting the composer's ideas'.[9] This had not seemed to trouble him when writing his two earlier biblical oratorios. An article in *The Musical World*, almost certainly written by Joseph Bennett, pointedly commented:

> The idea of words from the Sacred Book requiring a 'certain amount of conventional treatment . . . limiting the composer's ideas,' applied to the musician who wrote the *Prodigal Son* and *The Light of the World* is . . . moonshine. The truth is clearly that Mr. Sullivan is too busy to devote time to the preparation of an oratorio; and so in lieu of a *piece de resistance*, he tenders us a side-dish in the shape of a cantata.[10]

Having abandoned the idea of another biblically based work, for whatever reason, Sullivan turned instead to the story of an early Christian martyr, St Margaret of Antioch, as recounted in a long poem written in 1822 by Henry Hart Milman, a distinguished church historian and author who had been Dean of St Paul's Cathedral from 1849 until his death in 1868 and is now best remembered for his Palm Sunday hymn, 'Ride on, ride on in majesty!'. The poem recounted the story of Margarita (as Milman called her), the daughter of Callias, a pagan priest in Antioch, during the period of Christian persecution in the reign of the Roman Emperor Diocletian at the beginning of the fourth century AD. Although herself a pagan priestess, she converted to Christianity, leading her to reject the advances of her former lover, Olybius, a Roman prefect, who thereupon denounced her and condemned her to torture and death. Sullivan saw the dramatic possibilities inherent in the poem's contrast between pagan and Christian worship, and in Margarita's heroic sacrificial death for her faith. There was the added attraction that she was portrayed as the principal musician of the pagan temple, and the theme of religious music was at the core of the poem's dramatic and philosophical interest. A central dilemma for Margarita was whether she should take into her new faith the musical gifts that were previously 'hallow'd to an impious service'.[11]

It was almost certainly George Grove who suggested this poem as providing suitable material for a sacred cantata. He had been a good friend of Milman, who shared his liberal theological views. Arthur Jacobs states that Sullivan consulted Grove 'on matters of text and musical setting'.[12] Although this seems highly likely, I can find no definite evidence for Grove's involvement and, as with *The Prodigal Son*, no acknowledgement was given to him in the preface to *The Martyr of Antioch*. Sullivan seems rather to have turned to W.S. Gilbert, with whom he had just collaborated on *The Pirates of Penzance*, to help him condense Milman's lengthy poem into a manageable libretto. Gilbert took time off from working on the libretto of *Patience* to arrange the material and turn some of Milman's blank verse into rhyme. In his preface to the finished work, which he called a 'sacred musical drama', Sullivan wrote that 'the responsibility of the selection rests with the composer' and credited Gilbert with 'the change which in one or two cases has been necessary from blank verse to rhyme'. Gilbert is also thanked in the preface for 'many valuable suggestions' although Sullivan subsequently claimed credit for the overall text, telling his secretary that 'it took me a considerable amount of time and thought to make the libretto'.[13]

The Martyr of Antioch runs to one hour and twenty minutes and has four scenes. The first, set in the Temple of Apollo, opens with a lengthy chorus of sun-worshipping youths and maids, transferred virtually uncut from Milman's original. In its review of the first performance, the *Musical Standard* critic rightly described this as 'a complete scene in itself of Pagan rites and idolatrous worship' and went on to praise it as 'one of the most extraordinary pieces of workmanship that any composer, of any land, has ever produced.'[14] Olybius' opening song, 'Come, Margarita come', one of Gilbert's versifications which could do duty as a pagan parlour ballad and bears more than a passing resemblance to 'Come into the garden, Maud', calls on the priestess to take her appointed place and preside over the sacrificial rituals. When she fails to appear, Callias charges Olybius with being lukewarm towards the cult of Apollo, but the prefect responds with a clear statement of his determination to put Christians to death.

The second scene is set in a Christian cemetery at night where the funeral hymn 'Brother, thou art gone before us', taken straight from Milman's original, is being intoned as one of the persecuted Christian community is buried. Margarita stays behind alone after the ceremony to sing of her new faith in the hymn 'Thou didst die for me, O Son of God!' which is also taken straight from Milman's poem and provides both a more detailed and more harrowing account of Jesus' crucifixion and a much clearer statement of its salvific and atoning purpose ('To wash our souls from sin's infecting stain, To avert the Father's wrathful vengeance flame') than is found anywhere in *The Light of the World*. Her father enters and realizes that she has converted from paganism. They sing a duet extolling their respective gods. The third and briefest scene, set in the prefect's palace, begins with a chorus of maidens singing their evening song to Apollo, 'Come away with willing feet', and sounding not unlike the fairies in *Iolanthe* or the love-sick maidens in *Patience*. Olybius and Margarita sing a duet in which she attempts vainly to win his soul for Christ. He curses her faith and she leaves him for her prison cell.

The fourth and last scene takes place outside the prison where the Christians are kept. Heathen maidens on their way to the temple chant the glories of Apollo while the Christian prisoners hymn their God. Julia, one of the pagan sun worshippers, sings a frenzied chant to

Apollo, 'Io Paean!'. Margarita prepares to go to her funeral pyre—
Sullivan changed her manner of death from Milman's poem where it
was beheading. In a quartet written by Gilbert, Margarita, Olybius,
Callias, and Julia all cry for mercy but the crowd bay for Christian
blood. As the flames lick around her, Margarita has a vision of heaven,
the great victorious train of martyrs, and the Son of Man appearing:

> The Christ, the Christ, commands me to His home,
> Jesus! Redeemer! Lord! I come, I come, I come.

The piece ends with the chorus of Christians rejoicing that 'The Lord
almighty reigneth' and that 'He who forfeits earthly life a life celestial
gaineth'.

Although Christians get the last word, there is no doubt that taken
overall *The Martyr of Antioch* focuses as much if not more on pagan
beliefs and ritual. In terms of choruses, three times as much music is
given to the pagans as to the Christians. This is in marked contrast to
Milman's original poem where five pagan chants and seven Christian
hymns punctuate the blank verse. There is certainly no doubt that the
heathens get the best tunes. This is particularly striking in the double
chorus which opens the fourth scene where the Christian prisoners'
slow, dull dirge, 'Now glory to the God whose throne', contrasts with
the lively brightness of the pagan maidens' 'Now glory to the god who
breaks' with its thrilling trumpet accompaniment.

The contrast in the music given to the pagans and the Christians
was remarked on by several of the reviewers of the first performance in
Leeds on 15 October 1880. The *Musical Times* noted that it was a
sensible move on Sullivan's part to call the piece 'a Sacred Musical
Drama' as in that way 'no objection can be raised to a preponderance
of music which, from the Christian point of view, is not sacred at all'
and went on to observe:

> Comparatively speaking, the poor Christians are nowhere. We hear
> them singing a funeral hymn, and presently their voices reach us from
> the dungeons where they await their death. But Mr Sullivan is not
> happy in their company, and slips away at the earliest opportunity to
> the joyous flower-crowned votaries who worship the Lord of the lyre.
> I cannot find it in my heart to blame him.[15]

Joseph Bennett, writing in the *Daily Telegraph*, took a similar view:

Mr Sullivan is most charming when represented by the incense, flowers and songs of Apollo's maidens. With these are all his sympathies, and he invests them with so much musical beauty of form and colour that they command our sympathies likewise, and make the poor Christians and their lugubrious strains appear as uninteresting as they are sombre.[16]

It is certainly true that the brightest and liveliest music is given to the worshippers of Apollo. The most vigorous song in the whole piece is the contralto aria, 'Io Paean!' which excitedly calls on the pagan maidens to swing their smoking censers. However, I am not sure that we can deduce from this, as some have, that Sullivan's sympathies were with the pagans or that he felt he had to portray Christian worshippers in a restrained, sober, reverential way whereas he could let himself go and express his natural love of life when writing for the heathens. It was not so much a sense of inhibition, so often detected by critics in his sacred music, nor the stifling effect of Victorian religiosity which dictated Sullivan's music in *The Martyr of Antioch* but rather his desire to be faithful to the text that he was setting. The music that he writes for the Christians is restrained and serious because that is the condition in which they are portrayed in Milman's poem and in the drama that he constructed out of it with Gilbert's help. The two main Christian choruses are respectively a funeral anthem, 'Brother, thou art gone before us', a deeply affecting and pastorally very sensitive setting which rightly found its way into several church anthem books, and a prisoners' hymn. Both call for restrained and solemn music. By contrast, the pagan choruses cry out for bright, lively treatment. Milman himself wrote in the preface to his original poem: 'I have opposed to Christianity the most beautiful and natural of heathen superstitions—the worship of the Sun'.[17]

The critical reaction was mixed. The *Guardian* struck a positive note: 'Sullivan has risen in this work to a height which has astonished those who prophesied that he would never step out of the chains of comic opera'.[18] Several other critics, however, complained that the overall feeling of the work was lightweight and not serious enough. For the *Daily Telegraph*, 'criticism will always point to the fact that the drama is treated substantially as a pretext for charming choruses and airs'; the *Morning Post* felt it reprehensible that 'truths which affect the

foundation of Christian belief had not been considered as a matter
worthy of more exalted treatment than a mere dramatic one'; the
Athenaeum declared: 'It might be wished that in some portions
Mr Sullivan had taken a loftier view of his theme, but, at any rate,
he has written some most charming music' and noted that it was at
least 'an advantage to have the composer of *H.M.S. Pinafore* once more
occupying himself with a worthier form of art'.[19]

George Grove had no such reservations. After attending the Leeds
premiere he wrote a characteristically warm letter to 'dearest A',
saying that he regarded it as his best work to date and enthusing that

> in these days of ugliness, crudeness, and pretension, it is delightful to
> have a new work in which the words are fully expressed throughout, in
> which the feeling is as deep and as lofty as anyone would wish, and yet
> in which there is not one ugly or inconsequent bar from beginning to
> end.[20]

Grove lambasted those critics who attacked the work for being lightweight and reminded them how Mozart had shown how music could
be both 'light' and 'masterly'.[21] He had every reason to feel particularly warmly disposed towards his old friend at this time. Just a few
weeks before the premiere of *The Martyr of Antioch*, on the eve of his
60th birthday, Grove had been the recipient of a handsome testimonial in the form of a gold chronometer and a purse of 1,000 guineas in
recognition of his services to both biblical studies and music. The
presentation, held in St James' Hall on 29 July 1880 and chaired by
the Archbishop of Canterbury, Archibald Tait, was attended by over
300 leading figures from the worlds of theology, music, literature, and
public life. Arthur Stanley spoke about Grove's contribution to the
study of the Bible and Arthur Sullivan about his services to music and
literature. In his speech of thanks, Grove bracketed the two Arthurs as
pre-eminent among 'the dear faces and figures' who 'have known me
so long and so intimately . . . and studded the long corridor of my
life'.[22]

The Martyr of Antioch was widely taken up on the concert circuit.
Sullivan conducted its first London performance at the Crystal Palace
in December 1880 with further performances the following year at
St James's Hall and the Albert Hall. He also took it to Norwich in
October 1881 and again in October 1890, Brighton in November

1882, and Nottingham in March 1886. A performance in Bradford was conducted by Charles Hallé in December 1893 and one in Leeds by Hubert Parry in 1896.

The involvement of Gilbert in this 'sacred musical drama' provided much opportunity for parody on the part of the press. A piece in *Punch*, almost certainly by Francis Burnand, jokingly claimed that a telephone relay of a performance had contained a chorus with the refrain:

> In spite of all temptations
> From some denominations,
> I remained a Christian.
> I remained a Christian.[23]

In similar vein, *The Yorkshireman* speculated that Gilbert had attempted to insert another chorus beginning:

> When the lions hungry feel, Tarantara!
> And desire their mid-day meal, Tarantara!
> Then each martyr bears his chest
> To increase their hunger's zest, Tarantara![24]

In fact, Gilbert seems to have felt no urge to extract humour from this project and took it extremely seriously. When Sullivan gave him an eighteenth-century silver chalice, suitably engraved, as a thank you present, he responded with a letter which suggests, at least on the face of it (it is always difficult to tell with Gilbert) that he had found the whole experience both elevating and moving:

> It most certainly never occurred to me to look for any other reward than the honour of being associated, however remotely and unworthily, in a success which, I suppose, will endure until music itself shall die. Pray believe that of the many substantial advantages that have resulted to me from our association, this last is, and always will be, the most highly prized.[25]

The Leeds Festival

When Sullivan presided over the first performance of *The Martyr of Antioch* he did so as the new conductor of the Leeds Musical Festival. He succeeded Sir Michael Costa in this role in 1880 and was to hold it for a total of seven festivals.

The Leeds Musical Festival was founded in 1859 to raise funds for local health services. The most prestigious of the many British provincial music festivals established in the mid-nineteenth century, it brought together a locally recruited choir and an orchestra predominantly made up of London-based players for four days of intense music making every three years, with a programme largely made up of classical symphonies and big choral works. Although he had established his reputation as a leading conductor on the basis of his two seasons at the helm of the Covent Garden Proms and was easily the best known British figure in contemporary musical life, Sullivan was not the first choice of the festival committee. Their preference was for either Michael Costa, who had conducted the 1874 and 1877 festivals, or Charles Hallé. However, both men made demands deemed unacceptable by the committee, Costa requiring control over the selection of repertoire, refusing to perform Beethoven's choral symphony, and having a marked aversion to Bach; and Hallé insisting on using his own Manchester-based orchestra. So the 38-year-old Sullivan obtained the post by default, much to the satisfaction of those, including most of the local Yorkshire press, who wanted an English conductor for the festival, which had as one of its main aims the promotion of English music.

Sullivan took considerable care over his work for the festival, carefully rehearsing both the choir and the orchestra, whose members appreciated his approachability, humour, and openness, which contrasted with the distant and autocratic manner of Costa. In the words of the *Leeds Times*,

> The principals, band and chorus had faith in their conductor, Mr A. Sullivan. They found in him a gentleman whom they could esteem and respect. His kindly manner and style, and the excellent hints he gave them in the preliminary rehearsals, won for him the unbounded confidence of his forces.[26]

He was particularly committed to the sacred works which were the festival's main staple. Among those that he conducted were Mendelssohn's *Elijah* (programmed as the opening item in five of his seven festivals); Beethoven's *Missa Solemnis* (twice), *Mass in D*, and setting of Psalm 114; Haydn's *Creation* (twice); Handel's *Samson* (twice), *Messiah*, and *Israel in Egypt*; Spohr's *Last Judgment*; Dvorak's *Stabat Mater* and

St Ludmilla; Brahms' *German Requiem*; Palestrina's *Stabat Mater*; Mozart's *Requiem*; and Schubert's *Mass in E Flat*. Although the festival committee selected the programme, he had a say in it, championing fellow British composer George Macfarren's *King David*, of which he conducted the first performance, and vetoing Beethoven's oratorio *Christ on the Mount of Olives* on the grounds that 'it cannot be said to be inspiring'.[27] He introduced several Bach cantatas into the programme, giving the first British performance of *Thou Guide of Israel* in 1883; and conducted the first two parts of the *Christmas Oratorio* in 1895.

His most important contribution to the festival, and to the cause of sacred music more generally, was the performance which he conducted in 1886 of Bach's B Minor Mass, the first complete one in the United Kingdom. Despite being in excruciating pain from his kidney complaint, he took immense trouble to ensure that the Mass, which had hitherto been regarded in Britain as almost impossible to perform in its entirety, was performed as Bach had written it. He supervised the arrangement of an organ part and had trumpets specially manufactured to reproduce the tone and pitch of the instruments used in Bach's time. The chorus numbered 300 and the orchestra over 100. He made sure that both were well-rehearsed—the choir met more than fifty times and the orchestra had three solid days of rehearsal in London before choir, orchestra, and principals came together for three days in Leeds. On one occasion during the rehearsal period, Fred Spark found Sullivan lying on his couch scarcely able to raise himself on his elbow: 'Speaking of the *Sanctus*, his whole demeanour changed and he became quite animated, describing it as the grandest piece of music extant and declaring: "I would willingly give up all I have ever written it I could produce one piece like that".'[28]

The reviews of the performance were ecstatic. Noting that the 'choir became, for the first, time an immense organ', the *Musical Times* declared that the *Et resurrexit* and *Sanctus* 'attained the sublime—there is no other word to describe it'.[29] Other reviewers described the stupendous force of the choruses and the overwhelming effect that they had on the audience. Writing eight years later, Frederick Edwards, editor of the *Musical Times*, looked back on it as the crowning glory and culmination of all performances of Bach in nineteenth-century England and commented: 'It has been said that

"Sullivan nearly killed himself over that performance," so completely did he throw himself, body and soul, into the preparation and presentation of Bach's colossal work.'[30]

Family Deaths and Travels

On the personal front, the 1880s brought ever more foreign travel, some of it stimulating spiritual thoughts; the deaths of Mary Clementina Sullivan and Fred's widow, Charlotte; and a growing intensity in the relationship with Fanny Ronalds—all against a background of increasingly debilitating and painful illness.

In June 1881, Sullivan joined naval manoeuvres around the Baltic as the personal guest of the Duke of Edinburgh on his flagship, *H.M. S. Hercules*, an ironclad battleship. A diary entry reveals him taking part in one of his favourite activities: 'Yesterday being Sunday there was a church service and I played the harmonium. I was greatly delighted with the singing of the crew. They roared out the chants and the hymn tunes lustily and loved to dwell on the high notes.'[31] The voyage took in St Petersburg where he was profoundly moved by hearing the Imperial Chapel Choir, whose red and gold uniforms reminded him of his days in the Chapel Royal, perform at the Winter Palace:

> There were about 80 and, blasé as I am with music, I confess to a new sensation at hearing them. It was like nothing else. They have basses with the most wonderful voices going down to the low A and the effect of their singing their church music was thrilling. Sometimes it was exactly like an organ, only more beautiful. They sang for an hour and I could have heard them for a couple of hours more.[32]

This was not the only occasion when Sullivan showed his love for Russian church music. As has already been noted, he drew on it for his chorus 'The Lord is Risen' in *The Light of the World*. In 1874, he arranged two unaccompanied Russian church chants for a concert which he conducted in the Albert Hall in honour of the Czar who was visiting London. Herbert Sullivan noted, presumably on the basis of what his uncle had told him, that 'many of the unaccompanied quartets, etc., in his Savoy operas' were directly influenced by the chants that he heard on his visit to St Petersburg in 1881.[33]

A long trip to Egypt over the winter of 1881–2 allowed Sullivan to visit several mosques, experience both howling and dancing dervishes, and hear much Arab music which he found very affecting, and which he was able to bring into his later comic opera, *The Rose of Persia*. It also gave further opportunities for hearty hymn singing. On 23 January 1882, he wrote to his mother to tell her that he had been playing the organ at the English church in Cairo: 'Our gallant band sang very well, especially "Onward, Christian soldiers" (my tune).'[34]

This extended period abroad, which lasted from mid-December 1881 to mid-April 1882, was to be the last one on which Sullivan reported every detail so vividly to his mother. She died on 28 May 1882. Her death was undoubtedly a major blow to him. He had been devoted to her, taking her into his home after the death of his father, later setting her up with her own house and servants, visiting and entertaining her often, and writing to her almost daily when he was abroad. She in turn had acted as his valet and personal assistant before he acquired his own household staff. Several of his biographers have speculated that it was partly because of the intensity of his feelings for her that he found it so hard to have a lasting relationship with other women. I suspect that had more to do with his character and temperament, as identified early on during his relationship with Rachel Scott Russell. He stated his own view on the subject of marriage in a letter to his mother from Cairo in 1882 when he told her about having to get rid of a bad servant:

> Oh, the bother of servants . . . and I shall have to get a cook also, besides a man. It's enough to make one marry, but the cure would be more awful than the disease. I can get rid of servants, but not a wife— especially if she is my wife.[35]

Alongside his own commitment phobia, Sullivan was possibly influenced in this area as in others by the experience of George Grove who had a very unhappy marriage and took an increasingly jaundiced view of the whole institution, describing it as 'a terrible lottery' and reflecting:

> It really does seem to me that in the majority of cases marriages— viewed from any ideal—not a high ideal, but an ideal at all—are a failure . . . the real man or woman is found after marriage to be sadly

different to the image seen through the coloured glass of passion—what bad things some have to go through for that mistake! What hardships![36]

Sullivan's relationship with Fanny Ronalds undoubtedly intensified following his mother's death and as well as continuing as his lover she seems to have taken on some of the characteristics of a family member, often staying with him together with her own parents and with her two children. Theirs was not an exclusive relationship. Sullivan had other women and during his visit to Paris in early 1882 visited a brothel several times. There is clear evidence that, like Rachel Scott Russell, Fanny found his infidelity disturbing and complained about it more than once, but their relationship proved remarkably enduring, continuing until his death. From around the end of 1888, by which time Fanny was approaching 50, it seems to have ceased to be sexual and he took to describing her as 'Auntie', suggesting a rather different kind of relationship from that signified by his earlier references to 'L.W.' A new younger lover seems to have come on the scene. In what was perhaps a sign that Fanny took on at least something of the role of his mother, he wrote to her almost daily for the last twenty years of his life. When he took her on a trip to Cairo in 1890, they were accompanied by her mother, whom he referred to as 'Grandma'.

Another family death, this time of Fred Sullivan's widow Charlotte in January 1885, had a major effect on Arthur's life. She had married again in 1881 and emigrated two years later with six children to Los Angeles where her brother lived, leaving her oldest child, Herbert, in England. Following her death, her somewhat feckless husband decided to come home with their 2-month-old baby, leaving her other six children in the United States. Arthur, who had already taken responsibility for Herbert's schooling and well-being, and was supporting Charlotte with a yearly allowance, felt the need to go out and see his nephews and nieces to determine what would be best for their future. He set off for California in June, stopping off first in New York to deal with an unauthorized production of *The Mikado* and then visiting Salt Lake City where he was fascinated by 'the whole Mormon organisation' and went to a service in the Tabernacle where he was delighted to hear his arrangement of the hymn tune ST ANN being played on the organ.[37]

He spent over four weeks with his nephews and nieces in Los Angeles. The two oldest girls were 22 and 19, and he concluded that they were responsible enough to look after the rest of the family. He bought them a house and paid for a housekeeper with his own money. He had several adventures with them, including going to the Yosemite National Park where he attended a memorial service in a tiny chapel for Ulysees S. Grant, the American president who had just died. As so often, he was persuaded into playing the harmonium and reported that he had to endure 'an hour's prosy twaddle' from the minister who took the service.[38]

Sullivan's generosity to his extended family was exceptional. He treated his nephew Herbert (Bertie) like a son, sharing his home with him for several years, supervising his education and career and making him his principal heir on his death. He provided $3,000 a year for his other nephews and nieces in California plus extra allowances when they married. As well as supporting them financially, he sorted out family rows and took an interest in their spiritual welfare. When his niece, Cissie, was confirmed in May 1886, he wrote to her to tell her of his delight and asked, 'Who confirmed you? Was it a Bishop of the American Episcopal Church? Write and tell me all about it'.[39] His kindness to his extended family has led his great-great nephew, Scott Hayes, to reflect 'Sullivan must stand as one of the most generous and considerate of sons, brothers and uncles'.[40]

The Golden Legend, 1886

Following the success of *The Martyr of Antioch*, the Leeds festival committee approached Sullivan in 1884 for a new work for the 1886 festival. Initially they suggested an orchestral piece—a symphony had been promised for the 1883 festival but never delivered—but he responded that he would prefer to write 'a short choral work, not necessarily sacred, but of an earnest character'.[41] He informed the committee in December 1885 that he was considering three subjects none of which seemed wholly right. According to Joseph Bennett, it was Flora Chappell, daughter of Tom Chappell, the music publisher, who suggested that he look at Henry Longfellow's poem *The Golden Legend*. They worked on it together for some time before bringing in Bennett who fashioned it into a satisfactory libretto.[42]

Sullivan spent the summer of 1886 composing *The Golden Legend* side by side with *Ruddigore*.

Longfellow's poem, written in 1852, was based on a medieval German legend and also influenced by Goethe's *Faust*. It tells of a prince, Henry, who can only be cured of leprosy by a maiden giving up her life. Elsie, a pious farmer's daughter, resolves to make this sacrifice and Henry, under the influence of Lucifer, accepts it. As she is about to surrender her life, he is struck with remorse and saves her whereupon he is cured by the relics of St Matthew. In 1872, Longfellow incorporated his poem into a trilogy entitled *Christus* dealing with the three great Christian virtues of faith, hope, and charity. Within the trilogy, *The Golden Legend* stood for faith. He told a correspondent, 'I have endeavored to show in it, among other things, that through the darkness and corruption of the Middle Ages ran a bright, deep stream of Faith, strong enough for all the exigencies of life and death.'[43] Longfellow's story of self-sacrifice and redemption offered a theme of strong dramatic appeal in religious guise and as such was, in Arthur Jacobs' words, 'the very essence of the Victorian "sacred" choral work'.[44] Indeed, four composers before Sullivan had set it as a cantata in the early 1880s.

Sullivan's cantata, which runs to an hour and a half, begins with a prologue in which Lucifer is thwarted in his attempts to tear down the Cross on the spire of Strasbourg Cathedral by its saints and guardian angels and by the bells, represented by the male chorus singing in unison to the praise of God with organ accompaniment. Much use is made of dissonance and destabilizing tonality with the fall of the evil spirits represented by descending semitones set against the bells which constitute the one harmonically stable element. In the first scene, Prince Henry is corrupted by Lucifer through the medium of alcohol despite repeated warnings by a chorus of angels. The second scene contains an evening hymn, 'O gladsome Light', sung *a capella* by the villagers as they gather after their work in the fields, and a powerful invocation of Christ by Elsie who has had a vision of Jesus standing at the door of His Father's mansion and beckoning to her from afar. This leads her to sing a heartfelt prayer, 'My Redeemer and my Lord' asking that she may resemble Jesus by dying sacrificially. There is another choral hymn, extracted from a long Latin text attributed to St Hildebert, archbishop of Tours in the early twelfth century, sung by pilgrims on their way to Salerno in the third scene which ends with Elsie's ethereal aria 'The night is calm and cloudless' in which she hears snow white choirs singing '*Christe eleison!*'.

The fourth scene focuses on Elsie preparing to lay down her life as a choir of attendants reflect that the lilies which will spring from the dust of her body will have 'Ave Maria' written on their petals in characters of gold. In a brief fifth scene, her mother, Ursula, is told that her daughter has not died and sings a hymn of thanksgiving to the Virgin Mary. The sixth and last scene sees Elsie and Henry married and reflecting on their eternal love. A concluding choral epilogue, memorably characterized by Gervase Hughes as showing 'Berlioz shaking hands with Mendelssohn in a hearty atmosphere of muscular Christianity', describes Elsie as a messenger of faith sent to scatter freshness on the barren sands and solitudes of death with her unselfish hands in the same way that rain is sent by God to water arid plains.[45]

Although Lucifer has a prominent role in *The Golden Legend*, with some of Sullivan's most radical and daring harmonies being employed in his depiction of the demonic in the prologue, it is most definitely not a work where the Devil has the best tunes. The setting of the hymns, prayers, and other statements of Christian belief is sincere and affecting without being cloying. The strong religious overtones of the score, and their source in Sullivan's own musical upbringing, were not lost on the critics. The *Leeds Mercury* hailed 'O gladsome Light' as

a massive example of simple diatonic harmony, such as might have been written by Tallis or Farrant. Here Sir Arthur's church training serves him well, and, in estimating pieces of this kind, we must not forget that the composer was a chorister of the Chapel Royal, St James's, where he made a part of himself the best traditions of English church music, and steeped his whole being in the classics of our ecclesiastical art.[46]

With seventeen performances within a year of its triumphant premiere in Leeds Town Hall on 16 October 1886, *The Golden Legend* ousted Mendelssohn's *Elijah* as the second most performed work in Britain after Handel's *Messiah*, a position which it continued to occupy for the next twenty-five years or so. Its unashamed sentimentality and perceived religiosity made it hugely popular with the public, especially with the Nonconformist-dominated choral societies and chapel choirs up and down the land which effectively treated it as a sacred work. My own copy of the score in Novello's Original Octavo Edition was awarded as the first prize for musical composition in the Liverpool Sunday School Union Eisteddfod of 1896.

Contemporary critics hailed the cantata as Sullivan's greatest choral work and for once found themselves in agreement with popular opinion. In the *Daily Telegraph*, Joseph Bennett enthused about Sullivan's 'trust in the power of tune' in an age of musical 'confusion and incoherence', while, in *The Times*, Francis Hueffer noted how pleasant it was to be 'in full accord with the *vox populi*' and delivered a verdict which could apply to much of Sullivan's sacred music:

> Sir Arthur Sullivan has had the good sense to make no attempt at being what he is not; he has simply put on paper what he felt and how he felt it; hence his success. Popularity, in the true meaning of the word, which is a very different thing from vulgarity and by no means incompatible with refinement of form, is this composer's birthright.[47]

Even Sullivan's usual detractors in the musical establishment had to concede that this was a considerable achievement. John Fuller Maitland, who was London music critic for the *Manchester Guardian* from 1884 to 1889 and a key proponent of the notion of an English Musical Renaissance in the later nineteenth century (from which Sullivan was very definitely excluded), described it as his greatest work. The Renaissance had first been heralded in a review by Joseph Bennett of Hubert Parry's first symphony in September 1882 and centred particularly around the figures of Parry and Charles Villiers Stanford, both slightly younger than Sullivan and regarded as altogether more serious composers who devoted their talents to symphonies and concertos in imitation of the heroic German masters rather than parlour songs or comic operas. Neither of these younger men had much time for Sullivan's music, but Stanford had to concede that *The Golden Legend* would take its place 'not only among the permanent successes of our generation, but even on the shelves of the classics'. He could not forbear, however, from adding a few characteristic jibes against the composer who had squandered most of his life 'on a class of composition distinctly below the level of his abilities'. Expressing the hope that henceforth Sullivan would 'stay his hand from works which, however refined and musicianly, must of their very nature and surrounding be ephemeral, and pass away with the fashion which gave them birth', Stanford noted waspishly in respect of the 'too undiscriminating praise' lavished on *The Golden Legend* by the press:

> It is natural, nay more, it is right that in the Paradise of Music, as in other Paradises, there should be more rejoicing over Sullivan's great and legitimate success, than over the works of the ninety and nine just composers who have remained uninfluenced (perhaps because untempted) by consideration of profit and popularity.[48]

There was a similar sting in the tail of *The Times* review which concluded that *The Golden Legend* was 'a work which, if not one of genius in the strict sense of the word, is at least likely to survive till our long-expected English Beethoven appears on the scene'.[49] Good though it was, this was still not quite what the musical establishment had hoped for from the first Mendelssohn scholar.

Modern critics have generally agreed that this was Sullivan's finest work and that it was also highly innovative and influential on later composers. Percy Young is one of several who regard it as having been instrumental in liberating oratorio from its tight religious bands. He suggests that together with *The Martyr of Antioch*, it pushed oratorio in a more dramatic and operatic direction: 'In the general context of choral music of that era both works represented a departure from the overriding convention of religiosity, and by doing so helped to emancipate such music from the shackles by which it was bound'.[50]

Others have pointed to the considerable influence that *The Golden Legend* had on Edward Elgar, another composer who was to be cold-shouldered by several of the exponents of the English Musical Renaissance. There is no doubt that Sullivan's sacred work as a whole had a strong impact on Elgar. It is highly likely that as a 12-year-old Elgar attended the first performance of *The Prodigal Son* in Worcester for which both his father and uncle played in the orchestra. He later himself played in performances of *The Prodigal Son*, *The Light of the World*, and *The Golden Legend* in Worcester, Birmingham, and Hereford. Elgar's admiration of *The Golden Legend* is well-documented, as is Sullivan's support and help for the young British composer to whom he perhaps felt closest and admired most. David Russell Hulme has pointed to the striking similarity of the opening tenor phrases in *The Golden Legend* and *The Dream of Gerontius*; and Meinhard Saremba sees the lament of the dying Gerontius as recalling the sufferings of Prince Henry.[51] Saremba, indeed, argues that Sullivan's sacred work exercised a broader influence on Elgar and suggests that the prologue to *The Prodigal Son* may have paved the way for the younger composer's involvement in Biblical subjects. For Nigel Burton, who sees *The Dream of Gerontius* as the apogee of the tradition represented by *The Golden Legend*, 'Elgar was Sullivan's spiritual successor'.[52]

The most recent and the most detailed musicological analysis of *The Golden Legend* has come from Benedict Taylor who regards it as 'containing some of the most memorable and expressive music written by an English composer'.[53] For him, as for Young, Sullivan's great achievement lay in 'the move away from the old Baroque form of oratorio towards a more modern, secularised work'.[54] Seeing Sullivan's radical approach prefiguring avant-garde early-twentieth-century composers like Stravinsky as well as influencing Elgar, Taylor argues that Sullivan had found his creativity stifled by the constraints of setting Biblical texts and that *The Golden Legend*, like *The Martyr of Antioch*, freed him to be much more innovative, original, and profound.

More controversially, Taylor suggests that *The Golden Legend* expressed Sullivan's romantic, humanist, existentialist philosophy. He finds parallels between his exquisitely sensitive setting of Henry's solo 'It is the sea in all its vague immensity', where the melody of a melancholy cor anglais floats over the evocation of white ships 'with their ghostly sails unfurled' haunting 'the dim confines of existence' as 'phantoms from another world', and the sentiments expressed in Matthew Arnold's poem 'On Dover Beach' with its evocation of the 'long withdrawing roar' of the sea of faith. For Taylor, the overriding theme of the cantata, as brought out as much in the music as in the text, is 'the need for human, directed action rather than naïve, metaphysical religious belief'—it is a humanist message about 'the imperativeness of love'.[55]

Were Victorian audiences then wrong to see this as essentially a religious and indeed a Christian work? I don't think that they were. There are deeply spiritual, transcendent, mystical moments in the music of *The Golden Legend*. One occurs as the pilgrims' voices fade towards the end of their hymn and Sullivan interpolates a line for Elsie which floats above it and is not found at this point in Bennett's libretto:

'Hark those sounds whose accents holy fill the warm noon with music sad and sweet'. Elsie's prayer to Christ and Ursula's invocation of the Virgin both suggest simple but heartfelt faith. Was Sullivan perhaps thinking of his recently deceased mother and her Roman Catholic faith when he set them? His ravishing, ethereal treatment of lines from Prince Henry and Elsie's duet in the third scene touches on the sublime:

> This life of ours is a wild Aeolian harp of
>   many a joyous strain,
> But under them all there runs a loud perpetual wail,
>   as of souls in pain . . .
> All through life there are wayside inns, where man may
>   refresh his soul with love;
> Even the lowest may quench his thirst at rivulets fed
>   by springs from above.

Benedict Taylor sees this passage as perfectly expressing the outlook of 'the composer of popular strains, the chronic invalid, the perpetual womaniser, the humble Lambeth boy'.[56] It is true that it expresses a love of life and its pleasures, epitomized by 'the wayside inns, where man may refresh his soul with love'. But there is also an unmistakable acknowledgment here, expressed in the music as much as in the words, of the pain and suffering which are central to the human condition, and of the need to draw on the springs from above, clearly meant to indicate the grace and blessing which God pours out like the rain that falls from heaven.

The Golden Legend was Sullivan's last big serious composition. Benjamin Findon observed that 'from 1886 onwards he made no important contribution to the serious side of his art'.[57] In fact, as we shall see, he did contemplate writing another major sacred work in 1898, and had he lived longer it might well have seen the light of day. But the question remains why, given the enormous success and critical acclaim that greeted *The Golden Legend*, did the 44-year-old composer turn his back for at least ten years on this side of his work which he said meant so much to him, and why did he not go on to produce the big sacred choral piece that, in the eyes of critics, would have put him on a par with Mendelssohn and Brahms? Was it laziness and lack of commitment, was his heart just not in it, or did he lack the soul, the seriousness, and the religious gravitas for a work comparable to *Elijah* or the *German Requiem*? Some of his friends felt that oratorio was not where his gifts really lay. The composer Ethyl Smyth had the courage to tell him so:

> One day he presented me with a copy of the full score of the *Golden Legend*, adding: 'I think this is the best thing I've done, don't you?' and when truth compelled me to say that in my opinion *The Mikado* is his masterpiece, he cried out: 'O you wretch!' But though he laughed I could see he was disappointed.[58]

Others took the contrary view and felt that he should have written more oratorios. Joseph Bennett was perhaps the supreme exponent of this position. In his memoirs he noted that his friendship with Sullivan reached its climax in their collaboration on *The Golden Legend* in 1886. Thereafter, it declined.

> As far as I was responsible for the state of things, I attributed it in part to disappointment naturally felt at Sullivan's failure to go on to 'higher things' . . . I saw him immersed in West End life, which is never healthy for an artist; I saw him, as I thought striving for such poor honours as the Turf can bestow; in these pursuits wasting time which was precious not only to himself, but to the nation. Moreover, I felt that gifts so exalted as his were not turned to best account in the writing of comic operas, however popular and charming.[59]

Maybe there were other more pressing factors at work, including his increasingly debilitating illness and the need for money to fund his gambling and his support for his nieces and nephews. Perhaps, too, there was a growing realization that he could put his supreme talent for writing music with a softening and spiritualizing as well as an uplifting effect, that quality of divine emollient which George Grove had identified and benefitted from, into his comic operas as much as into more serious works.

Imperial Odes, 1886 and 1887

Sullivan's status as unofficial composer laureate led him to be called on twice in the mid-1880s to produce 'imperial odes' for major public occasions. The first involved a collaboration with Tennyson for an ode commissioned for the opening of the Colonial and Indian Exhibition in Hyde Park in May 1886. It proclaimed the ultra-patriotic message: 'One life, one flag, one fleet, one throne! Britons, hold your own!'. The second more elaborate ode was written to accompany the laying of the foundation stone of the Imperial Institute in South Kensington by Queen Victoria as part of her golden jubilee celebrations in July 1887. The words were supplied by Lewis Morris (1833–1907), a Welsh-born poet who penned several fulsome paeans of praise to Britishness and might well have become poet laureate were it not for his association with Oscar Wilde. His 1887 Imperial Institute Ode invoked the idea of Britain as a chosen nation.

> Our England at the call of Fate
> Left her lone islets in the sea,
> Donned her Imperial robe and state,
> Took the sole sceptre of the Free!

At Sullivan's suggestion, a verse encouraging emigration to the colonies was cut from the Ode and more focus was put on Queen Victoria, hailed as 'First Lady of our English race'. The composer ramped up the patriotic sentiment with plenty of brass and martial chords before moving into more spacious Elgarian mode, reminiscent of the closing chorus from *The Golden Legend*, for the final stanza:

> Oh, may the Hand which rules our Fate,
> Keep this our Britain great!
> We cannot tell, we can but pray
> Heaven's blessing on our work today.

Fervent monarchist and staunch patriot that he undoubtedly was, Sullivan was supremely happy setting texts such as these. It would be wrong, however, to see him just as a tub-thumping and essentially secular-minded imperialist. His spiritual sensitivities and religious faith took him beyond simple devotion to Queen, country, and Empire, important as this trinity undoubtedly was to him.

Address on Music, 1888

On 19 October 1888, Sullivan gave a lecture entitled 'About Music' in Birmingham Town Hall in his role as president of the Birmingham and Midland Institute. It reveals much about his beliefs, not least in respect of the divine character of music that he had first felt conscious of as a boy when hearing Jenny Lind sing:

> From the soft lullaby of the mother that soothes our cradle-life to the dirge that is sung over the grave, music enters into our existence. It marks periods and epochs of our life, stimulates our exertions, strengthens our faith, speaks both words of peace and of war, and exercises over us a charm and indefinite power which we can all feel, though we cannot explain.[60]

The bulk of his address is concerned with demonstrating music's usefulness, necessity for the mind, and influence in the world. Strikingly, the leading examples which he gives of these features are drawn from the Old Testament. In writing about its usefulness, he begins:

> In the account of the origin of mankind as given us in the book of Genesis, we find society divided into three great divisions, (1) Agriculturists, 'those that dwell in tents and have cattle'; (2) Manufacturers, 'artificers in brass and iron'; (3) Musicians, 'such as handle the harp and pipe,' i.e. strings and wind. Music is put on a level with such essential pursuits as agriculture and manufactures.[61]

This is a reference to Genesis 4.17–22 which describes three brothers, Jabal, Tubal-Cain, and Jubal, the direct descendants of Cain, as respectively the ancestors of farmers, metalworkers, and musicians. Sullivan comes back to this passage when considering the influence of music, referring specifically to Jubal, the father of all the musicians who have succeeded him, and reiterating how significant it is that 'his existence is announced in exactly the same terms as the discoverers of agriculture and of engineering'. He also mentions Jubal's father Lamech, whom he describes as 'the antediluvian hero' associated with 'what are perhaps the earliest lines of poetry in the world' and goes on to say that 'Lamech's poetry probably had its own melody'.[62] This is a reference to what is sometimes called the 'Song of the Sword' in Genesis 4.23–4 which refers back to the curse of Cain.

He goes on to cite another early biblical reference in his consideration of the constant association of music with eventful episodes in the ancient world:

The greatest of the great wells which supplied the Israelites during their wandering in the wilderness is expressly stated to have been dug to the sound of a solemn national music, of the extent of which we can form little idea from the concise terms of the ancient narrative; but from the mention of the fact that, at the special command of Jehovah, the great Lawgiver himself, the leaders of the people and the whole congregation took part in the singing, there can be little doubt that it was a most imposing and impressive musical ceremonial. We have the words, the very words themselves: 'Spring up, O well, sing ye unto it; The well which the princes digged, Which the nobles of the people delved With the sceptre and their staves.' Would that the music had also been preserved![63]

This is a reference to Numbers 21.17 which describes the people of Israel singing as they dug a well at Be-er on their way to the promised land.

By any stretch, these are obscure biblical references which would only be known to someone with a very thorough knowledge indeed of the Old Testament. Maybe George Grove had made Sullivan something of a biblical scholar, or perhaps the composer consulted his old friend when preparing this address and together they searched the Scriptures for early references to music. It is perhaps significant that Grove made reference to the Genesis 4.17–22 passage about Jabal, Tubal-Cain, and Jubal in a letter to a Scottish friend in 1895, asking him 'Did you ever notice that at the first enumeration of the inhabitants of the world they are divided into three great sections— herdsmen, *musicians* and engineers? It struck me as very interesting when I first observed it'.[64] Whether they were suggested by Grove or not, Sullivan's prominent use of these passages from the Old Testament to make his argument about the usefulness and influence of music is striking. They are not the only biblical references in his address. Citing Thomas Carlyle's life of Oliver Cromwell as his source, he recalls the battle of Dunbar in 1650 and 'the emotion which forced that silent and undemonstrative man into urging his soldiers forward by shouting and making them shout the 117th Psalm to the version still used in the Church of Scotland, and to a still existing tune'.[65] It is an intriguing and somewhat surprising choice of example to illustrate the power of music for one who was such a staunch Royalist and Anglican.

Less unexpectedly, Sullivan makes several references to the power of hymnody and the importance of church music in his address, singling out for special mention Martin Luther's '*Ein feste Burg*' and his other chorales 'which are well known to have precipitated the conversion of whole towns to the reformed faith', as well as the anthems of his beloved sixteenth-century English composers.[66] There is much historical and patriotic material in the address, but ultimately his argument is a spiritual and moral one:

> Herein lies one of the divine attributes of music, in that it is absolutely free from the power of suggesting anything immoral. Its countless moods and richly varied forms suit it to every organisation, and it can convey every meaning except one—an impure one. Music can suggest no improper thought, and herein may be claimed a superiority over painting and sculpture, both of which may, and indeed do at times depict and suggest impurity. This blemish, however, does not enter into music; sounds alone (apart from articulate words, spectacle, or descriptive programme) must, from their indefinite nature, be innocent. Let us thank God that we have one elevating and ennobling influence in the world which can never, never lose its purity and beauty.[67]

In making the case for music on moral grounds, Sullivan was echoing a widespread Victorian idea, supremely expressed by Hugh Haweis, a London vicar in his very popular and influential book *Music and Morals* (1871). Sullivan's own tendency, displayed perhaps above all in *The Golden Legend* and in *The Light of the World*, to use orchestral passages to paint spiritual word pictures and scenes, could be read as an illustration of his point about the purity of music, unadulterated by 'articulate words or spectacle'. In an interesting letter that he wrote to his old mentor Thomas Helmore in 1889 he went even further than this, describing his striving for an even purer and more mystical kind of music that went beyond notes as well as words:

> It sounds paradoxical, but there are times to me when the music would be more beautiful and complete without notes . . . How often have I felt myself hampered by having to express all I wanted to say by voice and instruments of limited means, and definite, unchangeable quality. After all, it is only human to be longing and striving for something more than we have got.[68]

Perhaps the most revealing remark that Sullivan makes in his 1888 Birmingham address is right at the beginning when, after noting that it has been his incessant occupation since the age of 8, he states: 'Music is to me a mistress in every sense of the word; a mistress whose commands I obey, whose smiles I love, whose wrongs move me as no others do.'[69] This is of course precisely what Rachel Scott Russell had rightly discerned all those years ago and what other women were to realize. Maybe it tells us why he never married but rather remained wedded to his demanding but utterly absorbing muse.

Sullivan's language here as in other parts of his address closely echoes that of Martin Luther who similarly saw music as a divine gift next only to theology, and spoke of Lady Music (*Frau Musica*) as a mistress (*domina*) as well as a ruler (*gubernatrix*) of the affections. There are other striking similarities in the two men's thinking and writing on the subject. Luther believed that music even without words could preach the Gospel and that the heart rather than the head was the organ through which the human relationship with God was shaped. He felt that music more than any other divine gift set humans free from the bondage in which they were enslaved. Even if Sullivan did turn down the first organist's post that he was offered because it was in a Lutheran rather than an Anglican church, he perhaps had imbibed more of Luther's ideas during his time in Leipzig than he had realized.[70]

Collaboration with Gilbert, 1877–1889

Sullivan's dominant professional occupation throughout the period covered in this chapter was writing comic operas with W.S. Gilbert. Although their names are inseparably linked and they are remembered for forming the most successful theatrical partnership in history, theirs was not an easy relationship and it needed all Sullivan's charm, forbearance, and tact to keep it going.

The two collaborators could hardly have been more different in upbringing, temperament, and philosophy of life. Perhaps partly because of a very unhappy and lonely childhood, Gilbert took a distinctly jaundiced view of the world and the human condition. For him, life was arbitrary, unfair, and unjust, the world being ruled by the fickle forces of fate rather than a benign and omnipotent deity. His outlook on life was well-expressed in Dick Deadeye's utterance in *H.M.S. Pinafore* that 'it's a cruel world' and the Mikado's observation: 'It's an unjust world and virtue is triumphant only in theatrical performances'. Perhaps influenced by Darwin's theory of the survival of the fittest, Gilbert held that 'Man was sent into the world to contend with man, and to get the advantage of him in every possible way.'[71] Alongside this negative and pessimistic world view went an obsession with cruelty, torture, and death, seen clearly in *The Mikado* which for all its brightness has an inescapably dark underside.

By nature Gilbert was irascible and argumentative. As he himself put it, 'I am an ill-tempered pig and I glory in it'.[72] The actor and playwright Seymour Hicks wrote that 'he always gave the impression that he got up in the morning to see with whom he could have a quarrel'.[73] His most recent biographer, Andrew Crowther, notes that 'throughout his life, Gilbert gave the impression of being a fundamentally angry man'.[74] It was perhaps in an effort to escape the grim reality of the world and his own misanthropic musings that he developed his penchant for topsy-turvydom, inverting the usual and expected conventions and inventing ridiculous, surreal characters and situations. In many ways he was the founding father of the theatre of the absurd.

Sullivan's character and outlook could not have been more different. Unlike Gilbert, he had had a very happy childhood and was by nature optimistic, trusting, and generous in his assessment of people's motives and in his own instincts. Gregarious and full of charm, his whole demeanour was ingratiating and engaging. He loved life, not least its pleasures and distractions. Every day was a delight to be savoured, even when he was wracked by pain. An unashamed sentimentalist, he was moved by appeals to the heart rather than to the head, and this quality came over in his work. If Gilbert was something of a Darwinist, sharing the bleak philosophy of Thomas Hardy, Sullivan was much closer to the Pre-Raphaelites and the Romantics. It is no coincidence that his favourite authors were Dickens and Thackeray who shared his own idealistic sentimentalism. Arthur Lawrence reported that 'More than once Sir Arthur has told me of his antipathy to fiction of a morbid or decadent character'.[75]

Sullivan had a simpler, surer, and more straightforward faith than his collaborator, and much more respect and fondness for the church.

Gilbert directed a good deal of his satirical fire-power at the clergy, pointing up their self-righteousness and narrow legalism. His original plot for *Patience* involved two rival Anglican curates, the Rev Clayton Hooper from Spiffton-extra-Souper and the Rev Hopley Porter from Assesmilk-cum-Worter, who vied with one another in mild-mannered insipidity, but to avoid offending Victorian sensibilities he changed them to aesthetic poets. The one clergyman whom he did put into the Savoy operas, Dr Daly, the vicar of Ploverleigh in *The Sorcerer*, is an engaging and loveable figure, made all the more attractive by Sullivan's wistfully lyrical melodies for his two arias which recall his days as a pale young curate and his failure to gain a wife when all the village seems to be getting engaged under the influence of a magic love potion. Gilbert confessed more than once that his favourite piece of literature was the Book of Job and he also declared that no work could be compared to the historical books of the Bible for 'simplicity, directness and perspicuity'; but these judgements seem to have been made on literary rather than theological grounds.[76] He was not a church-goer and when he expressed a wish to be buried in the churchyard of an Anglican church near his home because he found its quietness attractive, the vicar declined his request on the grounds that his congregation did not want the churchyard crowded with strangers. In the event, a compromise was reached with Gilbert's widow and his cremated ashes were laid to rest near the church door, guarded over by a white marble angel.

Sullivan came close on several occasions through the 1880s to ending their partnership. He complained repeatedly about his collaborator's fixation with topsy-turvydom and the absurd, and requested 'a story of human interest and probability' to set. He also expressed his distaste at Gilbert's stereotypical and somewhat grotesque stock characters like 'the middle aged woman with fading charms'.[77] He longed for something more romantic, lyrical, and uplifting from the pen of his cynical partner. Yet he stuck with him, cajoled by Richard D'Oyly Carte who used all his smooth diplomacy to keep his two cash-cows together, and placated by Gilbert who made sufficient concessions, including abandoning his desire for more plots involving magic lozenges and potions, to keep him on board. For all his protestations, there was a part of Sullivan that enjoyed the buzz of the stage, and the glamour and social status, as well as the money, all of which went with being part of what was the most successful and sustained partnership in theatrical history. As early as 1884, in addition to companies playing at the Savoy Theatre in London and in New York, D'Oyly Carte had six companies touring the United Kingdom.

What did Sullivan bring to his collaborations with Gilbert apart from all those marvellously memorable melodies which still retain their freshness and infectious gaiety today? He was largely responsible for their distinctly 'churchy' feel, as noted by George Bernard Shaw who found the Savoy operas 'most unexpectedly churchy after Offenbach' and, indeed, by Gilbert who reproached his collaborator for writing tunes that were altogether too serious and 'fitted more for the Cathedral than the Comic opera stage'.[78] Even had he wanted to, which he did not, Sullivan could never get away from his upbringing in and deep love of church music. Several of the most characteristic musical features of the Savoy operas show its influence. The contrapuntal double choruses have their origins in church counterpoint, the madrigals that feature so prominently have something of the character of the Tudor church anthems to which he was so attached, and the distinctive patter songs, with their repeated notes and precise syllabic setting hark back to the tradition of plainchant in which he had been so thoroughly schooled.

The key role given to the chorus was one of the most important innovations that the Savoy operas brought into the world of musical theatre. It is no coincidence that they emerged and thrived on the back of the great choral revival in mid-nineteenth-century Britain which saw thousands of people attending classes in tonic sol-fa and part singing, and the emergence of hundreds of choral societies up and down the country whose repertoire centred around sacred works like Mendelssohn's *Elijah* and Stainer's *Crucifixion*. Sullivan was himself steeped in this world, and he wrote for his stage choruses in four-part harmony as if he were writing for church choirs or composing oratorios. Indeed, there are choral passages in his comic operas which would not sound out of place in an oratorio—'I hear the soft note' from *Patience* and much of the Act 1 finale of *The Yeomen of the Guard* with its echoes of the '*Dies Irae*' come to mind. The fact that so much of the music for the chorus in the Savoy operas has close similarities with Victorian anthems and sacred pieces is one of the reasons why they were so avidly and widely taken up by church choirs. Many of the earliest amateur Gilbert and Sullivan performing societies on both sides of the Atlantic began as offshoots of churches and Nonconformist chapels, with choir members forming the nucleus.

Another reason for the popularity of the Savoy operas among churchgoers was their wholesome, respectable character which appealed to those who shunned both the musical hall and the opera house as being decadent and immoral. This quality was made much of in Richard D'Oyly Carte's marketing strategy. A flyer advertising a provincial tour of *H.M.S. Pinafore* in 1879 boasted 'My theatre in London is visited largely by the clergy, who have given to it a support which they withhold from many others'.[79] Following the success of the same show in the United States, the *American Review* expressed the hope that the work of Gilbert and Sullivan 'might be the means of starting the great work of regeneration of the modern stage in our native land' and approvingly cited wide ecclesiastical endorsement: 'Clergymen have approved it. Church choirs have sung it. Church members have gone to see it and have been conscious of no moral degradation in the act.'[80]

Sullivan was at least as responsible as Gilbert for creating this ethos which sprang in many ways from those qualities of innocence and purity in music that he had identified in his 1888 address. He elevated their joint works into something at once more soul-enhancing and life-affirming than was provided by the topsy-turvy plots and the clever word play in the libretti. Even Stanford conceded that 'the world of music has to thank him for a purification of the operetta stage'.[81] From *Cox and Box* onwards, critics often noted that his music for his comic operas was somehow too serious, too good even, for the words to which it was set. Gilbert felt the same, complaining that the scoring of the ghost scene at the opening of Act 2 of *Ruddigore* was far too grand and serious for a comic opera: 'It is as though one inserted fifty lines of *Paradise Lost* into a farcical comedy'.[82] As well as finding Sullivan too serious and 'churchy', Gilbert also felt that he was too sentimental. He proposed cutting Sergeant Meryll's song in Act 1 of *The Yeomen of the Guard*, 'A laughing boy but yesterday', in which a father looked back wistfully on the boyhood of his son, on the grounds that there were already too many numbers of a serious, grim or sentimental character for a professedly comic opera. In the same opera, he rejected the first two tunes that Sullivan offered for Colonel Fairfax's song 'Is life a boon?' on similar grounds. Gilbert basically wanted tunes that followed the words and ensured that every syllable would be clearly heard. He did not want music that added a more reflective or sentimental dimension. Again and again, Sullivan protested that he was a mere syllable-setter, subordinating his music to Gilbert's words and very much playing second fiddle in their partnership. He largely provided what Gilbert wanted, because he was a consummate word setter—it was the same quality that made his hymn tunes so good— but he also managed on many occasions to break the constraints of mere syllable setting, to give his music wings and let it soar.

Sullivan's music nearly always has the effect of softening and brightening the often rather grim and cynical messages conveyed in Gilbert's lyrics. This quality can properly be described in spiritual terms as having a redemptive, transforming, and ultimately transfiguring dimension. With his own faith, philosophy of life, and innate humanity and sensitivity, Sullivan was incapable of writing music that expressed a nihilistic or misanthropic outlook. Where Gilbert often seeks to caricature his characters and take them down, Sullivan instinctively wants to build them up and give them a certain nobility and dignity. This is evident in the contrasting treatment on the part of librettist and composer of the unfortunate 'elderly, ugly daughters' like Katisha in *The Mikado* and Lady Jane in *Patience* where the music redeems and softens their unappealing portrayal in terms of words, as demonstrated in their respective arias 'Hearts do not break' and 'Silver'd is the raven hair'. In both songs, Sullivan introduces a note of pathos and sympathy which is not there in the rather cold and cruel words. The way in which he transforms and redeems Gilbert's lyrics is particularly evident in the quartet 'The world is but a broken toy' in *Princess Ida*. As written on the page, the words are clearly meant to be satirical, with Princess Ida's lofty and disdainful renunciation of the world and its ways being mocked and parodied by Hilarion, Cyril, and Florian. Sullivan transforms their meaning by his serene and sublime lyrical setting into a poignant statement of the reality of pain and sorrow. In a rather different way, he softens the opening female chorus in *The Mikado* 'Comes a train of little ladies', giving it a much more appealing and positive message than lines like 'Is it but a world of sorrow, sadness set to song?' would suggest yet without losing its poignancy and wistfulness.

Sullivan's contribution in this regard has been recognized by the authors of several modern studies of the Savoy operas. Andrew Crowther writes that 'Sullivan's music was able to give Gilbert's words a warmth which they often lacked'.[83] David Eden puts it in Freudian terms, observing that 'the life instincts of Sullivan overcame the death instincts of Gilbert'.[84] It is not too much to say, I think, that Sullivan spiritualizes the overwhelmingly secular outlook of his collaborator. Meinhard Saremba gets close to acknowledging this when he writes:

> Influenced by the humanity of Freemasonry and his friendship with Dickens and Trollope, Sullivan translated the anfractuosities of Gilbert's literary world—bleak, sparkling or grotesque—to the musical stage. He sees the good side even in the evil characters and his music transcends mechanical topsy-turvydom . . . If his writings are to be believed, Gilbert never trusted love; Sullivan, on the other hand, did.[85]

Just occasionally, there are moments in the Savoy operas where one feels that their two creators are completely aligned in expressing a deeply shared conviction. One such is the unaccompanied anthem 'Hail, Poetry!' expressing both men's agreement with the Pirate King's rhetorical question which introduces it, 'What, we ask, is life without a touch of poetry in it?'. Critics have tended to see this as a lampoon or parody of a certain kind of religious sentiment. Arthur Jacobs described it as 'a burlesque of an operatic prayer scene . . . but the words of prayer could not be burlesqued, nor could the Deity be invoked in satire. So the abstraction of "Poetry" takes its place, an awkward substitute.'[86] Gervase Hughes wrote in similar vein: 'Sullivan's share has been decried as a lapse into "churchiness", and he may or may not have had his tongue in his cheek, but he knew that his audience, steeped like himself in the tradition of English choral singing, would applaud it to the echo.'[87] In fact, I do not think that either librettist or composer had their tongues in their cheeks when they wrote 'Hail, Poetry!'. I believe that Gilbert, accomplished poet as he was, was utterly sincere in his tribute to poetry as 'a heaven born maid' and indeed as 'Divine emollient' which is perhaps as near as he ever gets in any of his writing to directly invoking the Deity. Sullivan was equally sincere in providing an anthem-like setting for this hymn to the flowing fount of sentiment in which he believed so strongly.

Another song which brings librettist and composer together in an expression of shared belief is the quintet 'Try we lifelong' in *The Gondoliers* with its philosophy of *Carpe Diem*, its reminder that 'life's a pudding full of plums, care's a canker that benumbs', and its injunction to 'string the lyre and fill the cup lest on sorrow we should sup' and to take life as it comes. It is preceded by what is the nearest there is to a theological statement in the whole Gilbert and Sullivan canon, the Grand Inquisitor's observation that 'Life is one closely complicated tangle: Death is the only true unraveller'. Did those words strike a particular chord with Sullivan, whose own life was somewhat tangled and who was so lacking in fear of death? He certainly set them with particular power and sensitivity, as he did the subsequent quintet which so perfectly sums up his own philosophy of living for the moment and enjoying every day to the full.

The Gondoliers represented the culmination of Gilbert and Sullivan's partnership and was their closest and most harmonious collaboration. It was preceded by a typically fractious correspondence, in which each man argued that he had sacrificed himself to the other over the past twelve years and did not want to continue the partnership. Relations gradually improved, thanks partly to the intervention of Richard D'Oyly Carte who suggested that Sullivan might work on a grand opera with a different librettist while collaborating on another lighter work with Gilbert. A Continental holiday, which took place in Venice, improved Sullivan's mood and when he returned home in April 1889 he responded positively to Gilbert's suggestion of a Venetian setting for a typically topsy-turvy plot involving Republican-inclined gondoliers finding themselves jointly ruling an island kingdom. Both men spent longer on *The Gondoliers* than they had on any of their previous joint works. Gilbert took the best part of five months to write the libretto and Sullivan was occupied on the music for the whole of the summer of 1889 which he spent largely at Weybridge in Surrey. Following their usual practice, after discussion on the overall shape of the work, Gilbert sent the songs to Sullivan one or two at a time, and numerous letters passed between them about redrafting or dropping particular numbers.

Despite this comparatively long period of preparation, the run-up to the opening performance was, as always, a frantic rush. Sullivan did not have his first orchestral rehearsal until five days before the London first night. After taking the rehearsal, he worked until three the following morning composing the overture. He was up again after only a few hours' sleep to agree with Gilbert the title of the piece, which had, characteristically, been left to the last minute. Two days later the dress rehearsal lasted for a marathon seven hours.

The Gondoliers opened at the Savoy Theatre on 7 December 1889 and ran for 554 performances until 20 June 1891. The critics were almost unanimous in their praise, with the *Daily Telegraph* applauding 'the all pervading character of brightness and unaffected delight' and noting '*The Gondoliers* conveys an impression of having been written *con amore*. It is as spontaneous as the light-hearted laughter of the sunny South and as luminous as an Italian summer sky'.[88] The public's reaction was equally ecstatic. When Chappells published the vocal score, twelve men were employed packing it from morning till night and on the first day 20,000 copies were dispatched in eleven wagon loads.

The opera's success prompted from both librettist and composer rare but heartfelt tributes to each other's talents. Gilbert wrote to Sullivan on 8 December: 'I must thank you for the magnificent work you have put into the piece. It gives one the chance of shining right through the twentieth century with a reflected light.'[89] Sullivan replied, 'Don't talk of reflected light. In such a perfect book as *The Gondoliers* you shone with an individual brilliancy which no other writer can hope to attain'.[90] At last, it seemed, librettist and composer were acting, like Marco and Giuseppe Palmieri, 'in perfect unity'. Alas, this rare state of affairs was to be short-lived.

Notes

1. Augustine Godwin, *Gilbert & Sullivan: A Critical Appreciation of the Savoy Operas* (London: Dent, 1926), p.50.
2. Derek Scott, *The Singing Bourgeois: Songs of the Victorian Drawing Room*, 2nd edn. (Aldershot: Ashgate, 2001), p.211.
3. Michael Ainger, *Gilbert and Sullivan: A Dual Biography* (Oxford: Oxford University Press, 2002), p.220.
4. Arthur Jacobs, *Arthur Sullivan*, 2nd edn. (Aldershot: Scolar Press, 1992) p.262.
5. *The Globe*, 5 August 1878.

6. Jacobs, *Sullivan*, p.167.

7. Fred Spark and Joseph Bennett, *History of the Leeds Musical Festivals 1858–1889* (Leeds: Fred Spark & Son, 1892), p.146.

8. Spark and Bennett, *History*, pp.146–7.

9. Spark and Bennett, *History*, p.147.

10. *Musical World*, 19 June 1880, p. 385.

11. Henry Milman, *The Martyr of Antioch* (London: John Murray, 1822), p.42.

12. Jacobs, *Sullivan*, p.146.

13. Arthur Sullivan [hereafter AS], *The Martyr of Antioch* (London: Chappell & Co., 1880), p.iii; AS to Wilfred Bendall, 20 January 1898: Pierpont Morgan Library, New York [hereafter PML].

14. Spark and Bennett, *History*, pp.199–200.

15. Ian Bradley, *Lost Chords and Christian Soldiers* (London: SCM Press, 2013), pp.131–2.

16. *Daily Telegraph*, 18 October 1880.

17. Milman, *The Martyr*, p.vii.

18. Spark and Bennett, *History*, p.200.

19. *Daily Telegraph*, 16 October 1880; *Morning Post*, 16 October 1880; *Athenaeum*, 23 October 1880.

20. George Grove to AS, 16 October 1880: PML.

21. *Pall Mall Gazette*, 16 October 1883.

22. Graves, *Grove*, pp.253–4.

23. *Punch*, 23 October 1880.

24. *The Yorkshireman*, 4 September 1880, quoted by Simon Moss in *SASS Magazine* 93 (Spring 2017), p.26.

25. Jacobs, *Sullivan*, pp.151–2.

26. *Leeds Times*, 23 October 1880, p.2.

27. Jacobs, *Sullivan*, p.235.

28. Harold Orel, *Gilbert & Sullivan: Interviews and Recollections* (Iowa City: University of Iowa Press, 1994), p.118.

29. *Musical Times*, 27:525 (November 1886), pp.654–5.

30. *Musical Times*, 37:646 (December 1896), p.800.

31. AS to his mother, 27 June 1881: PML.

32. AS to his mother, 6 July 1881: PML.

33. Herbert Sullivan and Newman Flower, *Sir Arthur Sullivan* (London: Cassell & Co., 1927), p.117.

34. AS to his mother, 23 January 1882: PML.

35. AS to his mother, 26 February 1882: PML.

36. Percy Young, *George Grove* (London: Macmillan, 1980), p.231.
37. Diary, 19 July 1885, quoted in Scott Hayes, *Uncle Arthur: The California Connection* (Retford: Sir Arthur Sullivan Society, 2009), p.21.
38. Hayes, *Uncle Arthur*, p.47.
39. AS to his niece, 22 May 1886: PML.
40. Hayes, *Uncle Arthur*, p.65.
41. Spark and Bennett, *History*, p.284.
42. Joseph Bennett, *Forty Years of Music* (London: Methuen, 1908), p.78.
43. Henry Longfellow to Emma Martin, 17 January 1852, in *Letters of Henry Wadsworth Longfellow*, ed. Andrew Hilen, Vol.III (Cambridge, MA: The Balknap Press, 1972), p.326.
44. Jacobs, *Sullivan*, p.232.
45. Gervase Hughes, *The Music of Arthur Sullivan* (London: Macmillan, 1960), p.66.
46. Spark and Bennett, *History*, p.309.
47. *Daily Telegraph*, 18 October 1886; *The Times*,18 October, 1886.
48. Charles Villiers Stanford, *Studies and Memories* (London: Archibald Constable, 1908), pp.156, 168–9.
49. *The Times*, 18 October 1886.
50. Percy Young, *Sir Arthur Sullivan* (London: J.M. Dent, 1971), p.218.
51. David Russell Hulme, sleeve notes to *Golden Legend* CD, Hyperion, 2001; Meinhard Saremba, 'Unconnected with the Schools—Edward Elgar and Arthur Sullivan', *Elgar Society Journal* 17:4 (April 2012), pp.9–10.
52. Nigel Burton, 'Oratorios and Cantatas' in Nicholas Temperley (ed.), *Music in Britain: The Romantic Age 1900–1914* (London: Athlone Press, 1981), pp.229–30.
53. Benedict Taylor, *Arthur Sullivan: A Musical Reappraisal* (London: Routledge, 2018), p.166.
54. Taylor, *Sullivan*, p.149.
55. Taylor, *Sullivan*, p.164.
56. Taylor, *Sullivan*, p.164.
57. Benjamin Findon, *Sir Arthur Sullivan: His Life and Music* (London: James Nisbet, 1904), p.200.
58. Orel, *Gilbert & Sullivan*, p.117.
59. Bennett, *Forty Years*, p.86.
60. Arthur Lawrence, *Sir Arthur Sullivan: Life Story, Letters and Reminiscences* (London: James Bowden, 1899), p.276.
61. Lawrence, *Sullivan*, p.275.
62. Lawrence, *Sullivan*, p.278.

63. Lawrence, *Sullivan*, p.278–9.
64. George Grove to James Maxtone Graham, 22 April 1895, published in *Strathearn Herald*, 27 April 1895.
65. Lawrence, *Sullivan*, p.285.
66. Lawrence, *Sullivan*, p.279.
67. Lawrence, *Sullivan*, p.287.
68. AS to Thomas Helmore, 26 December 1889: PML.
69. Lawrence, *Sullivan*, p.261.
70. On Luther's approach to music, see Christoph Schwöbel, 'Mutual Resonances: Remarks on the Relationship between Music and Theology', *International Journal for the Study of the Christian Church* 20:1 (March 2020), pp.12–15.
71. 'Men We Meet' by the Comic Physiognomist, *Fun*, 9 March 1867.
72. Reginald Allen, *W.S. Gilbert: An Anniversary Survey* (Charlotte, VA: Bibliographical Society of University of Virginia, 1963), p.78.
73. Seymour Hicks, *Between Ourselves* (London: Cassell, 1930), p.49.
74. Andrew Crowther, *Gilbert of Gilbert & Sullivan* (Stroud: The History Press, 2011), p.62.
75. Lawrence, *Sullivan*, p.223.
76. Jane Stedman, *W.S. Gilbert* (Oxford: Oxford University Press, 1996), p.274.
77. Ainger, *Gilbert and Sullivan*, p.288.
78. Jacobs, *Sullivan*, p.16; Sullivan and Flower, *Sullivan*, p.187.
79. Regina Oost, *Gilbert and Sullivan: Class and the Savoy Tradition 1875–1896* (Farnham: Ashgate, 2009), p.28.
80. *American Review*, 19 May 1879.
81. Stanford, *Studies and Memories*, p.162.
82. Ainger, *Gilbert and Sullivan*, p.261.
83. Crowther, *Gilbert*, p.119.
84. David Eden, *Gilbert and Sullivan: Creative Conflict* (Madison: Farleigh Dickinson University Press, 1986), p.196.
85. Meinhard Saremba, '"We Sing as One Individual"? Popular Misconceptions of Gilbert and Sullivan', in David Eden and Meinhard Saremba (eds), *The Cambridge Companion to Gilbert and Sullivan* (Cambridge: Cambridge University Press, 2009), p.63.
86. Jacobs, *Sullivan*, p.140.
87. Hughes, *Music*, pp.86–7.
88. *Daily Telegraph*, 9 December 1889.
89. W.S. Gilbert to AS, 8 December 1889: PML.
90. Letter from AS quoted by W.S Gilbert in letter of 8 May 1890: PML.

6

The 1890s

The Final Decade

The 1890s was a difficult decade for Arthur Sullivan. It began inauspiciously with the so-called 'carpet quarrel', when W.S. Gilbert took umbrage at the deduction from the partners' earnings of £500 for a new front of house carpet at the Savoy Theatre and took Richard D'Oyly Carte to court. Sullivan tried to avoid getting dragged into their acrimonious dispute but, as the *Musical Standard* put it, 'the eminent and genial composer of *The Gondoliers* found himself in a warm place just because he happened to be seated near a fire'.[1] He refused to support Gilbert's action against Carte, to whom he was close, having been best man at his recent wedding to Helen Lenoir at the Savoy Chapel. This provoked a string of furious letters from the librettist, denouncing him and vowing never to work with him again. Although their working relationship was eventually restored, it was on a much looser and more occasional basis than before and the creative spark went out of it. Both men did most of their subsequent work with different collaborators.

Sullivan told Gilbert that the 'wretched business' of the carpet quarrel had left him physically and mentally ill.[2] Increasing ill health dogged him throughout the 1890s, with bouts of pneumonia and neuralgia adding to his longstanding kidney problems. He also suffered periods of depression, one of the first occurring in July 1891 when he told his brother-in-law, 'all my energy and strength have been taken out of me . . . I stick in my chair and read to the very last line of the advertisements in *The Times* because I haven't the moral strength to see about doing what I propose to do'.[3] He came close to death while staying in a villa near Monte Carlo in April 1892, apparently only being saved when his nephew Bertie and his servants plunged him into a warm bath, and had to be carried on to the boat train at Calais for his return home to London where he remained incapacitated for several months with depression as well as physical weakness. His diary entry for 31 December that year reads: 'Saw New Year in; hoped and prayed that it might be a happier one for me than this last, half of which was lost through illness. *Health* is the secret of happiness'.[4] There were further bad bouts of depression in 1895 and 1898, exacerbating the effects of the increasingly recurring and painful flare-ups of his kidney complaint. Alongside ever stronger and more frequent injections of morphine he sought relief by taking cures in Continental spas which he found excruciatingly boring. In the midst of a thirty-day cure in Contrexéville in the Vosges region of France, he reported: 'There is a constant delirious whirl of dullness here, the counterpart of which is only to be found in England at a Young Men's Christian Association weekly evening recreation.'[5]

A further irritation came in the form of the continuing hostile and derogatory comments from those music critics, led by John Fuller Maitland, chief music critic of *The Times* from 1889, who were strong proponents of the new English Musical Renaissance. For this increasingly influential and vocal lobby Sullivan was a shallow populist, conservative and unadventurous in his musical approach, and prostituting his talent by writing light and undemanding pieces. The animus against him was particularly strong in academic circles. The Royal College of Music, which had been set up in 1883 to replace the National Training School for Music where he had been the first principal, became particularly associated with the English Musical Renaissance. Thomas Dunhill, the twentieth-century composer, recalled that when he was a student there in the mid-1890s, Sullivan's name was anathema and it was unwise to say a good word about him, so strong was the influence of his detractors, led by Stanford who was professor of composition. Sullivan remained the darling of the public, and of his many well-connected fans, led by the Queen herself, but the carping criticism from the new musical establishment undoubtedly stung him and further sapped his strength.

It was perhaps to escape his critics as well as for the sake of his health that he took to spending even more time abroad, often staying for several months on the Riviera in addition to his regular spa cures. In the eyes of his detractors, these lengthy vacations confirmed his fundamental laziness, a condition which he himself admitted to when he commented during one of his stays in Nice: 'my natural indolence aided by the sunshine prevent my doing any real work'.[6] He continued to gamble heavily on the roulette tables and also began buying race horses. His first purchase in 1894 was a thoroughbred called Cranmer. Whether it was named after the prominent English Reformer and architect of the Book of Common Prayer and whether this was a factor in his purchase is not recorded, although its bloodline included mares called Heresy and Satiety, suggesting a less evidently ecclesiastical provenance. He subsequently bought another horse, Blue Mark, after it beat Cranmer at Newmarket. Financial problems continued to loom large, compounded not just by the horse-racing and gambling but also by his considerable generosity. He regularly gave gifts of £50 (over £6,000 today) to those whom he heard were in trouble, by no means all of them close friends or even acquaintances. In 1894, he found himself in debt and asked Helen D'Oyly Carte to lend him £1,700 to tide him over.

Despite these setbacks, what turned out to be Sullivan's last decade was not without its achievements. They included his one and only grand opera, *Ivanhoe*, two more collaborations with Gilbert, and four other light operas for the Savoy Theatre. He worked with Tennyson on a poetic drama entitled *The Foresters* and wrote music for a play about King Arthur, which he toyed with turning into a full scale opera. There were also further song settings, a ballet, and a hymn for Queen Victoria's Diamond Jubilee, and a *Te Deum* to be sung at the end of the Boer War. Other promised works, including another cantata for the Leeds Festival, went unwritten, however, and his untimely death at the age of 58 in 1900 left several projects uncompleted and an undeniable sense of unfulfilled potential, especially in the sphere of sacred music which he had described as his greatest love.

Ivanhoe

Sullivan liked to suggest that his one and only grand opera came about as the result of a direct royal commission. Following a command performance of *The Golden Legend* in the Albert Hall in May 1888, Queen Victoria apparently told him, 'You ought to write a grand opera, you would do it so well'.[7] In fact, he hardly needed this royal prompt to embark on something that he had been wanting to do for years. His first attempt at a grand opera had been the unperformed *The Sapphire Necklace* back in 1864. Some years later he had discussed with the poet Lionel Lewin the possibility of collaborating on an Arthurian opera. What provided the catalyst for him to return to this area of composition in 1890 was not so much the Queen's suggestion as the financial support and commitment of Richard D'Oyly Carte who felt that Sullivan had the potential to be the founding father of a new school of English opera. The impresario conceived the idea of emulating the success of the comic operas at his Savoy Theatre by establishing the Royal English Opera Company and building a magnificent new theatre on Cambridge Circus with the highest and deepest stage in London as its home. His vision was that it would host a string of new operas composed by English composers and so at last establish a British presence in a field hitherto dominated by Italians, French, and Germans.

Such a patriotic project was calculated to appeal to Sullivan, who was given carte blanche to choose the subject and the librettist for the opera which would open the theatre and launch the company. He chose Walter Scott's famous novel, *Ivanhoe*, which had come out in 1829 and greatly stimulated the Victorians' love affair with the Middle Ages, which Sullivan himself shared. He had already set several of Scott's poems and drawn inspiration from two of his other novels in the *Kenilworth* masque and the *Marmion* overture. Like Longfellow's *The Golden Legend*, Scott's *Ivanhoe* provided an idealized romantic medieval mixture of heroic faith and chivalry, pious monks, and self-sacrificing maidens. It additionally offered a strong national narrative, constructing an English origin legend in the mixing of Saxon and Norman blood, symbolized by the marriage of the Saxon knight of Ivanhoe to the Lady Rowena.

Choosing as his librettist the American-born but Eton-educated novelist and poet Julian Sturgis, who stuck pretty close to Scott's original story to produce nine tableaux-like scenes in three acts, Sullivan called *Ivanhoe* a romantic rather than a grand opera, in part to distinguish it from the Wagnerian operas that he so disliked. Its historical basis furnished a cast of convincing real-life characters of the kind that he complained Gilbert had so seldom provided.

In a newspaper interview in 1885, giving further vent to his anti-Wagnerian sentiments, he had said:

> I do not believe in operas based on gods and myths. That is the fault of the German school. It is metaphysical music—it is philosophy. What we want are plots which give rise to characters of flesh and blood, with human passions. Music should speak to the heart and not the head.[8]

But if *Ivanhoe* eschews Wagnerian metaphysics and provides a more naturalistic and realistic canvas for its composer to work on, it is by no means bereft of deeper spiritual themes. Indeed, the libretto puts religion at the centre of the opera, most notably in contrasting the pure and trusting faith of Rebecca, the Jewish heroine, with the casual and coarse Christianity of her seducer Sir Brian de Bois-Guilbert, a Norman knight who is Commander of the Order of Knights Templar. More broadly, there is an underlying emphasis on religious tolerance, displayed in the attitude towards Jews on the part of the English Saxons, on the importance of forgiveness, and on the triumph of good over evil which is given a patriotic twist in terms of the struggle between Saxons and Normans. There is also a touch of patriotic Protestantism at the end with the banishment from England of the Templars with their appeal to Rome. All were themes calculated to appeal to Sullivan and they elicited sensitive and appropriate musical treatment.

From a religious point of view, the most interesting scene comes at the end of the second act when Rebecca prays to Jehovah and then engages in a powerful duet with the Templar knight Sir Brian in which she resists his wooing and chastises him for his blasphemy in appealing to the Christian cross to aid him. Rebecca's aria 'Lord of our chosen race' bears many similarities in terms of both words and music to Margarita's song as she prepares to face the funeral pyre in *The Martyr of Antioch*. Prefaced by the invocation 'O Lord Jehovah, aid me in this hour', it is a haunting statement of deep religious faith with the wide intervals in the melodic line producing an atmosphere of melancholy and longing. Hermann Klein, the music critic of the *Sunday Times*, who was himself Jewish, was struck by the oriental character of the harmonies and intervals in the aria, and 'thought nothing could be more distinctively eastern or Hebraic in type'. Sullivan told him that for the phrase 'Guard me, Jehovah, guard me', which serves as a refrain at the end of each verse, he had borrowed the striking progression in the minor which he had heard chanted in the synagogue in Leipzig when he was the Mendelssohn scholar there more than thirty years earlier and which 'occurred so frequently that I have never forgotten it.'[9]

The subsequent duet between Rebecca and Sir Brian, which is among the most dramatic that Sullivan wrote, has distinct echoes of the exchange between Margarita and Olybius in the third scene of *The Martyr of Antioch*. In this case, however, instead of trying to win her wooer's soul for Christ, the Jewess Rebecca chastises him for his failure to live up to Christian standards and the blasphemous way in which he invokes the Cross while behaving in a wholly selfish and repellent way:

> I hold my father's faith, and if I err,
> May God forgive me—and He will forgive.
> But thou, a Christian knight, wilt thou appeal
> To thine own Cross to aid thee in thy sins?

Sullivan set those lines, which speak so eloquently of faith, forgiveness, and Christian hypocrisy, in a way that is as spiritually sensitive and powerful as anything in his sacred oratorios and cantatas. Indeed, the music that underscores Rebecca's faith and her utter trust in 'the God of Abraham' is noticeably more powerful and expressive than anything that is given to the Christian characters in the opera and it is not surprising that *Ivanhoe* led to a revival of the seemingly erroneous suggestion that Sullivan himself had Jewish ancestry (see p. 16). By contrast, his musical treatment of the most obviously Christian character, the genial Friar Tuck, is humorous and light-hearted although never disrespectful. The friar's first entrance is accompanied by a hint of medieval plainchant which is reintroduced for his subsequent appearances. Arthur Lawrence took this as a nod to the church music in which Sullivan had been steeped in his youth and which 'even in his operas we find sprouting forth, sometimes with a peculiarly touching effect and at others with that subtle strain of humour that is ever enchanting without being offensive':

> No better example of this latter can be found than in the ecclesiastical accompaniment which attends the presence of Friar Tuck through

Ivanhoe. Here the broad harmonies and cadences of the church are
employed with such refined taste, with such dramatic appropriateness,
that it is impossible for the most fastidious to take offence.[10]

If the music of *Ivanhoe* suggests strong empathy with Judaism and
genial affection for Christianity, more intriguing and ambiguous is
the treatment accorded to the knights templar. One might expect that
as a Freemason himself, Sullivan would have been highly sympathetic
in his portrayal of them. The problem for him is that, following Scott,
Sturgis' libretto casts the order, and especially its commander,
Sir Brian de Bois-Guilbert, in a thoroughly unattractive light. It is
the Jewess Rebecca who has to remind him that the order was founded
on the principles of poverty and chastity and not for the purposes of
self-aggrandisement. When Sir Brian first enters in the opening scene
of the opera, Sullivan delineates his character with a menacing passage
in A flat major. The chorus 'Fremuere principes' with which the
knights templar make their entrance in the closing scene is suitably
robust, clean-limbed, and masculine, and there is more than a hint of
the sonority of Sarastro, the high priest of the temple of wisdom in *The
Magic Flute*, in the music that Sullivan gives to Lucas de Beaumanoir,
the master of the knights templar. But overall the templars are not
portrayed very sympathetically by either librettist or composer.

Ivanhoe had its premiere in the Royal English Opera House on
31st January 1891. Both the Prince of Wales and the Duke of Edinburgh were in the audience and reported their enthusiasm to their
mother who expressed her particular satisfaction to Sullivan 'as she
believes it is partly owing to her own instigation that you undertook
this great work'.[11] Although Queen Victoria allowed Sullivan to
dedicate his opera to her, she never saw it. *Ivanhoe* ran for 160
performances over the next six months, during which time *The Gondoliers* was still playing at the Savoy Theatre. On the evening of 28
February, *The Golden Legend* was performed at Covent Garden. George
Grove wrote to *The Times* pointing out that never before had three
works by one composer been performed on the same evening in major
venues in central London. Despite *Ivanhoe*'s long opening run, which
was unprecedented for a serious opera, Carte's plans for his Royal
English Opera Company subsequently fell apart. None of the other
works that he had commissioned from English composers was ready

when *Ivanhoe* came to the end of its initial run, and it was replaced by a French opera in translation which attracted poor audiences. He was forced to sell his new theatre just a year after opening it. It became the Palace Theatre of Varieties and subsequently the Palace Theatre, which in recent years has hosted long runs of *The Sound of Music*, *Jesus Christ Superstar*, and *Les Misérables*, and since 1983 has been owned by Andrew Lloyd Webber.

Ivanhoe was not one of Sullivan's strongest works, something which he himself seems to have accepted. In a magazine interview in 1913, the American composer, Reginald de Koven, said that he had told Sullivan on the opening night how much he liked it, eliciting the response, 'That's more than I do. A cobbler should stick to his last'.[12] This is almost certainly an apocryphal story, but it is significant that there is no mention of *Ivanhoe* in Arthur Lawrence's biography, in the preparation of which Sullivan himself was closely involved. George Bernard Shaw felt that it was altogether too 'smooth, orderly and within the bounds of good breeding'.[13] This was not entirely the fault of the composer who was presented with a series of rather static tableaux without any great build-up of tension or dramatic power. But it is hard to avoid the conclusion that in this particular work Sullivan's distinctive quality of divine emollient was not really what was needed. There is a lack of passion and anguish. Benedict Taylor, who does see several redeeming features in the music and identifies 'an undefinable stamp of a lyricism unique to Sullivan at this time' also points out that the characters are too stereotypical: 'Religiously, the Jewish Rebecca is the only serious figure in the whole story. The Saxon Christian Friar Tuck is a lovable rogue, an honest drinking fellow who doesn't take his religion too earnestly, and the Normans (read Catholics) lascivious foreign rapists.'[14]

More Savoy Operas

Sullivan composed six works for the Savoy Theatre during the 1890s. *Utopia, Limited* (1893) and *The Grand Duke* (1896) had libretti by Gilbert. The others involved collaborations with different writers: Sydney Grundy for *Haddon Hall* (1892), 'an original English light opera' with a historical theme; Francis Burnand for *The Chieftain* (1894) reworked from the earlier *Contrabandista*; Arthur Pinero and Joseph Comyns

Carr for *The Beauty Stone* (1898), 'a romantic musical drama'; and Basil Hood for the *Rose of Persia* (1899) based on stories from the Arabian Nights.

As before, Sullivan found Gilbert's cruel characterizations of ageing women particularly offensive. Yet another one in the mould of Katisha and Lady Jane appeared in the person of Lady Sophy in *Utopia, Limited*. Sullivan complained that he found her 'unsympathetic and distasteful' and that 'the elderly spinster, unattractive and grotesque . . . is a character which appeals to me vainly, and I cannot do anything with it'.[15] Gilbert responded that Lady Sophy was not 'very old, raddled or grotesque' but rather 'a dignified lady of 45 or thereabouts, & no more ugly than God Almighty has made the lady who is to play her'.[16] Her character was toned down a bit but Sullivan continued to find Gilbert's characterizations crude and it was a relief for him to turn to his other librettists, even if they lacked Gilbert's wit and brilliant word play.

There are several religious resonances in these later light operas. *Haddon Hall* is set at the end of the English Civil War on the eve of the restoration of the monarchy in 1660 and contrasts the lifestyle and attitudes of the Puritan Roundheads and Royalist Cavaliers. As one might expect, the music leaves no doubt as to which side had Sullivan's sympathies, with the Puritans being given a suitably lugubrious chorus for their entrance. *The Beauty Stone* involves a Faustian compact with the Devil who arrives in a fifteenth-century Flemish village bearing a magic stone which confers perfect beauty on any girl who wears it around her neck. He first appears in the guise of a friar to an ugly, crippled girl, Laine, apparently in response to her prayer to the Virgin Mary that she might be allowed to die as she is never to attain beauty or love. Sullivan sets Laine's prayer in a particularly sympathetic manner that echoes his treatment of Ursula's hymn of thanksgiving to Mary in *The Golden Legend* and can similarly perhaps be read as an acknowledgement of his mother's Roman Catholic faith and his own Catholic ancestry. In contrast, he makes the Devil, played in the opening production by the D'Oyly Carte principal comedian and 'patter man', Walter Passmore, a rather low key and almost comical figure. Sullivan himself described his music for the Devil as 'characterized by a certain "grim levity"'.[17] Several critics felt that this rather bloodless treatment compared unfavourably with the portrayal of Lucifer in *The Golden Legend*, with *The Times* commenting:

> It would not hurt the effect of the production in the least if the part were to be recast, and musically the opera would gain enormously if Sir Arthur Sullivan would treat the character with some of the *diablerie* exhibited so happily in the Lucifer of *The Golden Legend*. It is, perhaps, the greatest disappointment in the new production that there should be so little of the supernatural element conveyed in the music, and more particularly so when Sir Arthur Sullivan is the composer.[18]

Perhaps the most intriguing religious element in these later works is the portrayal of Islam in *The Rose of Persia*. Sullivan's previous encounter with this faith, in his 1871 cantata *On Shore and Sea*, had involved writing a stirring call to prayer and a Moorish dance. Now Basil Hood had presented him with an uncompromising exposition of the Muslim faith in an aria sung by the high priest Abdallah, 'When Islam first arose, a tower upon a rock' with its chilling message:

> For Islam's gates are strong against a friend or foe;
> Her gates of Right and Wrong none passeth to and fro;
> For foes are they without and friends are they within;
> The postern-gate's the Gate of Doubt, that leads
> to the Camp of Sin!

It is difficult to know exactly what to make of this song. Abdallah is in many ways the villain of the piece and is here chastising the wealthy philanthropist Abu-el-Hassan for consorting with riff-raff and preferring 'the society of beggars to the beggars of society'. It comes over in print as a pretty black and white statement of the intransigent nature of the Muslim faith. Sullivan appears to take it seriously and does not ham it up in any way. He begins with six repeated notes, suggestive of the opening of several of his hymn tunes and sacred pieces, and adopts an increasingly lyrical and sonorous tone, with the last four lines (quoted above) about doubt leading to the camp of sin being treated very reverently and seriously. In the second verse, an ethereal chorus is introduced in a way that makes the whole song even more anthem-like. Is this a musical joke at Islam's expense? It does not sound like that. Is it an ecumenical gesture showing respect for another faith and even signalling a certain admiration for it, as he had done for Judaism in *Ivanhoe*? Is Sullivan being very careful not to offend Muslims and send them up in any way; or is he doing what he always does and seeking to enhance the meaning and message of the text before him? Whatever lies behind his seemingly respectful and even reverential setting of this exposition of Islamic faith, it stands as an intriguing musical statement by a liberally inclined Broad Church Christian.

Renewal of Friendship with Grove and Last Love Affair

The 1890s saw a renewal of Arthur Sullivan's friendship with George Grove on almost as intimate a level as it had been in the 1860s. Their relationship had continued through the intervening decades but not with quite the same intensity. It seems to have been illness which brought them closer together again in 1892. They met briefly in Paris when Sullivan was on his way home after his near-fatal illness in April. Grove, who was himself plagued by severe rheumatism and depression, noted that while he was concerned by Sullivan's condition, 'to me he's always what he was in 1863, when I first knew him—the same simple, good, gay creature that he was then'.[19] In December, Sullivan invited his old friend to come and stay with him in Cabbé-Roquebrune, near Monte Carlo, where he was spending the winter: 'I have a lovely villa with a very large garden right down to the sea, and you can go to bed and get up when you like—you can be alone, or with me; we can walk or drive, or not do any mortal thing'. He went on to warn 'If you do not take a rest now, you are acting little short of criminally . . . No man, whether Christian, Mahometan, Jew, or Buddhist, has the right to treat his existence here on earth in a reckless, careless manner'. Offering to send him a first-class ticket, he concluded:

> Don't, dearest G., read this lightly and put it aside with a smile and answer 'Bless your dear heart, I can't come.' You *must* come. I am very much in earnest about this, and mean that you should have a rest—and a real rest, which shall cost you nothing. It is divine down here—such sea, sky, and sunshine. Ever your loving A.[20]

Grove at first hesitated to take up this invitation, partly, according to his biographer Percy Young, 'because of his unease at the thought of the amoral and bohemian habits into which Sullivan had now fallen.'[21] However, he overcame his reservations and travelled down to the Riviera, from where he wrote in January 1893 that he found Sullivan 'a perfect host—as simple and natural as when we first met 30 years ago; full of information about everything, and as affectionate to me as I could wish or require'.[22] By contrast he found Gilbert, who was also a guest at Cabbé-Roquebrune for some days, having come there to talk to Sullivan about *Utopia, Limited*, to be 'a hard cynical man of the world . . . a bitter, narrow, selfish creature'.[23] In another letter during his stay Grove reported: 'Sullivan and I get on like two brothers—we are resuming the close intercourse which we enjoyed twenty years ago: we agree perfectly.'[24] There was just one matter on which the two friends did not see eye to eye. Grove found the gaming tables of Monte Carlo to which Sullivan dragged him 'dark and uninviting . . . indeed anything more dull and miserable I never saw'.[25]

Although he deeply disapproved of Sullivan's gambling, Grove continued to find a divine quality in his music. Returning to a theme which he had expressed before, notably in his comments on the *Martyr of Antioch* (p. 130), he wrote to their mutual friend Nina Lehmann about his admiration for this quality which he felt put Sullivan at odds with many of his contemporaries:

> The fact is that in music now composers and hearers worship ugliness . . . There has come a turn or *kink* in the brains and heartstrings of composers; they have no affection—no love—for their music. That divine quality which made Mozart, Beethoven, Schubert, couch their thoughts in the most beautiful forms they could find, and return to their lovely phrases and subjects over and over again, giving the melodies to one instrument after another, with small appropriate changes, and loving it better every time they came back to it—that is now all dismissed in favour of sound and fury . . . And so the old school, with our dear Arthur as its latest product, must go, and wait in the background till the fad has passed, and reason comes back![26]

Lying behind this tribute to Sullivan for sharing the divine quality found in Mozart, Beethoven, and Schubert, was there, perhaps, an acknowledgement that he was providing something more than just his music at this time and once again bolstering Grove's waning faith as he had so many years earlier? Grove's diaries and letters through the 1890s show a growing spiritual anguish and uncertainty, especially over the question of life after death. 'Oh dear, if one could only believe—not only feel but believe—in the next world!', he wrote in 1892, 'I often wish that I could look on the other world with that definite and undoubting view that some of my friends do. But I can't. I often try. I have not that happy simple faith'.[27] Sullivan was one of those friends who did still have that happy simple faith in the next world and he must surely have tried to assuage Grove's doubts on this score in the many conversations that they had at this time.

Grove expressed his religious doubts in a stream of letters that he wrote to Edith Oldham, a woman forty-five years his junior, with whom he had become infatuated when she was a student at the Royal College of Music. Over the last fifteen years of his life he pursued an ever more intense but seemingly non-physical relationship with her, pouring out his feelings of love, candidly describing his unhappy marriage, and telling her that if he could he would ask her to marry him. Sullivan, too, developed an infatuation with a woman much younger than himself around this time, although it was destined to be a much shorter-lived affair. While in Lucerne in August and September 1896 he fell in love with a 22-year-old English girl, Violet Beddington, whom he had known as a child when he had been introduced to her family by the pianist, Anton Rubinstein. She seems to have reciprocated his feelings and he proposed marriage to her. More than fifty years later she recalled:

> He was very frank with me. He said he had two years to live. Could I not give him two years of my life? Could I find the love that would renew him? After that—I should still have my own life before me. He would leave me all he possessed. He said it would have to be a secret wedding—'In London. Round the corner, Hyde Park Square. Registry Office.'
>
> But I thought it over, and I knew it wouldn't do.[28]

Broken-hearted by her rejection of his proposal, Sullivan left Lucerne the following morning. Violet went on to marry the novelist Sidney Schiff (pseudonym Stephen Hudson), who put Sullivan's infatuation with her into his 1925 novel *Myrtle*, and who died in 1962.

In the midst of this strange episode, Sullivan wrote a tortured letter to Violet's sister Sybil describing his obsession with Violet, chastising himself over it and seemingly invoking a higher power:

> My manhood and my whole past career cry out against me—cry shame upon me for my weakness, & yet though I see and know the right, I follow the wrong. And what does it all mean? When I say I will go away, Violet says 'No, you musn't', and tonight the tears were in her eyes. I have not much chance of talking to her alone, but even with such little opportunity, I discover in her far deeper feelings—far more sensitiveness than either you or I gave her credit for. She is not strong enough to fight. She can offer passive resistance, but she has not the energy to attack. God forbid that I should dull her young life by trying to force her into such an attitude; it would be criminal. All I can do in the future is to pass my life in solving the question 'What am I to do'? unless a Higher Power steps in and solves it for me, one way or the other.[29]

Yet again, there are distinct echoes of the prodigal son in this outpouring. How much should be made of that strange and striking reference to 'a Higher Power' at the end of the letter it is difficult to say. Sullivan seldom invoked the deity, other than in the 'God bless' with which he customarily signed off letters to his family. He did also occasionally use the phrase 'Thank God' when he had completed a major piece of work—it occurs in his diary entry for 11 September 1892 after noting that he had finished the orchestral score of *Haddon Hall* at 11.40pm. But the somewhat masonic invocation of 'a Higher Power' at the end of this letter is of a very different order and is not found anywhere else that I am aware of in his diaries or letters.

Queen Victoria's Diamond Jubilee, 1897

As the unofficial court composer, it was only to be expected that Sir Arthur Sullivan should contribute to the celebrations of Queen Victoria's Diamond Jubilee in 1897. Of the two pieces that he wrote for it, the first and more substantial, *Victoria and Merrie England*, came about as the result of a commission from Alfred Moul, manager of the Alhambra Theatre, Leicester Square, for a patriotic ballet consisting of seven historical tableaux. The first scene, 'Ancient Britain', set in an oak forest, featured a Druid high priest discovering the sleeping figure of Britannia and prophesying her future greatness. This was followed by two scenes illustrating 'May Day festivities in Queen Elizabeth's Time' with Morris dancers, appearances by Robin Hood, Maid

Marion, and Friar Tuck, and dancing round a maypole. Scenes four and five, set in Windsor forest, told the story of Herne the Hunter, with nymphs, huntsmen, mummers, and peasants dancing round a yule log before dragging it homeward. The sixth scene showed Christmas festivities in the hall of an old castle during the reign of Charles II, including the carrying in of a boar's head and a baron of beef, the appearance of Father Christmas, a game of blind man's buff, and a dance under the mistletoe. The final scene brought this pageant of British history and folklore up to date with a *tableau vivant* of Queen Victoria's coronation in Westminster Abbey. English, Irish, and Scottish soldiers marched past, followed by volunteers and colonial troops. Britannia made a triumphant reappearance and the final scene depicted the four groups of allegorical sculpted figures representing Europe, Asia, Africa, and the Americas around the base of the Albert Memorial in Hyde Park.

Sullivan noted 'that we have tried to make our ballet as British as possible . . . a frame for a series of pictures of English "jollification" in various ages, with just a glimpse of fairyland in the middle and a burst of patriotism at the end'.[30] Among the well-known national airs that he quoted were 'Rule, Britannia', 'The boar's head carol', 'The roast beef of Old England', and 'A fine old English gentleman'. The final scene included a lengthy quotation of 'Home, sweet home'; and the entry of the English, Irish, and Scottish soldiers was accompanied by a medley of 'The British grenadiers', 'St Patrick's Day', and 'Scots wha hae'. There was no Welsh air, nor any Welsh military presence, because, as he explained, 'Something stood in my way, and I didn't know what. At last daylight came to me. It was the "Men of Harlech" who resolutely barred my passage. So I swept them clean away—gallant little Wales has been sacrificed and I am triumphant.'[31]

His other contribution to the Diamond Jubilee celebrations came about as a result of his own direct lobbying of the palace. In a letter to the Prince of Wales on 1 April 1897 he expressed his desire 'to receive the Queen's command to compose something special for this wondrous occasion'. He specifically suggested a hymn tune to be sung with military band accompaniment at the open-air service at St Paul's Cathedral which the Queen herself would be attending on 22 June after processing through the streets of London: 'I think I should reach *the hearts of the people* best in a hymn tune, such a one as 'Onward,

Christian soldiers'.[32] It is significant and characteristic that Sullivan felt that a hymn tune would be the best way of reaching people and, indeed, that he emphasized reaching their hearts rather than their heads.

Sullivan was summoned from Beaulieu-sur-Mer on the French Riviera, where he had spent the winter, to Cimiez, the up-market suburb of Nice where the Queen was staying. Sir Arthur Bigge, her private secretary, told him that the Queen wanted any hymns used at the St Paul's service to be popular and well-known, but that she would welcome something new to be sung in churches throughout the land on 20 June, the day that marked the sixtieth anniversary of her accession. Sullivan suggested that his old friend William Walsham How, now bishop of Wakefield, should be asked to write a new hymn which he himself would set to music. While in Cimiez, and at his suggestion, he played the harmonium at the Easter Sunday service which Victoria attended in one of the rooms in her hotel.

It is not surprising that Sullivan chose How, with whom he had collaborated so happily on *Church Hymns and Tunes*, as his partner for the jubilee hymn. The two men shared a liberal theological outlook and were both staunch monarchists and populists—How was known as 'the omnibus bishop' because he scorned an episcopal carriage and preferred to travel round his newly created urban diocese on a horse-drawn public bus. They were the perfect pair to catch the celebratory mood of the nation. In a letter sent to Sullivan on the same day that he was playing for the Queen's Easter devotions, How confessed that he was feeling 'awfully dry and dusty' and finding inspiration difficult, but was consoled by the fact that 'you have promised to write a tune for it. That may possibly redeem it'.[33] In the event, he produced four verses beginning 'O King of Kings, Whose reign of old hath been from everlasting' which brimmed over with heartfelt patriotism and por-trayed the Queen as the much-loved mother of the nation. Forward-ing the text, which had been submitted to Victoria for royal approval, Bigge told Sullivan, 'As the Bishop says, "Sir Arthur Sullivan's genius will light it up a little!"'.[34] When he received the verses, Sullivan told How: 'I have rarely come across so beautiful a combination of poetry and deep religious feeling'.[35] He composed a stirring march tune not unlike ST GERTRUDE with a similar use of repeated notes at the beginning. Characteristically modest about his effort, he told How in a letter informing him that copies of the hymn would go out to all beneficed clergy throughout the land and also be dispatched to the colonies, 'My only regret is that I don't think the music is quite up to the level of the words, but I did my best, and it is not easy to be devotional, effective, original *and* simple at the same time'.[36]

In fact, his catchy tune BISHOPGARTH, named after the Bishop of Wakefield's residence, was perfectly calculated to reinforce How's triumphalist and exhortatory message. 'When you sing it properly in church', How told a young boy who had written to say how much he liked the hymn, 'you must try to think you are singing it to God, and thanking him for giving us so good a Queen'.[37] For his part, Sullivan defended the robustly vulgar quality of BISHOPGARTH, maintaining: 'It is not a part song, nor an exercise in harmony. It is a tune which everyone will, I hope, be able to pick up quickly and sing heartily'.[38] There could not be a better summation of his credo as a hymn tune writer. 'O King of Kings' was first sung on the morning of Sunday, 20 June 1897 at the thanksgiving service in St George's Chapel, Windsor, attended by the Queen herself and by congregations in churches across the land and the empire. It was not used, as Sullivan had originally suggested, at the brief thanksgiving service held two days later outside the west door of St Paul's Cathedral's while the Queen, who felt too frail to climb up the steps, remained in her carriage. The only hymn sung there was 'All people that on earth do dwell' to the OLD HUNDREDTH, a tune which, according to the reminiscences of a friend, Sullivan consistently maintained was '*the* grandest tune which was ever composed by mortal man'.[39]

The jubilee hymn on which How and Sullivan had collaborated was instantly popular with the public. At the composer's suggestion, all royalties from the sale of copies went to the Prince of Wales Hospital Fund. Another Victorian bishop, this time of an Evangelical persuasion, Edward Bickersteth of Exeter, was so taken with the vigorous, muscular quality of BISHOPGARTH that he wrote a stirring gospel hymn 'For my sake and the Gospel's, go and tell redemption's story' especially for it, so ensuring that the tune would not be lost once the jubilee celebrations were over but would continue to do its evangelistic work for many years to come, as, indeed, it has.

The Queen sent for Sullivan once the jubilee celebrations were at an end. He was invited for an audience at Windsor Castle on 5 July at which he had a twenty-minute conversation with her. Newman Flower and Herbert Sullivan note that in addition to having long recognized him as the premier British musician of her reign, 'she recognized, too, how completely national had been his composing during the Jubilee preparations; he had caught the history of England and charmed it into notes'.[40] He was to fulfil one last royal commission the following year, writing 'Wreaths for our graves' by command of the Queen for a service at the Royal Mausoleum at Frogmore, Windsor, on 14 December 1897 to commemorate the anniversary of the death of Prince Albert. The text, by Mrs L.F. Massey, is a classic example of Victorian funerary verse, sentimental, morbid, and maudlin. Sullivan invested it with a suitably reverential, subdued, and gloomy tune.

'Wreaths for our Graves' made a subsequent appearance in a staged version of *The Martyr of Antioch* which was mounted by the Carl Rosa Opera Company. It opened at the Lyceum Theatre, Edinburgh on 25 February 1898 in a double bill with *Cavalleria Rusticana* and subsequently toured the country. The recently composed funeral anthem replaced 'Brother, Thou art gone before us' to accompany the burial of the Christian martyrs at the start of the second scene. Noting the enthusiastic response from the audience to this staged version, the *Scotsman* commented that 'if it helps to bring home to an audience the bitter trials of the early converts to the Christian religion and at the same time to make them acquainted with a noble work by the greatest of English composers, the experiment has its justification'.[41]

1898 Leeds Festival

Sullivan commented several times during the 1890s that the conductorship of the Leeds Festival was 'the one musical pleasure of his life'.[42] Although he twice came close to pulling out, first in 1892 when Joseph Barnby was appointed as his deputy without any consultation; and then in 1898 on health grounds, he always rose to the occasion and relished conducting the great choral works, his interpretation of which earned plaudits from audiences and most critics alike.

He had a particularly strong rapport with the orchestra and with the chorus, which was recruited from across West Yorkshire. After the

1892 Festival, which followed his long period of severe illness, one of
the choristers, who came from Bradford, wrote to him:

> My primary thought just now is of yourself, and how you have inspired
> the deep love and affection of the chorus towards yourself. I have heard
> it on all hands, and it has grown until it culminated in tears in many
> eyes on Saturday night. I wish I could gather up some of the heartfelt
> expressions I have heard. I do not know how weak physically you have
> felt during the week just gone. I hope you have not been as weak as
> some of us have feared, but your noble strength as a conductor has
> made a deep impression on us all. There are no more loving hearts in
> the kingdom than those of the Leeds Festival Chorus towards you, and
> none will rejoice more than us to hear of your complete restoration to
> health and strength.[43]

Sullivan's restrained style of conducting continued to come in for
some criticism from his detractors but most critics praised his meticu-
lous care and attention to detail, and compared his unostentatious
approach favourably with the histrionics displayed by other conductors. Joseph Bennett wrote after the 1895 Festival: 'Sir Arthur Sullivan
should be heartily congratulated upon his share of the common task.
The qualities of a great conductor are sometimes denied in him
because he does not wear long hair or gesticulate like figures moved
by putting a penny in the slot.'[44]

Sullivan had not written a new work for the Leeds Musical Festival
since the *Golden Legend* in 1886 and there was much excitement when it
was announced in December 1897 that he had agreed to write a new
cantata for the 1898 festival. Writing in the *Illustrated Sporting and
Dramatic News*, Benjamin Findon looked forward to a popular work
with a strongly English and Protestant flavour, noting that

> Sir Arthur shows his wisdom in taking subjects which have a general
> interest, instead of confining himself to works whose suitability for
> public performance is marred in the first place by the words being in
> a foreign tongue and secondly by their being associated with a form of
> divine service people in this country know little about.[45]

This was almost certainly a dig at Stanford who had recently produced a Latin Requiem for the Birmingham Musical Festival.

In fact, there was a somewhat foreign and Catholic feel to the first
subject that Sullivan considered for the Leeds cantata. His diary for

6 December 1897 contains the entry 'seeing if anything could be done with "Saint's Tragedy" for Leeds'. This was a poem by Charles Kingsley, the Anglican clergyman best remembered as the author of *The Water Babies*, about St Elizabeth of Hungary, the thirteenth-century princess who was widowed at the age of 20 and devoted the rest of her short life—she died at the age of 24—to charitable works. He concluded that it was 'not dramatic enough, I fear'. Newspaper reports suggested that he also looked at a play on King Arthur by Joseph Comyns Carr, with whom he was already collaborating on *The Beauty Stone*, and at Oliver Goldsmith's poem, 'The Vicar of Wakefield'. He seems to have got rather further with the powerful penitential hymn entitled 'Recessional' that Rudyard Kipling had written for Queen Victoria's Jubilee, calling for humility in the midst of Britain's imperial triumphs and warning of the ephemeral nature of military success and national glory. The February 1898 edition of the music magazine, *The Minim*, announced that Sullivan had almost completed setting it for chorus and orchestra. This seems to have been something of an exaggeration, however, as Sullivan subsequently wrote to Kipling saying he had found it impossible to set as a cantata, eliciting the response: 'I quite recognise the difficulty you find about Recessional. The thing is a hymn in spirit and method and it seems to me should be dealt with on hymn lines.' The poet went on to show his considerable respect for Sullivan as a word setter: 'No one has come up with an appropriate setting. Please accept the thing as yours if you care to use it . . . There will be no other setting authorized by me'.[46]

Sullivan seems to have worked longest on a text which he commissioned from Paul England, a prolific librettist responsible for English language versions of operas by Wagner and Berlioz, Bach cantatas, and songs by Brahms and Richard Strauss. Unfortunately, there is no evidence as to its subject. The programme for the 1898 Festival, announced in April, included a new cantata by Sullivan, as yet without a title. In a very low state both mentally and physically for much of the early part of the year, he struggled to make anything of England's libretto and devoted what little energy he had to his collaboration with Joseph Comyns Carr on *The Beauty Stone*. Carr went out to visit him in Beaulieu-sur-Mer, where he had again retreated, and reported:

Sullivan was already a sick man. Sufferings long and painfully endured had sapped his powers of sustained energy, and my recollection of the days I passed with him at his villa at Beaulieu, when he was engaged on setting the lyrics I had written, are shadowed and saddened by the impression then left upon me that he was working under difficulties of a physical kind almost too great to be borne . . . The old genial spirit was still there, the quick humour in appreciation and the ready sympathy in all that concerned our common task, but the sunny optimism of the earlier days shone only fitfully through the physical depression that lay heavily upon him.[47]

Sullivan himself realized that he was struggling and in a letter to his recently appointed secretary, Wilfred Bendall, which underlined just how much of his composing over the past twenty-five years had been undertaken in pain, he expressed his grave doubts about his ability to undertake the Leeds Festival commission:

Six months of writing, organising and rehearsing will I fear bowl me over, and bring on the physical trouble just when I need all my strength most. I cannot travel to Leeds and back and rehearse when I am in pain, and I have had enough of writing when in pain. The 'Pinafore', 'The Martyr of Antioch', part of 'Iolanthe' besides various smaller things, were all written in bodily suffering, varied and relieved by anodynes, and I cannot do it anymore.[48]

Fearing that he could not retain the conductorship of the festival if he did not write a new work, Sullivan offered his resignation to the members of the Leeds committee. They prevailed on him to change his mind, having discussed the desirability of lining up Charles Villiers Stanford as a stand-by. After confirming that he would not be able to produce a new cantata, Sullivan headed off to the Austrian spa of Bad Gastein for a cure in an effort to relieve his physical and mental malaise. For three weeks in July and August, he diligently undertook daily baths and massages, went for long, solitary walks in the Alpine meadows, made the acquaintance of the former Liberal prime minister, Lord Rosebery, who was also taking a cure, and conducted a concert of his own music. He found the cure beneficial, noting in his diary entry on the last day of his stay: 'my stay has been very quiet, and I think very beneficial. I feel much fresher and better.' It prompted him to reflect on the ways in which he had neglected and damaged his own health. He wrote to his nephew Bertie,

> Don't grow up into a livery, jaundiced, probably querulous old man . . . Do try to live regularly—as plainly as you like, but not a feast one day and a fast the next. I only wish I had attended more to my eating and drinking when I was young—what trouble, pain and worry I should have avoided.[49]

Apparently recovered from his earlier ailments, Sullivan put in a characteristically committed performance at the Leeds Festival in October 1898. It began, as so often, with Mendelssohn's *Elijah* which he insisted on carefully rehearsing even though it was well-known. The Bach B Minor Mass, which he had first conducted at the 1886 Festival and reprised in 1892, received a further outing, occupying the whole of one morning, although greatly to his annoyance the committee insisted on cutting three movements. There was also a very well-received performance of Beethoven's Choral Symphony. Although it lacked a new piece by him, the 1898 Festival was notable for premieres of new works by younger English composers, including C.V. Stanford's *Te Deum*, Edward Elgar's *Caractacus*, Alan Gray's *A Song of Redemption*, and Frederic Cowen's *Ode to the Passions*. It also featured Hubert Parry's *Blest Pair of Sirens*, the first performance of which in 1887 was widely regarded as marking a seminal stage in the English Musical Renaissance. All these composers conducted their own works. Sullivan was particularly helpful to Elgar who found it difficult to communicate his wishes to the orchestra. Elgar noted that while rehearsing *Caractacus*, he had urged Sullivan to rest 'but he remained and made notes of anything which struck him, in that most charming and self-sacrificing way which was always his'.[50] Elgar subsequently wrote a warm letter to Sullivan thanking him for his particular kindness and support in 'making my "chance" possible and pleasant' and observing with reference to the stigma that both men suffered as outsiders from the academic world of the English Musical Renaissance, 'it contrasts very much with what some people do to a person unconnected with the schools, friendless and alone'.[51]

As always, it was the members of the chorus who were most enthusiastic about Sullivan's performance as conductor of the 1898 Leeds Festival. Eleanor Davison, a chorister who had sung under his baton at every festival since 1889, recalled the approbation that greeted him after the final item, Mendelssohn's *Lobgesang*: 'When it was over, the chorus rose to him . . . Sullivan was overcome with emotion. He stood there with his back to the audience and then he suddenly put his head down on the score he had been using and broke down.'[52] It was to be Sullivan's last appearance at the Leeds Festival. In September 1899, he received a letter from Frederick Spark telling him that the committee had resolved to find another conductor for the next festival in 1901. Although the reason given was his state of health, which was actually by now much better than it had been the previous year, it is clear that other factors were at work, among them his failure to produce the promised cantata and the fact that he seemed rather to have put his energy into yet another comic opera. The sustained campaign against Sullivan by those championing the English Musical Renaissance also undoubtedly influenced the Leeds Festival committee in their decision to replace him. As Anne Stanyon writes in her thesis on the 1898 Festival, 'it is difficult not to conclude that there were those among the Provisional Committee who had decided to launch a coup against him in favour of Stanford.'[53]

Sullivan was mortified by this blow and felt that he had been treated very shabbily after seven very successful seasons. He refused to go on the grounds of ill health and simply resigned from the conductorship on 5 October 1899 without giving any reasons. A draft of his resignation letter to Spark suggests that he had one last project in mind for the 1901 Festival which he was sorry that he would not now be able to fulfil:

> In 1901, I shall have been 40 years before the public (as I date my career from the time I returned from Leipzig in 1861) and I intended making the festival an occasion of publicly retiring from the active pursuit of my profession, and to do this with éclat I meant to produce a work (which I am engaged on now) which would I hope be a worthy successor to *The Golden Legend* and form a dignified close to my personal public appearances. The words are from one of the (in my humble opinion) finest poems in the English language, and it has taken a strong hold upon me. This was my project and I confess to feeling some disappointment that it is not to be carried through.[54]

It is tempting to speculate as to the identity of this (presumably lengthy) poem that Sullivan rated so highly and which he was hoping to set as his swansong. Was it a sacred work, perhaps coming from the pen of Milton or Tennyson, maybe even *Paradise Lost* or *In Memoriam*, either of which might reasonably be described as one of the finest poems in the English language? There is some evidence that Sullivan also considered writing another Biblical oratorio at this time. In her reminiscences following his death, Mary Carr indicated that he had shown interest in a libretto which she sent him about Daniel.[55] As it was, his untimely death on 22 November 1900 meant that this last serious work which would form 'a dignified close' to his public career went unwritten. Just a month later Stanford was formally appointed as the next conductor of the Leeds Musical Festival.

The *Boer War Te Deum*

In October 1899, the South African Republic and Orange Free State declared war on the United Kingdom, triggering the bloody and protracted conflict that would become known as the Boer War and stimulating a wave of patriotic and jingoistic feeling across Britain. Sullivan did his bit for the war effort, and for the national mood, by setting Rudyard Kipling's poem 'The Absent-Minded Beggar', written as part of an appeal by the *Daily Mail* to raise money for soldiers and their families. Both Kipling and Sullivan declined any financial recompense for the song, the chorus of which exhorted its audience to 'pass the hat for your credit's sake, and pay—pay—pay!'. Although he found the irregular metre of Kipling's verses difficult to set, and commented that, 'if it wasn't for charity's sake, I could never have undertaken the task', Sullivan completed the music in four days and conducted the first performance of the song at the Alhambra Theatre, London, on 13 November 1899, to a 'magnificent reception'.[56] With characteristic grace, he wrote to Kipling, 'Your splendid words went with a swing and enthusiasm which even my music cannot stifle'.[57] For his part, the poet commended the composer for 'a tune guaranteed to pull teeth out of barrel-organs'.[58] The song was hugely popular throughout the war, being performed in music halls and at concerts up and down the land and across the empire. The *Daily Mail* estimated that it raised a total of around £340,000, equivalent to over £4 million today. Kipling travelled to South Africa to help distribute supplies bought with the funds raised.

Reactions to this song showed just how differently Sullivan was regarded by the popular compared to the serious press. *The Daily Chronicle* cnthuscd that 'It has not been often that the greatest of English writers and the greatest of English musicians have joined inspiring words and stirring melody in a song which expresses the heart feelings of the entire nation'.[59] By contrast, Fuller Maitland fulminated in *The Times* about the vulgar music-hall style of the composition, prompting Sullivan to comment, 'Did the idiot expect the words to be set in cantata form, or as a developed composition with symphonic introduction, contrapuntal treatment, etc.?'[60] On the back of their joint success, on 27 May 1900, Kipling once again sent 'Recessional' to Sullivan and expressed the hope that 'the spirit will move you to set it', but as before the composer found the task impossible.[61]

On the same day that he got Kipling's request, Sullivan received a letter from Sir George Martin, organist of St Paul's Cathedral, asking him on behalf of the Cathedral's Dean and Chapter to consider writing a thanksgiving *Te Deum* for use at a future service of celebration on the conclusion of the Boer War. He readily accepted and set to the task with unusual speed, doubtless hoping that the conflict in South Africa would soon end—in fact, it was to drag on for another eighteen months—and also conscious of his own poor health and that his composing days might be limited. Putting to one side *The Emerald Isle*, the operetta on which he was working for Richard D'Oyly Carte in collaboration with the librettist Basil Hood, he concentrated on the sacred rather than the secular commission.

The *Boer War Te Deum*, which was completed within two months, is a much more restrained and dignified work than the *Festival Te Deum*, without its florid fugues and operatic echoes. Running to just fifteen minutes, it is through-composed rather than divided into separate movements, giving it a less disjointed feel than the earlier work. Set for chorus, orchestra, and organ, there is no soloist or military band, although there is plenty of use of bright brass. What the two works have in common is the prominent use of a hymn tune. In the case of the *Boer War Te Deum* this is Sullivan's own ST GERTRUDE which is introduced subtly in the opening bars and then employed to considerable effect towards the end when it is played by the orchestra with increasing volume as the choir sings 'O Lord, in Thee have I trusted, let me never be confounded' and finally returns to the opening verse 'We praise Thee, O God'.

Reviewers were united in praising the work's simplicity, directness, and reverence. Many pointed to the way in which its largely diatonic rather than chromatic harmonies harked back to an earlier age and placed it firmly in the great tradition of English church music. The *Yorkshire Daily Post* noted that 'it is easy to recognise the influence on the composer of his early grounding in Anglican Church music at the Chapel Royal' and the *Daily Telegraph* rejoiced that 'the Te Deum honours the traditions of English church music. It is grave, restrained, solid, with enough of sentiment to satisfy modern taste. The work is everywhere pervaded by the refinement and distinction never absent from the composer's productions.'[62] There was particular praise for the devotional way in which the lines beginning 'To thee all angels cry aloud' had been set.

Modern commentators have tended to focus on the prominent use of ST GERTRUDE while disagreeing about its effect. Jeffrey Richards argues that in building his *Te Deum* around the tune of 'Onward, Christian soldiers', Sullivan was 'imbuing the Boer war with the idea of a Christian struggle against the infidel'.[63] For Benedict Taylor, on the other hand,

> the effect of the closing section is majestic but not remotely bombastic, the sense of control and quiet dignity continually present. There is a lyricism and sweep to this conjunction of fugal working-out and chorale-like hymn tune which is quite moving, leading to the final merging of opening chorus and hymn as the work's culmination.[64]

Overall, Taylor sees the *Te Deum* as containing 'some of Sullivan's 'most inward and devotional writing' and concludes that 'while seemingly more devout and restrained than much of his previous religious music, it is nevertheless readily comprehensible and accessible to the wide public at which it is aimed.'[65] The overall impression is certainly one of calm confidence and trust in God rather than bombastic and jingoistic triumphalism. Once again, Sullivan shows his love of hymn tunes and his belief that they are the way to get through to the hearts of people.

Sullivan prioritized the *Te Deum* over his comic opera, *The Emerald Isle*. Helen D'Oyly Carte complained to him about this and told him that it was a mistake that he had undertaken to write it. He replied jocularly 'I couldn't help smiling at the little dig at the *Te Deum*—it was so thoroughly womanly', but assured her that writing it had been no mistake.[66] The fact was that he was still committed to composing serious and sacred music. His simple, open, trusting faith shines out in the way he set the lines: 'O Lord, in Thee have I trusted' and 'Thou hast opened the kingdom of heaven to all believers'. Less than two months after his exchange with Helen, and less than four months after completing the *Te Deum*, Sullivan was dead. With the Boer War still raging, it was left to Sir George Martin to announce the work to the world in a letter to *The Times*:

> This was his last completed work. Thus the lad who received most of his early musical education in the Church, and who afterwards won such phenomenal popularity, not only where the English language is spoken, but in other countries, devoted his last effort to his Queen, to his Church, and to his country.[67]

Death, Funeral, and Tributes

The last six months of Arthur Sullivan's life were spent in increasing physical pain and mental depression, and in the now customary travels around the spas of Europe as well as the resorts of the Riviera. He managed to compose about half of *The Emerald Isle*, including a haunting finale to Act 1 which invoked a Celtic other-world of fairy voices and the mythical caves of Carrig-Cleena. The last piece of music that he wrote, it has an ethereal spiritual quality unlike anything else from his pen. It was a depressing time, with the loss of several close friends, most notably George Grove, who died on 28 May 1900, having signed off one of his last letters, 'Goodbye and God bless, ever your affectionate old friend'.[68] Sullivan made his last public appearance on 21 July conducting a brass band performance of 'The Absent-Minded Beggar March' in the Crystal Palace, the venue where, thanks largely to Grove, he had first made his mark as a composer nearly forty years earlier.

The last spa that Sullivan visited in a vain attempt to cure his many ills was Tunbridge Wells from where he wrote in his diary on 14 October: 'Have been here just a fortnight, and what have I done? Little more than nothing, first from illness and physical incapability, secondly from *brooding*, and nervous terror about myself'. He left for London the following day, noting 'I am sorry to leave—such a lovely day'. It is the last ever entry in his diary. At the end of October Helen D'Oyly Carte wrote to ask if he would appear with Gilbert on stage for the opening night of a revival of *Patience* which was being planned for late November or early December at the Savoy Theatre. He replied, 'if it would really please Gilbert to have me there and go on with him I will come. Let us bury the hatchet and smoke the pipe of peace'.[69] The two men had last met when they appeared on stage together on 17 November 1898 for the opening night of a revival of *The Sorcerer*, twenty-one years to the night since its first performance at the Opéra Comique which had inaugurated their period of close collaboration. They did not exchange a word.

With Gilbert crippled by gout and Richard D'Oyly Carte also far from well, Helen told Sullivan that it would please his old partner very much if he did join him for the *Patience* opening and suggested that the three men should come on stage in bath chairs. On 2 November, Sullivan visited his mother's grave, as he always did on her birthday. It was bitterly cold and he spent a long time arranging flowers, as a result catching a chill which turned into pneumonia. On 7 November, he wrote to Helen telling her that he would be unable to make the reunion at the Savoy, asking her to let Gilbert know how disappointed he was and reflecting 'Three invalid chairs would have looked very well from the front'. Written in a shaky hand, and headed 'in bed', it was the last letter he wrote.[70] He died suddenly at his home in Queen's Mansions in the early hours of 22 November.

Arthur Sullivan had expressed his wish to be buried alongside his mother and father in Brompton Cemetery. However, a group of church musicians, led by Sir George Martin, suggested that he should have a public funeral at St Paul's Cathedral, and this was enthusiastically endorsed by the dean and chapter. The Queen commanded that there should also be a service at the Chapel Royal, St James' Palace, before the burial at St Paul's.

The floral tributes which filled four carriages of the funeral cortege as it made its way through the streets of London from his home in Victoria Street to St James' Palace and then on to St Paul's Cathedral on 27 November 1900 showed the extent to which Sullivan was remembered and revered for his sacred music as well as for his more worldly pleasures. Alongside a wreath of pink and mauve roses indicating his racing colours were a banner of white chrysanthemums with the first two bars of 'Onward Christian soldiers' picked out in violets, a white cushion of chrysanthemums decorated with the notes of 'I shall hear that grand Amen' from 'The Lost Chord', and a Bible made up of white chrysanthemums and violets with rosebud clasps, purple ribbons and bouquets inscribed 'O Gladsome Light', the evening hymn from *The Golden Legend*. The tribute from Fanny Ronalds consisted of a large heart of white lilies with branches of pink roses inscribed 'that one lost chord divine, 1870–1900'.

The funeral obsequies further confirmed Sullivan's standing as a church musician. The pallbearers included Sir John Stainer, Sir George Martin, and Sir Frederick Bridge, organist of Westminster Abbey. Sullivan's own music featured prominently. In the Chapel Royal the choristers sang 'Yea, though I walk through the valley of the shadow of death' from *The Light of the World* and his recent funeral anthem 'Wreaths for our graves'. The service there concluded with the organist playing 'In Bethany' from the Lazarus scene in *The Light of the World*. At St Paul's Cathedral 'Yea though I walk through the valley of the shadow of death' was sung again before the coffin was lowered into its resting place under the floor of the crypt, close to the caskets of William Boyce, Henry Hart Milman, Henry Liddon, and Sir John Millais. Following the dean's closing benediction, 'Brother, thou art gone before us' from *The Martyr of Antioch* was sung *a capella* by members of the chorus of the Savoy Theatre. For the *Daily Telegraph* reporter,

> In much that was solemn and impressive, this, perhaps formed the most effective act of homage, the choicest and most eloquent prayer. For we seemed to realise the two sides of Sir Arthur Sullivan's brilliant nature, the two Sister Muses by whose inspiration he wrote. There was not so much contrast or discord between them as some have been in haste to imagine. In the lighter music of opera and burlesque there was the touch of noble and masterful purpose; in the solemn chant or anthem

there was a feeling for melody and tune, serving to link the religious mood with the hours of everyday. Here at least, as the well-trained chorus of the Savoy Theatre, the female voices almost choked with emotion, sang the sweet words of sorrow and faith and hope, there was a complete fusion of brightness and gloom, of the grave and the gay, of the happy and the solemn. It was right that this should be the last chaplet laid on the musician's bier, harmoniously welding together the varied triumphs of the operatic composer with the strains of religious feeling and awe.[71]

Of all that was written in the immediate aftermath of Sullivan's death, those words were among the most perceptive and fitting. They encapsulated the two sides of his personality and his artistry which were complementary rather than at variance, providing both the spiritual emollient that infused his comic operas and the emphasis on melody and accessibility which characterized his sacred work.

Sullivan's religious and sacred music was highlighted in a lengthy obituary in the *Musical Times* which ended with a paean of praise to his work for the church, described as being 'distinguished by a happy and original beauty hardly surpassed by the greatest masters':

His early upbringing in the school of English church music was of the greatest value to him in after years. His anthems are characterised by pure melody and dignified harmony. The same may be said, even in a more marked degree, of his hymn tunes, which are sung by worshippers of all denominations wherever the English language is spoken.[72]

Fulsome as it was, this tribute was considered insufficient and a subsequent issue of the *Musical Times* carried a substantial article on 'Sir Arthur Sullivan as a Church Musician', prompted by concern that 'in the many biographical notices of Arthur Sullivan that have recently appeared, comparatively little attention has been paid to the church-musician side of his genius' and by the fact 'that the gifted composer returned to his first love—church music—in the last completed composition he has left'.[73]

It was also as a serious and sacred musician that Sullivan was remembered in the concerts held in his memory. A memorial concert at the Crystal Palace conducted by August Manns on 8 December 1900 included the *In Memoriam* overture and selections from the *Festival Te Deum*, *The Golden Legend*, and *The Martyr of Antioch*.

A subsequent concert conducted by Sir Henry Wood at the Queen's Hall on the first anniversary of his death featured *In Memoriam, The Golden Legend*, and a selection from the second act of *Ivanhoe*. There was not so much as a bar of his comic operas or parlour ballads in either of them.

His detractors similarly lost no time in denouncing him. An unsigned article which appeared on the day after his death in *The Times* and was almost certainly penned by Fuller Maitland, raised the all too familiar gripe of the proponents of the English Musical Renaissance:

> Many who are able to appreciate classical music regret that Sir Arthur Sullivan did not aim consistently at higher things, that he set himself to rival Offenbach and Lecocq instead of competing on a level of high seriousness with such musicians as Sir Hubert Parry and Professor Stanford . . . If he had followed this path, he might have enrolled his name among the great composers of all time.[74]

This snide jibe aroused the ire of Frederick Bridge who wrote from Westminster Abbey to protest that neither Parry nor Stanford would surely 'claim to have produced work which will rank higher or live longer than *The Golden Legend*, the *In Memoriam*, and other overtures, the Shakespeare music and his many beautiful songs'. He went on to say that 'Sir Arthur Sullivan's church music is a worthy continuance of the best Cathedral traditions'.[75]

Fuller Maitland continued his attack with a stinging signed obituary in the *Cornhill Magazine* which castigated Sullivan for displaying 'the spirit of compromise' and 'deference to the taste of the multitude' and rubbished his oratorios as 'lamentable examples of uninspired and really uncongenial work' with choruses which 'only succeeded in being pompous and dull' and solos which 'turned out to be trivial in the last degree'. Comparing him to 'Jumbo', the lumbering, over-hyped, and popular elephant who was the biggest attraction for the masses who flocked to London Zoo, Fuller Maitland declared that 'the great renaissance of English music, which took place in the last quarter of the nineteenth century, accomplished itself without any help or encouragement from Sullivan'. He ended by asking: 'How can the composer of "Onward Christian Soldiers" and "The absent-minded beggar" claim a place in the hierarchy of music among the men who would face death rather than smirch their singing-robes for the sake of a fleeting popularity?'[76] Edward Elgar described this obituary as 'foul' and representing 'the shady side of musical criticism'.[77] It was not Fuller Maitland's last salvo against the composer whom he regarded as morally and spiritually bankrupt. In his 1902 book, *English Music in the Nineteenth Century*, he dismissed Sullivan as a peddler of 'light music' who merely satisfied the taste of the masses and 'took no part whatever in the work of the renaissance'.[78]

There were other snubs. The only word of thanks that Sullivan received from the Leeds Musical Festival committee for his twenty years at the helm was a curt formal letter sent more than twelve months after his enforced resignation which arrived four days before his death. The 1901 Festival did not feature any of his music beyond the brief *In Memoriam* overture played on the opening morning. A proposal to include *The Golden Legend* had been turned down, prompting a strongly worded complaint from William Boosey, who was about to be appointed managing director of the music publishers, Chappell's. Commenting that 'it would be interesting to know how far the omission is intentional', Boosey observed that it was no secret that

> some among those in highest authority at the Royal College of Music have always refused to acknowledge Arthur Sullivan as a musician serious enough to be admitted into their solemn ranks. Only quite recently a well-known professor at the Royal College suggested to some of his fellow professors the desirability of putting up in the College a small bust or tablet in memory of Arthur Sullivan. He was informed that he better desist.

It was almost certainly Stanford, the professor of composition, who was particularly vehement in vetoing a memorial to Sullivan. Boosey went on to say that 'The fact is that to a certain class of musician Sullivan's name is as a red rag to a bull, because his music spells melody'. He could not resist pointing out that 'the Royal College of Music is a national, state-aided institution for the education of future Arthur Sullivans and not future Dryasdusts' and that those running it 'do not except in their own opinions necessarily represent the only musical intelligence in this country'.[79]

Boosey suggested that it was 'musical snobbishness' that lay behind this snub to Sullivan. In fact there was an element of social snobbishness as well. Unlike the upper-class Parry (Eton and Oxford) and Stanford (private school in Dublin and Cambridge), Sullivan was a lower-middle-class boy who had won the hearts of the public. In addition to being deprecating about his lowly origins and his vulgarity, his detractors were also jealous of his popularity and his earnings, even though by the end of his life the combination of high living and generous giving had whittled them down somewhat. He left £55,000 in his will, compared to Gilbert's £120,000 and D'Oyly Carte's £248,000.

While the highbrow critics and composers spread their calumny, the public enjoyed his two final works. *The Emerald Isle*, which had been completed by Edward German, opened at the Savoy Theatre on 27 April 1901 and ran for 205 performances. The *Boer War Te Deum* was first performed in a national service of thanksgiving in St Paul's Cathedral on 8 June 1902, just a week after the Boer War had finally ended with the signing of the Peace of Vereeniging. The service began with 'Onward, Christian soldiers' sung as a processional hymn to ST GERTRUDE. *The Times* enthused:

> Nothing more stately can well be imagined than the Royal procession advancing to the inspiring hymn, which so stirringly gives voice to the faith and enthusiasm of the Church militant and the Church triumphant. It seemed as if here, as indeed, was the case, one was in the presence of the most supreme act of acknowledgement of the Divine favour and mercy which the nation could perform.[80]

Two months later, the coronation service for Edward VII in Westminster Abbey included a setting by Sir Frederick Bridge of Psalm 5 to the concluding part of the chorus 'Men and brethren' from the *Light of the World*. Hymns specially written for the occasion to Sullivan's tunes BISHOPGARTH and BOLWELL featured in an order of service prepared for use in the Church of England and throughout the Empire on Coronation Day, providing a fitting epitaph to one who had devoted so much of his effort to extol the causes of monarchy, church, and country.

On 10 July 1903, Queen Victoria's daughter, Princess Louise, Duchess of Argyll, unveiled a memorial to Sullivan on the Thames Embankment not far from the Savoy Theatre. Gilbert, who had been approached about a suitable text, chose lines from *The Yeomen of the Guard*:

> Is life a boon?
> If so, it must befall
> That Death, whene'er he call,
> Must call too soon.

Even though he did not dread it and remained staunch in his belief of another life to come, death had indeed called too soon for the 58-year-old composer who was on the brink of writing what might have been his greatest sacred work. If Sullivan's was to some extent a life of unfulfilled potential, it was also one that brought spiritual comfort, uplift, and consolation as well as sheer joy to many.

Notes

1. Arthur Jacobs, *Arthur Sullivan*, 2nd edn. (Aldershot: Scolar Press, 1992), p.324.
2. Arthur Sullivan [hereafter AS] to Gilbert, 8 September 1896: BL Add MS 49,333 ff 77–80.
3. AS to William Lacy, 18 July 1891: Pierpont Morgan Library, New York [hereafter PML].
4. Herbert Sullivan and Newman Flower, *Sir Arthur Sullivan* (London: Cassell & Co., 1927), p.219.
5. AS to Ethyl Smyth, 10 August 1891, quoted in Jacobs, *Sullivan*, p.337.
6. Jacobs, *Sullivan*, p.154.
7. Diary, 8 May 1888: BRB.
8. 'A Talk With the Composer of *Pinafore*', *San Francisco Chronicle*, 22 July 1885.
9. Hermann Klein, *Thirty Years of Musical Life in London* (London: William Heinemann, 1903), p.336.
10. Arthur Lawrence, *Sir Arthur Sullivan: Life Story, Letters and Reminiscences* (London: James Bowden, 1899), pp.299–300.
11. Princess Louise to AS, 2 February 1891: PML.
12. R. Wolf, 'A Composer with a Monocle and a Mansion', *Green Book Magazine*, December 1913, p.396.
13. *The World*, 4 February 1891.

14. Benedict Taylor, *Arthur Sullivan: A Musical Reappraisal* (London: Routledge, 2018), p.193.

15. AS to W.S. Gilbert, 1 July 1893, quoted in Michael Ainger: *Gilbert and Sullivan: A Dual Biography* (Oxford: Oxford University Press, 2002), p.342.

16. W.S. Gilbert to AS, 3 July 1893, quoted in Ainger, *Gilbert and Sullivan*, p.342.

17. *Daily Mail*, 17 May 1898.

18. *The Times*, 30 May 1898.

19. Charles Graves, *The Life & Letters of Sir George Grove* (London: Macmillan, 1903), p.392.

20. Graves, *Grove*, pp.392–3.

21. Percy Young, *George Grove* (London: Macmillan, 1980), p.227.

22. George Grove to Edith Oldham, 8 January1893, quoted Young, *Grove*, p.228.

23. Young, *Grove*, p.228.

24. George Grove to Edith Oldham, 12 January 1893, quoted Graves, *Grove*, p.393.

25. George Grove to Edith Oldham, 12 January 1893, quoted Graves, *Grove*, p.394.

26. George Grove to Nina Lehmann, 17 November 1896, quoted in Graves, *Grove*, p.434.

27. George Grove to Edith Oldham, 24 June 1892, quoted Young, *Grove*, p.221.

28. Leslie Baily, *The Gilbert & Sullivan Book*, revised edn. (London: Cassell & Co, 1956), p.392.

29. AS to Sybil Seligman, August 1896: BL MS Mus.133 F.

30. *Daily Telegraph*, 24 May 1897.

31. Jacobs, *Sullivan*, p.379.

32. George Buckle (ed.), *Letters of Queen Victoria*, 3rd series, Vol.III (London: John Murray, 1932), p.147.

33. William How to AS, Easter Day 1897: PML.

34. Arthur Bigge to AS, 24 April 1897: PML.

35. Frederick How, *Bishop Walsham How: A Memoir* (London: Isbister, 1898), p.352.

36. AS to How, 27 May 1897: PML.

37. How, *How*, p.359.

38. James Lightwood, *Hymn Tunes and their Story* (London: Charles Kelly, 1906), p.311.

39. Baily, *Gilbert & Sullivan*, p.137.
40. Sullivan and Flower, *Sullivan*, p.242.
41. *Scotsman*, 26 February 1898.
42. *Yorkshire Evening Post*, 11 October 1898, p.4, quoted in Anne Stanyon, 'Sir Arthur Sullivan, the 1898 Leeds Festival and Beyond' (Leeds University PhD thesis, 2017), p.228.
43. *Bradford Observer*, 28 October 1892, p.271, quoted in Stanyon, 'Sullivan and Leeds Festival', p.95.
44. *Daily Telegraph*, 5 October 1895, p.7, quoted in Stanyon, 'Sullivan and Leeds Festival', p.96.
45. *Illustrated Sporting and Dramatic News*, 18 December 1897, p.645.
46. Rudyard Kipling to AS, 14 May 1898: PML.
47. Joseph Comyns Carr, *Coasting in Bohemia* (London: Macmillan, 1914) pp.246, 252.
48. AS to Wilfred Bendall, 26 March 1898: PML.
49. AS to Herbert Sullivan, 10 & 12 August 1898, quoted in Jacobs, *Sullivan*, p.389.
50. Edward Elgar to Herbert Sullivan, 29 December 1926, quoted in Percy Young, *Sir Arthur Sullivan* (London: Dent, 1971) p.216.
51. Jacobs, *Sullivan*, p.390.
52. *Yorkshire Post*, 24 May 1952, p.5, quoted in Stanyon, 'Sullivan and Leeds Festival', p.227.
53. Stanyon, 'Sullivan and Leeds Festival', p.267.
54. Jacobs, *Sullivan*, p.395.
55. *Musical Times*, 1 February 1901, p.101.
56. Jacobs, *Sullivan*, p.396.
57. John Cannon, 'The Absent-Minded Beggar', *Gilbert and Sullivan News* 11: 8 (March 1997), p.17.
58. Rudyard Kipling, *Something of Myself* (Harmondsworth: Penguin Books, 1977), p.113.
59. Cannon, 'The Absent-Minded Beggar', p.16.
60. Jacobs, *Sullivan*, p.396.
61. Rudyard Kipling to AS, 27 May 1900: PML.
62. *Musical Times*, 1 July 1902, p.497.
63. Jeffrey Richards, *Imperialism and Music, Britain 1876–1953* (Manchester: Manchester University Press, 2001), p.38.
64. Benedict Taylor, 'Musical Aspects of Sullivan's Boer War Te Deum', *SASS Magazine* 66 (Winter 2007), p.15.

65. Taylor, *Arthur Sullivan*, pp.209, 212.

66. Young, *Sullivan*, p.257.

67. *The Times*, 29 November 1900.

68. Young, *Sullivan*, p.262.

69. AS to Helen D'Oyly Carte, 2 November 1900, quoted in Ainger, *Gilbert and Sullivan*, p.386.

70. AS to Helen D'Oyly Carte, 7 November 1900, quoted in Ainger, *Gilbert and Sullivan*, p.387.

71. *Daily Telegraph*, 28 November 1900, p.10.

72. *Musical Times*, 1 December 1900, p.787.

73. *Musical Times*, 1 January 1901, p.21.

74. *The Times*, 23 November 1900, p.8.

75. *The Times*, 24 November, p.10.

76. *Cornhill Magazine*, March 1901, pp.300–9.

77. Jerrold Moore, *Edward Elgar: A Creative Life* (Oxford: Oxford University Press, 1984), p.479.

78. John Fuller Maitland, *English Music in the Nineteenth Century* (London: Grant Richards, 1902), p.170.

79. *Sheffield Independent*, 29 July 1901, p.2.

80. *The Times*, 9 June 1902.

Conclusion

Arthur Sullivan was no saint and he was certainly no ascetic. He enjoyed life to the full and was an unashamed pleasure seeker, adding gambling to the usual trinity of women, wine, and song. It is not surprising that he related so closely to the Biblical figure of the Prodigal Son whom he resembled both in terms of his somewhat profligate lifestyle and in his bouts of remorse and regret, as expressed in his particularly sensitive setting of the phrases 'I loved the garish day' and 'remember not past years' in John Henry Newman's 'Lead, kindly light'. The God in whom Sullivan believed and whom he portrayed so clearly in his two biblical oratorios had the attributes of the father in the parable of the Prodigal Son: forgiveness, understanding, reassurance, and overflowing love. Sullivan had a strong sense of divine assurance and comfort, especially in respect of death and what followed it, which he conveyed in his *In Memoriam* overture, the closing bars of 'The Lost Chord' and his choice and setting of texts such as 'Weep ye not for the dead' and 'God shall wipe away all tears from their eyes' in *The Light of the World*.

Sullivan did not wear his Christianity on his sleeve, and his faith was not of an abstract, speculative, philosophical nature. Rather it was expressed in his lifelong attachment to the church in which he had grown up and in in his considerable generosity to his family and to many beyond the circle of his close friends. George Martin's remark that his last work, the *Boer War Te Deum*, demonstrated his devotion to his Queen, his church, and his country could be applied to his life as a whole. His deep affection for the Crown bordered on the besetting English sin of monarcholatry. He never lost his sense of belonging to the Church of England and his affection for its liturgy and its central place in the nation's life. It was ironic that one who did not have a drop of English blood in his veins should be such a great enthusiast for all things English, constantly championing the country's musicians against their Continental counterparts, and seeking to create a national school of opera. It was doubly ironic that one whose ancestral roots were so firmly planted in Irish Catholicism should become the prime musical exponent of the patriotic Protestantism that was at the heart of the national identity of Victorian Britain.

There could, of course, hardly have been anything more English than his upbringing as the son of an army band sergeant at Sandhurst and a chorister in the Chapel Royal. This latter experience, far from inducing the 'spiritual bankruptcy' suggested by David Eden, had a positive effect on both his character and his music that was profound and lasting. It reinforced the natural qualities of innocence and graciousness that struck so many of those who had dealings with him. As Benjamin Findon pointed out, it also contributed significantly to the spontaneity, simplicity, clarity, and directness which character-ized his music and made it so accessible and popular:

> Not a little of this singular directness and gracefulness of expression is owing to the early bent of his studies while a chorister at the Chapel Royal, for there Arthur Sullivan had the opportunity of becoming intimately acquainted with the compositions of the great church writers of the seventeenth century, and with his quick gift of perception, his ready power of assimilation, it is not surprising that he obtained a complete mastery of their lucid style, and a ripe familiarity with the canon, fugue, and imitation which form so important a part in their compositions.[1]

If the distinctively Anglican tradition of the Chapel Royal left its mark on Sullivan, not least in giving even his lighter music a certain restraint and ecclesiastical feel, the influence of his Irish and Italian genes also made itself felt in his character and spiritual make-up as well as in his appearance. This was perhaps what lay behind the deeply romantic, soulful, and sensuous side to his personality which was well captured by an American journalist when he and Gilbert made their first visit to New York in 1879:

> In his appearance, gentle feeling and tender emotion are as strongly expressed as cold, glittering keen intellect is in that of Mr Gilbert . . . he is as dark as his *collaborateur* is fair, with a face of wonderful mobility and sensitiveness, in which the slightest emotion plays with unmistakable meaning, with eyes which only the Germanic adjective of 'soulful' would fitly describe and the full, sensuous lips of a man of impas-sioned nature.[2]

It was, of course, precisely these characteristics that made him so irresistible to women, and led to his various amorous encounters and entanglements. Maybe there was, too, a certain Irish (or even Italian?) capriciousness in his make-up which explains his reluctance to commit and settle down to married life. His Celtic and Continental genes perhaps also underlay his insistence that music should speak to the heart and not the head, a conviction that made him all the more unacceptable to the academically inclined apostles of the English Musical Renaissance.

In many ways Sullivan's character, like his music, was distinguished by simplicity, straightforwardness, and utter sincerity. This was what particularly struck his first biographer, Arthur Lawrence:

> It has been my lot, as a disciple in the modern development of interview-journalism, to come into contact with many men and women, eminent in their respective professions, but I have never met anyone who excelled Sir Arthur Sullivan in sincerity, whole-heartedness, and simplicity—as indicated in the sense of an entire absence of the least jot or tittle of mannerism, affectation, or ostentation. His entire absence of pose and prejudice, his catholicity of taste and equitable poise of temperament, must have been disappointing to those who regard any form of genius as an abnormal development which implies a sort of lop-sidedness.[3]

Yet for all this simplicity and straightforwardness, his life was not without its apparent contrasts and contradictions. He radiated happiness and genial bonhomie despite the inner demons of the chronic kidney disease which caused him pain for much of his life and the depression which gripped him especially in his last decade. He loved life with a passion but had no fear of death. He extolled his chosen mistress of music for its high moral purity while leading a lifestyle that some might consider rather immoral. He was a regular visitor to the casinos of Monte Carlo and yet he could be moved to tears by the sound of a boys' choir singing in Cologne Cathedral.

Most enigmatic, perhaps, was the apparent mixture of the frivolous and the serious in both his character and his music. When Ethyl Smyth first met him, she was struck by his 'perfect blend of chaff and seriousness (the exact perfection of cadence there is in his work)'.[4] Were there really two completely different sides to his personality? His life was certainly full of apparently clashing activities, swinging from the solemn to the hedonistic. To take just one example, on his trip to the west coast of the United States in 1885 he was attending a service in the Mormon Tabernacle Church in Salt Lake City one day and going on a tour of what he gleefully called "the vilest dens" of San Francisco's Chinatown the next. But such juxtapositions were indications not of a split personality but rather of one where inner seriousness and spirituality were combined with outer joie de vivre. In the perceptive words of William Parry: 'It was absolutely possible for Sullivan to lead a life in which a personal spirituality could co-exist with utter exuberance. We should not misunderstand that outward personality to mean that Sullivan was hypocritical, or that the inner religious feeling, while largely unexpressed, was not strongly felt.'[5]

Some of his contemporaries felt that when it came to his music there were actually three Sullivans. The German pianist and composer Jacques Blumenthal wrote after hearing *Ivanhoe*: 'You are most generous towards the English nation for giving it three composers by the name of Sullivan: the comic, the sacred and the highly dramatic'.[6] Benjamin Findon suggested that Sullivan's life and work could be divided into three periods: the sacred, the secular, and the dramatic.[7] Many of his critics felt that Sullivan started out serious, intent on fulfilling his potential as the *Wunderkind* of British music who would one day equal if not even excel Brahms, but then got diverted into lightweight comic operas and songs, either through a combination of the lure of easy financial gain and his habitual laziness or because he was not really up to the serious stuff and his heart was never in it. They varied in their view as to when this decisive and dangerous change of direction took place. For Joseph Bennett, it was as early as 1867 when Sullivan 'drifted to the butterflies' and became 'a darling of the drawing-rooms' (p. 84). For others it happened ten years later with *The Sorcerer* and the inauguration of the regular partnership with Gilbert churning out the Savoy operas; while Benjamin Findon suggested that it was only in 1886 after *The Golden Legend* that he turned his back on serious music (p. 143).

It is true that Sullivan composed more serious and sacred music in the earlier than in the later years of his professional career. It is also true that he did not fulfil his potential in this sphere and promised several major works that never materialized, notably the David and

Jonathan oratorio commissioned for the Norwich Festival in 1875, the cantata for the 1898 Leeds Festival, and the composition that he hoped would be his swansong in the 1901 Festival. Yet the fact remains that he did produce serious works in the second half of his composing career, *The Golden Legend* being the pre-eminent example, and that at the very end of his life he prioritized the sacred over the secular, laying aside *The Emerald Isle* to concentrate on the *Boer War Te Deum*.

Overall, I calculate that around 25 per cent of Sullivan's total output was made up of sacred pieces and music for church worship. This is a much lower proportion than for his Tudor heroes, Thomas Tallis and William Byrd, for whom the comparable figures are respectively 90 and 70 per cent, but it is very similar to what might be called the 'sacred score' of Henry Purcell (around 25 per cent of whose output was music for worship) and rather more than that of George Frederick Handel (roughly 18 per cent).[8] Yet we do not hear of either of them being criticized for dissipating their talents and being seduced by the lure of the theatre and concert hall.

In fact, I am not sure that it is right to divide Sullivan's compositions into the serious and the lightweight, temporally or otherwise, any more than it is right to split his personality between the sacred and the secular. As the *Daily Telegraph* correspondent so perceptively noted in the context of his funeral, 'there was not so much contrast or discord between them as some have been in haste to imagine' (pp. 189–90). There was an essential unity to all his music, both grave and gay, arising from those qualities of simplicity, sincerity, spontaneity, clarity, and directness which have already been mentioned, together with his exceptional gifts for melody and orchestration. They gave his serious and sacred compositions a limpid as well as a lyrical quality, and they lifted his comic operas and parlour ballads from the formulaic and shallow style displayed by many of his contemporaries. Sullivan's genius was to achieve an accessibility which made his music so popular, without sacrificing inventiveness and sometimes quite daring innovation in terms of tonality and harmonization. He was not interested in writing for academic musicologists or highbrow critics. What he wanted to do was to reach people and touch their emotions, moving them to laugh, to cry, to be cheered and inspired, to have a spring in their step, and not least to express their faith. It was no coincidence that he was so fond of hymn tunes, seeing them as the best vehicle through which to reach the hearts of the people, weaving them into his two *Te Deums*, and reminding those who criticized his own stirring contributions to this genre that they were neither part songs nor academic exercises in harmony, but tunes which 'everyone will be able to pick up quickly and sing heartily' (p. 177).

There was one overriding quality which infused both Sullivan's character and his music. It is difficult to define precisely but it has been hinted at more than once in this book and it was identified by many who had dealings with him. It can perhaps best be described as a kind of emollience which had an effect that was uplifting and life-enhancing as well as softening and smoothing. Edward Dicey, a close friend who served as his executor, wrote that 'no man I have ever known had so perfect a genius for kindness'.[9] Edward Elgar, whom he did so much to help, described him as 'one of the most amiable and genial souls that ever lived'.[10] Arthur Lawrence wrote:

> He had an unfailing courtesy, which was of the manner that makes the man, and his keen and untiring sympathies were ever on the alert. His was a sunny disposition, and not the least of his qualities was the equability—the serenity of his temperament—which enabled him to display the best principles of an active philosophy in all the chances of life.[11]

This quality, which so attracted George Grove to Sullivan because it lifted his own spirits and assuaged his doubts, was perhaps best summed up by his cousin Benjamin Findon when he wrote: 'He inspired in all who came into contact with him or his work a spirit of tranquil happiness, and an exquisite appreciation of the joy of living.'[12]

It was above all in his music that this softening and uplifting strain was expressed. Once again, George Grove felt it keenly and identified it when he pointed to the divine quality that Sullivan shared with Mozart and Beethoven, and which so many modern composers had lost in their pursuit of ugliness. Sullivan said that it was when listening as a boy to Jenny Lind singing solos from Mendelssohn's *Elijah* that he first felt that music was divine. That feeling inspired his own music making, giving it that lyrical, life-affirming character conveying the promise of spring and the conviction that the world is new every morning which it is not too much to describe as profoundly redemptive in its effect. Never was this quality more clearly shown than in the way that he softened, brightened, and transfigured the often rather bleak, cynical, and pessimistic lyrics of W.S. Gilbert. It was supremely in the Savoy operas for which he will always be most remembered that he displayed that distinctive if not unique characteristic of divine emollient which made his a spiritual life.

Notes

1. Arthur Lawrence, *Sir Arthur Sullivan: Life Story, Letters and Reminiscences* (London: James Bowden, 1899), pp.292–3.
2. *New York Herald*, 6 November 1879.
3. Lawrence, *Sullivan*, p.218.
4. Ethel Smyth, *Impressions That Remained* (London: Longmans Green, 1919), p.79.
5. William Parry, 'Sullivan between Secularism and Christianity', in Albert Gier, Meinhard Saremba, and Benedict Taylor (eds), *SullivanPerspektiven* Vol.I (Essen: Odlib Verlag, 2012), p.132.
6. Herbert Sullivan and Newman Flower, *Sir Arthur Sullivan* (London: Cassell & Co., 1927), p.210.
7. Lawrence, *Sullivan*, p.299.
8. These figures are taken from Andrew Gant, *O Sing Unto the Lord: A History of English Church Music* (London: Profile Books, 2015), p.225.
9. Edward Dicey, *Fortnightly Review, Recollections of Arthur Sullivan*, January 1905, p.78.
10. *Strand Magazine*, May 1904, pp.541–2.
11. *The Masonic Illustrated*, January 1901, p.69.
12. Benjamin Findon, *Sir Arthur Sullivan: His Life and Music* (London: James Nisbet, 1904), p.3.

Selected Bibliography

Ainger, Michael. *Gilbert and Sullivan: A Dual Biography* (Oxford: Oxford University Press, 2002)

Baily, Leslie. *The Gilbert & Sullivan Book*, revised edn. (London: Cassell & Co, 1956)

Barnett, John Francis. *Musical Reminiscences and Impressions* (London: Hodder & Stoughton, 1906)

Bennett, Joseph. *Forty Years of Music* (London: Methuen, 1908)

Bradley, Ian. *Abide With Me: The World of Victorian Hymns* (London: SCM Press, 1997)

Bradley, Ian. *Lost Chords and Christian Soldiers: The Sacred Music of Arthur Sullivan* (London: SCM Press, 2013)

Bradley, Ian. *The Complete Annotated Gilbert & Sullivan* (New York: Oxford University Press, 2016)

Cockaday, Richard. *The Hymn Tunes of Sir Arthur Sullivan*, 4th edn. (Norwich: Norwich Gilbert and Sullivan Society, 2019)

Crowther, Andrew. *Gilbert of Gilbert & Sullivan* (Stroud: The History Press, 2011)

Dibble, Jeremy. *John Stainer: A Life in Music* (Woodbridge: Boydell Press, 2007)

Disher, Maurice. *Victorian Song: From Dive to Drawing Room* (London: Phoenix House, 1955)

Eden, David. *Gilbert and Sullivan: The Creative Conflict* (London: Associated University Presses, 1986)

Eden, David. *Kyrie Eleison: The Ancestry of Arthur Sullivan* (Retford: Sir Arthur Sullivan Society, 2016)

Eden, David, and Saremba, Meinhard, *The Cambridge Companion to Gilbert and Sullivan* (Cambridge: Cambridge University Press, 2009)

Findon, Benjamin. *Sir Arthur Sullivan: His Life and Music* (London: James Nisbet, 1904)

Gier, Albert, Taylor, Benedict, and Saremba, Meinhard (eds). *Sullivan Perspecktiven*, Vol.1 (Essen: Odlib Verlag, 2012)

Gier, Albert, Taylor, Benedict, and Saremba, Meinhard (eds). *Sullivan Perspecktiven*, Vol.2 (Essen: Odlib Verlag, 2014)

Gier, Albert, Taylor, Benedict, and Saremba, Meinhard (eds). *Sullivan Perspecktiven*, Vol.3 (Essen: Odlib Verlag, 2017)

Godwin, Augustine. *Gilbert & Sullivan: A Critical Appreciation of the Savoy Operas* (London: Dent, 1926)

Graves, Charles. *The Life and Letters of George Grove* (London: Macmillan, 1903)

Grove, George. *The Light of the World: Analysis* (London: J.B. Cramer & Co., 1873)

Hayes, Scott. *Uncle Arthur: The California Connection* (Retford: Sir Arthur Sullivan Society, 2009)

Hayes, Scott. *Your Affectionate 'A': A Collection of Sir Arthur Sullivan's Letters to His Family* (Retford: Sir Arthur Sullivan Society, 2015)

Hughes, Gervase. *The Music of Arthur Sullivan* (London: Macmillan, 1960)

Hughes, Meirion, *The English Musical Renaissance and the Press 1850–1914*, paperback edn. (London: Routledge, 2017)

Hutchings, Arthur. *Church Music in the Nineteenth Century* (London: Herbert Jenkins, 1967)

Jacobs, Arthur. *Arthur Sullivan: A Victorian Musician*, 2nd edn. (London: Scolar Press, 1992)

Klein, Hermann. *Thirty Years of Musical Life in London* (London: William Heinemann, 1903)

Larsen, Tim. *A People of One Book: The Bible and the Victorians* (Oxford: Oxford University Press, 2011)

Lawrence, Arthur. *Sir Arthur Sullivan: Life Story, Letters and Reminiscences* (London: James Bowden, 1899)

Long, Kenneth. *The Music of the English Church* (London: Hodder and Stoughton, 1972)

Oost, Regina. *Gilbert and Sullivan: Class and the Savoy Tradition 1875–1896* (Farnham: Ashgate, 2009)

Orel, Harold. *Gilbert & Sullivan: Interviews and Recollections* (Iowa City: University of Iowa Press, 1994)

Richards, Jeffrey. *Imperialism and Music: Britain 1876–1953* (Manchester: Manchester University Press, 2001)

Rogers, Clara. *Memories of a Musical Career* (Boston: Little Brown & Co., 1919)

Saremba, Meinhard. *Arthur Sullivan. Ein Komponistenlebem im Viktorianischem England* (Wilhelmshaven: Florian Noetzel-Verlag, 1993)

Saremba, Meinhard. *Elgar, Britten & Co. Eine Geschichte der britischen Musik in zwölf Portraits* (Zurich: Edition Musik & Theater 1994)

Scott, Derek. *The Singing Bourgeois: Songs of the Victorian Drawing Room*, 2nd edn. (Aldershot: Ashgate, 2001)

Spark, Fred, and Bennett, Joseph, *History of the Leeds Musical Festivals 1858–1889* (Leeds: Fred Spark & Son, 1892)

Stanyon, Anne. 'Sir Arthur Sullivan, the 1898 Leeds Festival and Beyond' (PhD thesis, Leeds University, 2017)

Stedman, Jane. *W.S. Gilbert* (Oxford: Oxford University Press, 1996)

Sullivan, Herbert, and Flower, Newman. *Sir Arthur Sullivan* (London: Cassell & Co., 1927)

Taylor, Benedict. *Arthur Sullivan: A Musical Reappraisal* (London: Routledge, 2018)

Temperley, Nicholas (ed.). *Music in Britain: The Romantic Age 1800–1914* (London: Athlone Press, 1988)

Walker, Ernest. *A History of Music in England* (Oxford: Clarendon Press, 1907)

Willeby, Charles. *Masters of English Music* (London: James Osgood, 1893)

Wolfson, John. *Sullivan and the Scott Russells* (Chichester: Packard Publishing, 1984)

Wren, Gayden. *A Most Ingenious Paradox: The Art of Gilbert and Sullivan* (New York: Oxford University Press, 2001)

Wyndham, Henry Saxe. *Arthur Seymour Sullivan* (London: Kegan, Paul, Trench, Trubner & Co., 1926)

Young, Percy. *Sir Arthur Sullivan* (London: J.M. Dent, 1971)

Young, Percy. *George Grove* (London: Macmillan, 1980)

Index

Note: Page numbers in **bold** indicate major entries on particular topics.